WITHDRAWN FROM CLARK UNIVERSITY
LIBRARY

THE WARSAW GHETTO REVOLT

STATEMENT OF PURPOSE

The *Holocaust Library* was created and is managed by survivors. Its purpose is to offer to the reading public authentic material, not readily available, and to preserve the memory of our martyrs and heroes untainted by arbitrary or inadvertent distortions.

With each passing day the memory of the tragedy of European Jews, the greatest crime in the annals of mankind, recedes into history. The witnesses and survivors of the holocaust are still alive, their memories remain vivid; yet, a malicious myth about their experience keeps rising before our eyes, distorting and misinterpreting evidence, perverting history.

As new generations arise, so grows the incredible ignorance about our tragedy. Millions of men and women, Jews and Gentiles, are unaware of the basic facts of the tragedy, many have never even heard the word "holocaust." This is a seed of a new disaster.

The holocaust story should be untiringly told and retold making the world aware of its lessons. This can contribute to that moral reconstruction which alone may prevent a repetition of the catastrophe in our hate- and violence-stricken world.

ADVISORY BOARD: Alexander Donat *(Chairman)*, Sam E. Bloch, William H. Donat, Hadassah Rosensaft, Leon W. Wells, Elie Wiesel

THE WARSAW GHETTO REVOLT

REUBEN AINSZTEIN

HOLOCAUST LIBRARY
NEW YORK

A revised and expanded version of
"The Warsaw Ghetto Revolt" in
Jewish Resistance in Nazi-occupied Eastern Europe

Copyright © 1979 by Reuben Ainsztein

Publication of this book was made possible by a grant
from Benjamin and Stefa Wald.

Cover design by Eric Gluckman
Printed in the United States of America
by Waldon Press Inc., N.Y.C.

To my friend Dr Louis L. Kaplan,
President Emeritus of the Baltimore Hebrew College,
whose unfailing support, encouragement and financial
assistance made my work possible.

Contents

The Road to Resistance	1
Himmler Defied	53
The Uprising	93
The Epilogue	173
Notes	203
Selected Bibliography	231
Index	233

The Road to Resistance

I

To say that Jewish armed resistance in the city-ghettoes found its fulfillment in the Warsaw Ghetto Uprising is to state the obvious. But what remains far from obvious is that *the revolt in the Warsaw Ghetto was in every sense a people's uprising*—that is, it was not confined to the actions of two military organizations but was made possible by the involvement of thousands of ordinary people. It is this participation of thousands of unarmed civilians that made the revolt a unique event not only in the story of Jewish resistance, but also in the general anti-Nazi resistance movement in occupied Europe.

In attempting an assessment of the nature and significance of the Warsaw Ghetto Uprising, one is confronted by a fundamental difficulty. The difficulty is in the fact that although the event is annually commemorated, the knowledge of what happened in Warsaw in April and May 1943 is so vague as to have already assumed the character of a myth. Consequently, one has to tell the story of the Warsaw Ghetto Uprising without assuming that even the basic facts are known and can therefore be omitted.

The Warsaw ghetto was officially created on October 2, 1940 by a decree issued by Dr. Ludwig Fischer, Governor of the Warsaw Distrikt. Surrounded by a wall sixteen kilometers long and three meters high, which was topped by broken glass and barbed wire, the ghetto became a concentration camp for Jews and also for several thousand Poles of Jewish origin, that is, for people who had cut off their connections with the Jewish people by becoming Christians or whose only link with Jews was a single Jewish grandparent.[1] As many of the Jews in the Warsaw ghetto lived there "illegally," it was impossible for the various ghetto statisticians to establish the exact size of the population. However, it is certain that at its peak the ghetto population exceeded 500,000—some put it as high as 550,000—and that this total included in April 1941 as many as 150,000 refugees, many of them from Lodz, and entire communities deported by the Germans from the provincial towns and townlets of the Mazowsze region.[2]

The slums inhabited by the Jewish poor in prewar Warsaw were among the worst in Europe. However, bad as they were, the density per room in the working-class streets of the Jewish quarter had been seven people, while in the ghetto as a whole the density per room was thirteen people[3] and reached unimaginable dimensions in the warehouses in Dzika and Stawki Streets, where thousands of refugees covered every inch of available floor space. The official inhabitants of the ghetto were entitled to a monthly ration of food which averaged two kilograms of bread and 250 grams of sugar per person. The bread, it should be added, contained a large proportion of potato peelings or sawdust. Calculated in calories, a German in Warsaw received daily 2,310 calories, a Pole 634 cal. and a Jew 184. Furthermore, while a German paid 0.3 zloty for one calorie and a Pole as much as 2.6 zlotys, a Jew paid 5.9 zlotys. In simple figures, in April 1942 the price of a kilogram of rye bread smuggled into the ghetto was 8–12 zlotys and of white bread as much as 18–25 zlotys, while a kilogram of lard cost as much as 250 zlotys.[4] That the blackmarket food was beyond the means of the overwhelming majority of ghetto inhabitants, and especially beyond the means of the refugees and deportees who had few if any personal belongings to sell, can be deduced from the following facts. Thus, the small minority employed permanently in the workshops and factories producing for the Germans earned between four and seven zlotys a day after slaving between nine and eleven hours. After the deduction of the cost of two bowls of watery soup a day, the better paid workers were left with two and a half zlotys, while the worse paid workers were lucky to have two zlotys left.[5]

On June 30, 1941, when according to some ghetto statisticians the population had reached its peak of 550,000, the gainfully employed, who could count on two bowls of soup a day, numbered 27,000. According to a Jewish chronicler, on May 30, 1941 50 percent of the ghetto dwellers were literally starving to death, 30 per cent were starving "normally," 15 per cent did not have enough to eat, and 10,000 lived well, some of them even better than before the war. A year later, in April 1942, the anti-Semitic Antyk Agency* of the Government Delegate's Office concluded in a report on the situation in the ghetto that only a few thousand Jews lived well—that is, had enough money to provide themselves with all the food they wanted. For the overwhelming majority hunger was so persistent that it is surprising that only one case of cannibalism was officially recorded. Namely, in April 1942 a woman at number 13, Krochmalna Street had eaten part of the corpse of a dead child.[6]

Epidemics of typhoid, typhus and paratyphoid were the inevitable result of the indescribable overcrowding and hunger. The epidemics combined with hunger were responsible for 5,500 deaths in July 1941 compared with 454 in May 1938 among the 270,000 Jews of Warsaw.[7] However, hunger and disease did not work fast enough to satisfy the Germans, especially as the Jewish doctors helped by the man in the street succeeded in controlling the epidemics. They therefore rounded up tens of thousands of paupers inhabiting the traditional streets and alleys of the Jewish poor and hauled them off to labor camps where they were employed on drainage and river regulation work. Issued with a daily ration of 200 grams of bread and without adequate clothing or footwear, the Jewish slaves died in their thousands. Some 25,000 were still alive in a number of labor camps in April 1941, but after the German attack on the Soviet Union the Nazis submitted them to a régime of outright physical annihilation and their numbers quickly melted away.[8] The result of the Nazi policies was that about 100,000 people, mostly refugees and members of the local proletariat, died in the Warsaw ghetto by June 1942.

The chief purpose of the Nazi policy of starvation was, of course, the annihilation of the Jews imprisoned in the Warsaw ghetto. Ludwig Fischer, the Warsaw District Governor, stated it in no unmistakable terms: "The Jews will die from hunger and destitution, and a cemetery will remain of the Jewish question."[9] But no less importance was attached by the Nazi leaders to the effects of hunger on the Jewish will to resist. At a meeting of Governor-General Frank's cabinet held on October 15 and 16, 1941, SS

---

* See p. 50.

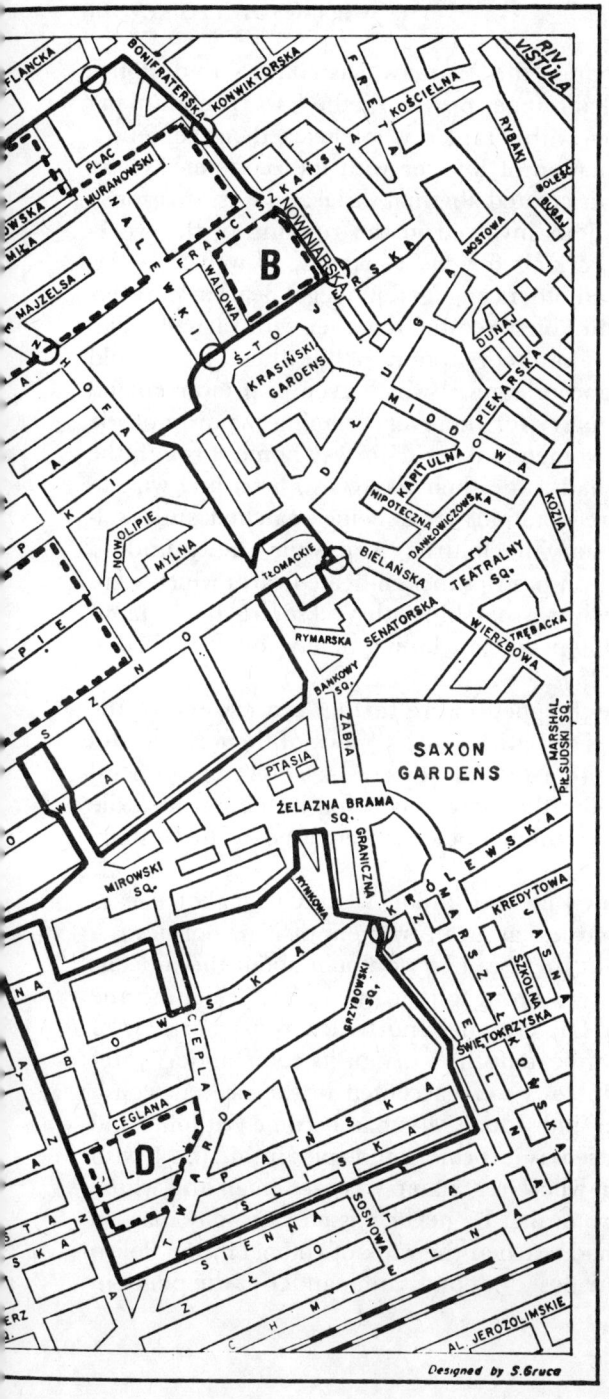

Brigadeführer Wiegand, the Warsaw Distrikt SS and Police Leader, pointed out that hunger prevented the Jews from thinking of resistance and met with Frank's wholehearted agreement.[10] Moreover, the combination of hunger with the economic system introduced by the Nazis created abysmal social and class divisions. The few thousand Jews involved in the running of the workshops and factories working for the Germans, as well as a few hundred smugglers and others engaged in illegal deals in partnership with Germans and Poles, became together with their families the chief element of moral corruption. While these Jews could afford to eat grapes and oranges,[11] which even in prewar Poland had been articles of luxury for the overwhelming majority of the population, ordinary women making their way home through the streets of the ghetto had to tie their baskets with barbed wire to secure their pitiful bread rations from being snatched and swallowed on the spot by starving children. And while a few hundred *nouveaux riches* gorged on pastries in well-heated cafés which were owned by Jews usually in partnership with Volksdeutsche, in January 1942 as many as 300 people, including ninety children, died in the streets of hunger.[12]

The divisions inside the ghetto were further exacerbated by the presence of 6,000 Poles of Jewish origins, many of them renegades and Judaeophobes, and German Jews, who showed a general propensity for regarding themselves as being in temporary exile from their fatherland. A number of them were used by the Gestapo as informers.[13]

Whether the Warsaw Judenrat under Adam Czerniakow's leadership could have acted less as an instrument of Nazi policies is a debatable question. But there can be no doubt about the hideous part played by the 2,000-strong ghetto police in facilitating the Nazis' Final Solution. The criminal and treacherous character of the police was to a large extent the work of its commander, Józef Andrzej Szeryński. No Jews were accepted in the prewar Polish police, except for a few individuals who had become Catholics and others who could be used as informers and spies inside the Jewish community. Szeryński, whose real name was Szenkman and whose Catholicism was so strong that he never missed a Sunday mass in the ghetto church,[14] had reached the rank of colonel in the Polish police and had held the post of deputy commander of the police in the Lublin Voyevodship at the time of the German invasion. An instrument of brutal class and national oppression until September 1939, the Polish police as a body became a willing and eager servant of the Nazis against their own people and especially against the Jews and Gypsies. Szeryński, helped by several Jewish converts with a similar background to his own, brought to the ghetto police the methods he had learnt in his former career and thus helped the Nazis in their policies of terror and moral disintegration.

II

Not content with the Judenrat and the ghetto police as instruments of control over the Jews, the Gestapo created two parallel agencies of treachery and corruption. Together the two agencies became a Mafia-like system of collaboration and gangster activities that had no parallel in any other ghetto.

The man whom the Nazis used to carry out their work was Abraham Ganzweich.[15] The son of a businessman, born in Częstochowa in 1904 or 1905, Ganzweich proved a gifted but lazy student, so that he left his Hebrew secondary school without matriculating. He joined Hashomer Hatzair and in 1923–4 was the head of the organization in his native city. For a time he worked as a teacher in a Hebrew primary school at Konin and during that period began to write for the provincial Jewish press in southwestern Poland. In the 1930s he moved to Belgium, where he continued to write for the socialist Zionist press, and from there to Vienna. In Vienna he worked for Irena Harand's anti-Nazi *Gerechtigkeit* until shortly before the Anschluss, when he returned to Lodz with his wife Miriam and son Samuel. Full of projects, he failed to obtain the financial backing of the wealthy Jews to whom he turned and became the editor of *Wolność (Freedom)*, a right-wing periodical owned by Poles, among them several priests. He also collaborated with a journal published by a British missionary society for the conversion of Jews. When the Germans occupied Lodz in September 1939, the Gestapo arrested the subscribers of *Wolność* but not Ganzweich, which according to Polish sources proves that he was already a Gestapo agent before arriving in Poland. On the other hand, it is also likely that the Gestapo recruited him as an agent after the occupation of Poland, for one of Ganzweich's colleagues on the staff of Harand's anti-Nazi periodical had been Dr. Ohlenbusch, an "Aryan" Austrian who soon after the German invasion appeared in Poland first as chief of the Propaganda Department in the office of the Nazi governor of the Cracow Distrikt and later as chief of the Propaganda Department in Dr. Hans Frank's government.

Thus the Gestapo already knew about Ganzweich before the occupation of Poland and probably enlisted him as its agent on finding him in Lodz. Ganzweich's brother-in-law was Moses Merin, whom the Nazis made the head of all the Judenrats in Upper Silesia and who was to play a role very similar to that of Gens in the Vilno region. Ganzweich explained to several Jews in the Warsaw ghetto that he owed his position to Merin's influence, but it is just as likely that it was Merin who owed his career to Ganzweich's status as a Gestapo agent.

From Lodz Ganzweich moved to Warsaw where in the spring of 1940 he first attracted public attention when, at a meeting of refugees from Lodz, he made a speech in which he said that the Nazi New Order had come to stay and that the Jews had to adjust themselves to it. This met with such a unanimously hostile reception that he did not try again to appear in public and confined himself to attempts to organize a circle of starving Hebrew writers and teachers for the alleged purpose of disseminating the knowledge of Hebrew and Hebrew culture among the youth in the ghetto. He had little success in this, but with the assistance of the Gestapo he collected a staff of collaborators recruited from members of his own family, friends and acquaintances, whom he brought to Warsaw from Lodz, Radomsk and Częstochowa.

To provide him with funds, the Gestapo made him administrator of 100 houses in the Warsaw ghetto, where until then all houses had been administered by the Judenrat. It also issued him every month with thirty passes allowing their bearers to travel on trains. As no Jew was allowed to use public transport, the possession of the passes conferred on Ganzweich and his men a unique privilege and also a unique source of income, for Ganzweich sold the passes and shared the profits with his Gestapo masters. Soon Ganzweich became known in the ghetto as the man who for payment could not only arrange the transfer of relatives from one ghetto to another, but also secure the release of people arrested by the Germans. And as unlike Czerniakow and other members of the Judenrat he was always ready to receive and listen to the troubles of any person, Ganzweich became by the end of 1940 a second force in the ghetto, which increasingly usurped much of the authority of the Judenrat.

On January 5, 1941, Ganzweich opened his Office for Combating Usury and Blackmarketeering at number 13, Leszno Street, which the ghetto subsequently dubbed The Thirteen. The need for such an office in the ghetto was great indeed, for although there was no usury in it, there was a vast blackmarket, which ensured the survival of a minority without helping to relieve the suffering of the proletarian and refugee elements. But it soon became obvious to most people in the ghetto that The Thirteen were not interested in combating blackmarketeering and profiteering.

Of the 318 people working for Ganzweich, 300 formed the "police force," eight were employed as drivers, motor-car mechanics and in similar honest occupations, and the rest were lawyers, who formed a court that went through the legal motions of trying people guilty of profiteering and blackmarketeering. In fact, only a few small bakers, butchers and smugglers were heavily fined or kept in The Thirteen's prison until they paid up. The 300 policemen performed the functions of an American gangster's hoodlums and with their help Ganzweich forced all the important businessmen in the ghetto, irrespective of whether they were honest or dishonest, to pay him protection money, which he shared with his Gestapo patrons.

As practically everything needed in the ghetto had to be smuggled in, Ganzweich's protection racket also extended to this vital activity. Before any article could be brought into the ghetto, bribes had to be paid to the Polish police, the ghetto police and to officials of the German Criminal Police, and even then there was no guarantee that it would reach the ghetto, for a German gendarme patrolling around its walls might seize it. However, if one paid protection money to The Thirteen, the article was certain to reach the ghetto without any other bribes being paid.

The Judenrat authorities attempted to oppose the growing power of The Thirteen, but without success. In April 1941 the Judenrat put out to public auction the concession for removing the ghetto garbage and received three offers, one from The Thirteen.

When the Judenrat failed to choose The Thirteen, three Gestapo officers paid a visit to the Judenrat offices, kicked the Chairman, Czerniakow, down the staircase and arrested him and two of his colleagues, Lichtenbaum and Herman. The three men were released only after the Judenrat has paid a bribe of 20,000 zlotys, which Szternfeld, the commander of Ganzweich's policemen, and his fellow-gangsters spent drinking in Casanova, the ghetto nightclub frequented exclusively by people of their ilk. Not satisfied with this victory, Szternfeld wrote to Szeryński demanding that the ghetto policemen should salute his own men. When Szeryński ignored the demand, Szternfeld's men arrested two ghetto policemen and one of them, who resisted arrest, was sent to Auschwitz by the Gestapo. Szeryński then agreed that the lower ranks of the ghetto police should salute the officers of Ganzweich's force.

Sharing in the proceeds of Ganzweich's rackets was, no doubt, an important element in the Gestapo game. But the most important factor was the usefulness of Ganzweich and his Mafia as an agency of espionage and subversion—in brief, as a classical fifth column. The espionage activities were not confined to the Warsaw ghetto or even to what was happening in the Polish underground outside. Until the German attack on the Soviet Union Ganzweich's agents travelled to Bialystok, Vilno and Lvov and no doubt carried out espionage assignments for their German masters. As for Ganzweich's subversive activities, which formed an integral part of the psychological warfare methods used by the Nazis against the Jews, they were of a complex nature. Two rabbis belonging to the Agudath Israel Party, Blumenfeld and Glicensztajn, made propaganda on his behalf among the Hassidic elements and saw to it that no resistance ideas should take root in the religious schools and colleges. But his attempts to control the intellectual life of the ghetto by bribing with food and better housing the many outstanding scholars and writers who had found themselves in Warsaw failed. Nevertheless, he managed to compromise a number of intellectuals, who to save their families and themselves from a hunger death accepted his money and food and thus lent an air of respectability to his activities.

On May 15, 1941, Ganzweich created another agency of subversion, the Ambulance Service, which was to play a particularly sinister role during the Great Liquidation. The members of the Ambulance Service claimed that the purpose of their organization was to provide medical assistance in an emergency and additional food rations for the poorest. In fact, Ringelblum recorded in his notes as an exceptional occurrence that on May 18, 1941 the Ambulance Service had distributed 110 loaves of bread, which The Thirteen had requisitioned from bakers. The Ambulance Service revealed its true face during the Great Liquidation when its members helped the ghetto police to round up the victims and drive them to the trains that took them to Treblinka. At the same time a few persons, who could afford the price demanded by the gangsters, were escorted to temporary safety in the ambulances.

Ganzweich visited the Gestapo every Tuesday with a report prepared by him and edited by a German Jew, a former member of the editorial board of the famous *Berliner Tageblatt*. The report contained a survey of the activities of the Judenrat, the Jewish Self-Help Organization and other Jewish institutions, a chronicle of events in the ghetto, and regular assessments of "What is said in the ghetto about the situation on the war fronts" and "What is reported in the ghetto on the course of the war." The last two sections of his weekly reports amounted to nothing better than denunciations. As Adam Czerniakow had to make his report to the Nazi ghetto commissar every Wednesday, Ganzweich's document served the Germans as a means of verifying whether the Judenrat was faithfully carrying out their orders. Ganzweich boasted that the Gestapo awaited his report with impatience, because they regarded it as the only reliable assessment of what was happening in the ghetto.

For reasons that remain unknown but can easily be guessed, the Nazi Security Service decided that it would be useful to have another agency of treachery and corruption and picked for the role of Ganzweich's competitors two of his lieutenants, Zelik Heller and Maurycy Kon, who had fled to the Warsaw ghetto from Lodz. Kon, who before the war had earned a living as an informer employed by the Polish tax authorities, and Heller separated from Ganzweich in April 1941 and soon proved themselves superior to their master in building up a financial empire. Ganzweich owned a covered market and made vast profits from the licenses for the importation of food into the ghetto given him by the Germans, but Heller and Kon soon outdid him by the size of their transactions. Apart from earning large sums of money by arranging the transfer of Jews from Lodz and, after September 1941, from Bialystok and other ghettoes in the former Soviet territories to the Warsaw ghetto, they obtained from the Germans a monopoly on the import of fish into the ghetto. As a result of their monopoly, fish which they purchased for one zloty a kilogram was sold inside the ghetto for six zlotys. On one occasion they obtained from their Nazi masters a license to import 40 railway truckloads of potatoes for which they paid 40 groszes a kilogram; they sold them at two zlotys a kilogram. Within a year they created a trust controlling thirty enterprises, including the only horse-drawn tram line in the ghetto.

While Ganzweich tried to act as the benefactor and sponsor of Jewish culture in the ghetto by helping financially the ghetto theater and paying a number of writers and artists regular monthly stipends, Kon and Heller devoted large sums of money to the maintenance of religious schools and institutions and extended their protection to many Hassidic rabbis. Before the war the same rabbis had been members of the Agudath Israel Party, which had been notorious for its readiness to collaborate with the most anti-Semitic Polish governments in return for personal or sectarian advantages. In the Warsaw ghetto the same people helped Kon's and Heller's work by telling their numerous followers that the ghetto was not only Lord's punishment for Jewish desertion of orthodoxy and atheism, but a blessing in disguise designed to bring the Jews back to the state of piety and isolation in which they had lived before the French Revolution.[16] As, unlike Bialystok, Vilno or other Jewish ghettoes in Lithuania and Byelorussia, the Hassidic element was relatively numerous in Warsaw, the effect of the views propagated by Kon's and Heller's protégés was most useful to the Nazis, for it helped to create an atmosphere of fatalism.

In the spring of 1942 Ganzweich created a fictitious resistance organization, whose purpose was to counteract the growing resistance movement inside the ghetto by producing confusion and also to discover, by various provocative moves, whether there were any links between the Judenrat and the resistance groups. The fictitious organization called itself *Żagiew (Firebrand)* and claimed to consist of Poles of the Jewish faith, who were faithful followers of Pilsudski and had served in the Polish Army. The ferociously anti-Soviet leaflets distributed in the name of *Żagiew* aimed at preventing the creation of a common front between the left-wing and non-socialist resistance groups in the ghetto.

No doubt convinced that The Thirteen had outlived their usefulness, the Nazis closed the Office for Combating Usury and Blackmarketeering on July 17, 1941. However, they forced the Judenrat to accept 200 of its members in the ghetto police, which made Ringelblum record: "It is justifiably feared that if there are still some honest people left in the ghetto police, they will become completely demoralized."[17] After the disappearance of The Thirteen Ganzweich's chief agency of subversion remained the Ambulance Service.

In April 1942 the Gestapo decided that Ganzweich's presence inside the ghetto was temporarily undesirable and ordered the Judenrat to hang out posters throughout the ghetto announcing that Ganzweich and his right-hand man, Szternfeld, were wanted by the Germans and that anybody who was sheltering them inside the ghetto or knew of their whereabouts but did not report them would be shot. In fact, Ganzweich and his closest collaborators were living safely in the "Aryan" part of Warsaw and continuing to work for the Gestapo. Such was not the case of Kon and Heller, whose usefulness ended during the Great Liquidation. They were both killed on August 4, 1942 in the building of the ghetto police. Ganzweich, however, reappeared in the ghetto after the Great Liquidation, when the Judenrat was ordered by the Gestapo to issue an announcement that there had been a mistake when its posters had described him as a wanted man.

By the end of 1942, aware of the new mood in the ghetto, the Gestapo entrusted Ganzweich with the task of winning over the surviving intellectuals to a policy of preaching fatalistic inactivity. On January 18, 1943, following the first armed act of resistance in the ghetto, Ganzweich invited the intellectual élite to a meeting, at which he proposed the creation of a committee that would undertake the task of saving the scholars, writers and artists. However, not one of the leading ghetto intellectuals turned up, although they were starving and the banquet prepared by Ganzweich's agents had cost 50,000 zlotys—a fabulous sum when one considers that Ganzweich's gift to all the starving intellectuals on his list at Passover 1942 had been 6,000 zlotys.

Having failed with the intellectuals, Ganzweich tried to sabotage the approaching uprising by reviving the Żagiew provocation and by creating an Anti-Soviet League, which the Nazis hoped would divide the Jewish underground as anti-Soviet feelings had divided the Polish resistance movement. The effect of his actions was nil, but Ganzweich remained useful to the Germans for several more months after the destruction of the Warsaw ghetto. According to some reports, he was liquidated by them on November 24, 1943, while according to others he went into hiding and was still being sought by the Gestapo in 1944.

Ganzweich, Kon and Heller and their collaborators together numbered some 500 people and of them only a few dozen were actually Gestapo agents. For a community of over half a million trying to survive in conditions unprecedented in human experience, such a number of traitors and degenerates, many of them former gangsters, thieves and pimps, was therefore not excessive. Among the Gestapo agents in the Warsaw ghetto there was, however, a man who, had he not been born a Jew, might have played the role of a Pétain or a Laval. Born in Lvov in 1864, Alfred Nossig was at first a fervent Polish nationalist and with a group of schoolboys founded in 1880 a periodical called *Ojczyzna (Fatherland)*, in which he preached the need for Jews to become Poles by their speech, way of life and, of course, their absolute loyalty to the cause of Polish freedom. Ten years later, Nossig, by then realizing that most Poles did not want the Jews to become Poles, emerged as the leader of the Zionist youth in Galicia.[18]

By the outbreak of the First World War Dr. Alfred Nossig's intellectual achievements and political activities had been so varied as to earn him more than a column in the eleventh volume of *Yevreiskaya Entsiklopediya* published in 1913. A student of law and natural sciences at Lvov University, a graduate in philosophy at Zurich University and a student of medicine at Vienna University, Nossig, to quote the encyclopaedia, had become famous by 1910 as "a playwright, poet, philosophical writer, political economist, sociologist, painter, drama critic and sculptor." The encyclopaedia recorded his works as two dramas, a volume of poetry and a libretto for an opera by Paderewski in the Polish language; four dramas in the German language; five works of a sociological and political nature on such problems as the agrarian question in Europe, socialism, world peace and social hygiene; three studies and a num-

Alfred Nossig
(1864–1943)

Abraham Ganzweich
(1904–?)

Emanuel Ringelblum
(1900–1944)

Dr. Ignacy (Isaac) Schipper
(1884–1943)

Henryk Iwański "Major Bystry"
(1901–1978)

Wiktoria Iwański

ber of articles on art, drama and aesthetics; a work on Spinoza's ethics; four studies dealing with statistical aspects of Jewish history; seven titles on Zionist subjects; and a number of sculptures on Biblical and other themes. As though this were not enough for one man, in 1903 Nossig organized in Berlin the Society for Jewish Statistical Studies and in 1906 the Society for Encouraging Jewish Art. In 1908 he founded the General Jewish Colonization Organization in Berlin and in 1911 the Orient Colonization Company in London—two organizations which propagated a non-Zionist territorial solution of the Jewish problem. It is also of interest that Sombart quoted Nossig's writings in his work *Die Juden und das Wirtschaftsleben* in support of his own racialist explanation of the Jewish role as bearers of capitalism throughout human history.

At the Ninth Zionist Congress in 1909 Nossig was publicly disowned by the president of the Zionist Organization and the delegates were warned to have nothing to do with the unauthorized activities of that "Jewish adventurer," as the Zionist historian Leonard Stein refers to him.[19] Nossig appeared in Constantinople soon after the Young Turks' Revolution with a plan for settling Jews both in Palestine and Mesopotamia under the auspices of his General Jewish Colonization Organization in Berlin. As in no part of the Turkish Empire were British and German imperial interests closer to the point of collision than in Mesopotamia, the British in Constantinople became convinced that Nossig was a German agent scheming, in the words of Sir Gerard Lowther, the British Ambassador there, to form a Jewish-Turkish alliance for the purpose of creating a pro-German state in Mesopotamia. Since the British in Constantinople, and *The Times* in London, already held that powerful Jewish interest were working to undermine the British position in the Arab world, Nossig's activities did great damage to the Zionist cause in London.[20] The British suspicions that Nossig was a German agent appear to have been justified, for during the First World War he again appeared in Constantinople where he unsuccessfully attempted to influence Henry M. Morgenthau, the United States Ambassador, to prevent the truth about the monstrous Turkish massacres of the Armenians becoming known in the United States.[21]

After the First World War Nossig engaged in pacifist activities and in 1928 founded a Jewish branch of the Peace Federation of the Religions. He returned to Poland after the victory of Nazism in Germany and found himself in the Warsaw ghetto at the age of seventy-six. Whether he volunteered to act as a Gestapo agent or whether the Nazis knew of his links with the German intelligence services and forced him to become their agent, we do not know. But there is no doubt that he worked for the Germans until February 22, 1943, the day when he was killed by three members of the Jewish Fighting Organization,[22] who were informed of his Gestapo connections by the Polish underground. His effectiveness as a Gestapo agent can only be surmised, but it is a fact that unlike Ganzweich, Kon and Heller his connections with the Germans remained unknown even to such a penetrating and well-informed observer as Ringelblum.

III

Such were the objective conditions in which the resistance groups had to work in the Warsaw ghetto. But they also had to contend with and overcome a subjective barrier that the resistance organizations in Minsk, Vilno and even in Bialystok did not face. The resistance organizations in those three cities were built by people who very early realized the nature of the Nazi plans with regard to Jews because of the unprecedented massacres and atrocities that happened before their very eyes. But until the summer of 1942 the horrors of the Warsaw ghetto were of a different dimension. The number of Warsaw Jews actually murdered by Germans until the Great Liquidation ran into hundreds and not into tens of thousands as was the case in Vilno or Minsk. Therefore, even to the most pessimistic Jews in the Warsaw ghetto the German aims in 1940 and 1941 appeared to be the extermination of the greatest possible number of Jews through hunger and disease. Against such plans it was natural to react by a determination to survive at all costs and to avoid all actions that could give the enemy an excuse for mass executions under the guise of collective reprisals.

That the Germans would exterminate millions of defenseless civilians by mass shootings and gas-chambers was something that no sane Jew in the Warsaw ghetto could envisage, let alone foresee, in 1940 and even in 1941. Thus, when in November 1941 the

Germans for the first time executed first two Jews and then another batch of eight Jews caught on the "Aryan" side of the ghetto walls where they had been searching for food, Ringelblum recorded on November 22: "The death sentences carried out on eight Jews, including six women, have shocked the entire city of Warsaw. We have experienced all kinds of things in Warsaw and other cities, in particular in Lithuania, where mass executions are taking place, but they all pall when compared with the fact that the eight people were shot for having left the ghetto."[23] When we consider that Ringelblum was one of the best informed persons in the Warsaw ghetto and that at the time when he made his entry the Einsatzgruppen, their local auxiliaries, the Wehrmacht and the Rumanians had for five months been busy exterminating the Jews in the seized Soviet territories, we realize how little the Jews imprisoned in the Warsaw ghetto knew of, or suspected, the fate that Hitler and his accomplices had prepared for them.

The first reliable reports of the Nazi methods of total annihilation were brought to the Warsaw ghetto by the emissaries from Vilno. Edek Boraks, Solomon Entin, Israel Kempner and Pińczewski were the first to reach Warsaw at the end of December 1941. They were followed in January 1942 by the sisters Sarah and Roza Zilber, who took with them eyewitness accounts of the massacres carried out in Lithuania and Byelorussia and the appeal of the United Partisan Organization (FPO) calling for armed resistance. The sisters were followed by Khaya Grosman, Tamara Sznajderman, Arye Wilner and Tenenbaum, who succeeded in meeting representatives of the most important political groups in the ghetto. What they had to tell was at first received by the older Jewish leaders with utter disbelief; when the facts could no longer be denied, they and others argued that the Germans could commit such crimes in occupied Soviet territories, but not in the General-Government and certainly not in Warsaw, one of Europe's capital cities, where the murder of half a million people could not be carried out without being noticed by the civilized world.

In February 1942 three men who had miraculously escaped being gassed at Chełmno[23a] arrived in Warsaw and brought news that 80,000 Jews from the Polish territories incorporated in the Reich and several hundred Gypsies from Bessarabia had been gassed there in November and December 1941. "The Warsaw ghetto did not believe in the reports," Marek Edelman, one of the leaders of the Warsaw Ghetto Uprising, recalled. "All who clung to life would not believe that their lives could be taken from them in such a manner. Only the organized youth, who had been carefully watching the growing German terror, accepted the likelihood and truthfulness of the reports and decided to carry out a large-scale propaganda campaign in order to acquaint the mass of the people with what was happening."[24]

At the end of April 1942 survivors from Lublin brought the news that the Lublin community of some 40,000 Jews had been liquidated in a few days and that the same fate had befallen the numerous provincial ghettoes in the region. Dr. David Wdowiński, the leader of the Revisionist organization in the ghetto, took two survivors to Adam Czerniakow to give him an eyewitness account of what they had seen in Lublin. But the head of the Judenrat reassured Wdowiński that he had the assurance of Governor-General Frank that three large ghettoes, in Warsaw, Radom and Cracow, would remain. Wdowiński then went with the terrible news to several Zionist leaders of his own generation only to be told by Dr. Isaac Schipper, the famous historian, that "It is impossible to liquidate a population of half a million souls. The Germans will not dare to exterminate the largest Jewish community in Europe. And, finally, there is the assurance of Governor-General Frank that Warsaw, Radom and Cracow will remain."[25]

Such was the great psychological barrier that the bearers of the truth that Jews had only the alternatives of dying with dignity or like trapped animals had to overcome. The work of building first a resistance movement and finally two military organizations devoted to the single aim of an armed revolt was carried out mostly by teenagers and people in their twenties belonging to four political groups: the Bund, the Zionist youth organizations ranging from the right-wing Revisionists to the extreme left-wing Hashomer Hatzair, and the Communists. As everywhere else in Poland, the most important role in bringing the hostile political groups together and building a unified resistance organization was played by the left-wing Zionists and, in particular, by Hashomer Hatzair.

Without a minimum amount of contact with the resistance movement outside the ghetto walls and some help from it, even if it amounted to little more than moral support, no resistance inside the city-ghettoes was possible. This was the chief reason why the Lodz ghetto, completely isolated in a city dominated and terrorized by a large German minority, could not produce an armed resistance organization despite the unique revolutionary traditions of its Jewish proletariat. On the other hand, in Warsaw, the political heart of Poland, the Jewish resistance movement received the support not only of the militarily weak Communists, but of three small but influential Polish resistance organizations and a number of noble individuals, who played a crucial part in making the Home Army Command provide the Jewish Fighting Organization with some arms.

IV

The first to establish links with the Polish resistance movement were the Revisionists and the Bundists.

The Revisionists had the very good fortune to establish relations of personal friendship with Henryk Iwański, a reserve captain in the Polish Army, as early as the end of 1939. Although a native of Warsaw, Iwański has taken part in the three Polish uprisings in Silesia in the years 1919–21 and therefore had to go into hiding as soon as the Germans occupied Warsaw. Under the name of Herbert Bystry he became the administrator of St. Stanislaw's Infectious Diseases Hospital in the Wola District of Warsaw, and as the Germans avoided entering hospitals dealing with epidemic diseases, his post provided him with excellent opportunities for underground activities. Both Iwański and his wife Wiktoria were deeply religious people without the bigotry that was all too common among Polish Catholics and as they had never had any sympathy with the pro-German policies pursued by Rydz-Śmigły and Beck, they became loyal supporters of Sikorski. Within months of the German conquest of Warsaw, Iwański organized a group of like-minded former participants in the Silesian uprisings, which subsequently became part of the Security Corps (Korpus Bezpieczeństwa or KB), which was commanded by Colonel Andrzej Petrykowski, whose *nom de guerre* was Tarnawa.

Petrykowski took a special interest in Iwański's assistance to Jews, no doubt because he himself was of Jewish origins—he was related to Nakhum Sokolow, the famous Zionist leader[26]—and in January 1941 made it officially part of the duties of Iwański's unit. Petrykowski and Iwański could act as they did because it was only in the autumn of 1942 that the Security Corps became officially part of the Home Army and it was only several months later, at the beginning of 1943, that it was actually incorporated in it. Its duties were to provide a cadre for the security forces to be organized in the German territories incorporated in Poland after Germany's defeat and as such it enjoyed a great deal of independence. No doubt because of the intelligence work carried out by the Security Corps, which made its leaders and members among the best informed men in the Polish underground, the organization found itself increasingly estranged from the Home Army Command after Sikorski's death and after the Warsaw Uprising Petrykowski and his men joined the Committee of National Liberation in Lublin.

It was in November 1939, when the Germans issued a decree ordering the registration of Polish reserve officers, that Iwański's Jewish acquaintances, David Mordecai (Moryc) Apfelbaum, Henryk Lipszyc, Bialoskura and Kalman Mendelson, asked his advice on what they should do. The four Jews, who held the ranks of reserve lieutenants or second lieutenants, told him that they and their friends wanted to join the Polish resistance movement. Iwański was unable to bring them into what was to become the Home Army and advised them to create their own organization. They did so and founded an underground organization, which they called *Świt (The Dawn)*. In January 1940 Iwański gave the Jews 29 VIS (Polish Colt) pistols and followed them up with a few more arms and some ammunition at the end of the month.[27] The organization did not engage in any military activities, but with the help of Iwański and his group it ran two shelters in the ghetto, which their Polish friend and patron helped to supply with bread, flour, fats and porridge.

After a few weeks the organization changed its name from *Świt* to the Jewish Military Union (Żydowski Związek Wojskowy or ŻZW) and at the beginning of 1942 it reached under Apfelbaum's leadership a strength of forty members organized in eight five-man teams. Although by then it had ceased to be an exclusively Revisionist organization and even had Communists as members, the ŻZW nevertheless remained a small clandestine group without any record of armed resistance. Consequently, it exerted very little influence on the shaping of the underground resistance movement in the ghetto.

In 1942, when the second PLAN was formed by a group of Polish radicals, Pawel Frenkel, one of the ŻZW leaders, established close links with Captain Cezary Ketling, one of the leaders of the organization. Why PLAN should have made assistance to Jews an integral part of its anti-German activities is of special interest, for the story of PLAN throws light also on other aspects of the resistance movement in the Warsaw ghetto.

The origins of PLAN (Polska Ludowa Akcja Niepodległościowa or the Polish People's Independence Action) go back to 1936–8, when after Pilsudski's death the openly fascist, anti-Semitic and pro-German elements led by Rydz-Śmigly and Beck took over the leadership of the Sanacja created by Pilsudski and transformed it into the OZN. Under Pilsudski, the Sanacja had been a conglomeration of various elements, including people who still believed that Pilsudski symbolized the radical and freedom-loving ideals, for which Polish freedom fighters had fought and died throughout the nineteenth century on many of the battlefields and behind most of the revolutionary barricades of Europe. In October 1937 these radical and romantic elements—a few hundred people all told—left the OZN and set up Democratic Clubs, which at the beginning of 1938 became the Democratic Party. The new party protested against the chauvinism, anti-Semitism and pro-Nazi policies of the OZN, called for an alliance with the Western Democracies against the Nazi menace and gave its support to Republican Spain, while a radical section called for a common front of all anti-fascist forces in Poland, including the Communists.

The example of their elders was followed by a group of young intellectuals, mostly university students, who left the youth organizations run by the OZN and with money provided by former leaders of the Sanacja, who had now become opponents of Rydz-Śmigly and his clique, founded the monthly *Orka (The Ploughing Time)* at the beginning of 1938. The monthly, which was edited by a handful of talented young people, among them several polonized Jews, proved a success and soon became a weekly called *Orka na Ugorze (Ploughing the Fallow Lands)*. In its first issue *Orka* quoted from an article written by Pilsudski forty years earlier, in which he had condemned Polish anti-Semitism, and as time went on it became increasingly radical. The authorities dealt with the critics who had come from their own camp by increasingly frequent confiscations, and when the weekly was on the point of collapse, offered to finance it on condition that the editors would undertake to combat "Communist influences" among Polish students. The editors refused and closed the weekly in March 1939.[28]

A number of the young intellectuals involved in the publication of *Orka na Ugorze* also belonged to KIMB, i.e., the Circle of Scoutmasters named after Mieczyslaw Bem (Koło Instruktorów imienia Mieczyslawa Bema). The creator of this unique circle was Juliusz Dąbrowski, whose father, Jan Dąbrowski, had been one of the organizers of the military organization of the Polish Socialist Party during the 1905 Revolution. Brought up as a socialist, Juliusz Dąbrowski found it impossible to accept that the Polish Boy Scout and Girl Guide movement should be controlled by the Catholic clergy and members of the right-wing and anti-Semitic National Party, in whose hands it had become an instrument for educating a very large proportion of Polish youth in a spirit of Catholic bigotry, chauvinism, militarism and anti-Semitism.

In 1931 Pilsudski's party wrested the control of the Boy Scout and Girl Guide movement from the hands of the Endecja and this led to a momentary liberalization, which allowed Dąbrowski and his like-minded scoutmaster-friends in Warsaw to form KIMB. In 1935 KIMB presented an aide-mémoire to the leadership of the movement asking for more democracy in the running the Polish Scout Union, the education of Boy Scouts and Girl Guides in an anti-militarist and humanitarian spirit, measures for combating anti-Semitism and chauvinism which were rampant in the movement, and the curtailment of the excessive role played by Catholic priests. As part of their fight against racialism and anti-Semitism, KIMB and their friends, including Aleksander Kamiński, a member of the Polish Scout Organization Headquarters, called for the creation of mixed Polish-Jewish troops, but after a long struggle only won the concession to form a number of segregated Jewish troops in Warsaw and Cracow, which although formally part of the movement, in fact remained without contacts with their Polish fellow-scouts.

The influence of the KIMB group on the education of the mass of 100,000 youths in the Polish Scout Union remained virtually nil, but where it was exerted, it affected Polish-Jewish relations. Thus in Vilno Antoni Wasilewski, the scoutmaster of the Black Thirteen Troop, was to demonstrate how much could be done in prewar Poland by a noble and courageous man determined to bring up young people against the current ideas of Jew-hatred and racialist madness. A Catholic influenced by the ideas of Jacques Maritain rather than those of Maurras, Chesterton or Belloc, Wasilewski did not hesitate to publish an article in the local *Słowo*, one of the two monarchist papers in Poland, in which he exposed the anti-Semitic activities of the Catholic clergy and called for less clerical influence in the Scout movement.[29] Influenced by Wasilewski, two local Girl Guides, Irena Adamowicz and Jadwiga Dudziec, both practicing and devout Catholics, became deeply involved in the work and ideology of the atheist Hashomer Hatzair and when the Nazis occupied their country, Adamowicz acted as a courier between the Jewish resistance organization in the Warsaw ghetto and the ghettoes of Vilno, Kaunas and Šiauliai, while Dudziec brought arms into the Vilno ghetto and saved a number of Jewish children.

Within weeks of Poland's fall, the KIMB and *Orka na Ugorze* groups formed, unknown to each other, two resistance organizations.[30] Among the ten men and women of the *Orka na Ugorze* group who founded PLAN, three—Andrzej Kott, Jan Sterling and Gustaw Herling-Grudziński—were Jews within the terms of Nazi legislation, even if they themselves did not regard themselves as Jews. In the second half of November 1939 Juliusz Dąbrowski and his group of about 100 members joined PLAN and among the leaders he brought with him were several more polonized Jews, including Andrzej Tuwim, a nephew of the great poet, Jolanta Forelle, whose father committed suicide when the Germans issued their first anti-Jewish decrees, and Stanislaw Bornstein, the nephew of a well-known Jewish psychologist.

PLAN was not only one of the first underground organizations to emerge in occupied Warsaw, but also the first Polish underground organization in the city to engage in actual acts of resistance against the Nazis. This was primarily the work of Andrzej Kott, the son of a Jewish optician who had left Judaism for Protestantism.[31] Right from the beginning of the organization, Kott insisted that its activities must not be confined to anti-German propaganda but assume the character of sabotage actions against German military transports and fuel dumps. According to Kazimierz Koźniewski, Kott's friend and one of the leaders of PLAN, Andrzej Kott was "a tall, strongly built dark young man with a slightly Negroid type of manly good looks."[32] Although baptized, he refused to study in Warsaw University in order not to have to witness the humiliation of Jewish students forced to occupy special Jewish benches and, against his parents' wishes, left for Liverpool to continue his studies there. At the outbreak of the war he returned to Poland via Sweden and Latvia, took part in the September Campaign and later became one of the organizers of PLAN, where he was put in charge of the fighting organization.[33]

The first anti-German slogans on the walls of Warsaw—they were pasted over Nazi decrees—were Kott's work. He and his men followed it up with the throwing of tear-gas bombs into a Polish cinema screening Nazi propaganda films and a dance hall mainly attended by Polish collaborators. Kott also organized the killing of Igo Sym, a popular Polish film star who had become a German agent. However, the Gestapo soon succeeded in placing a Polish traitor in the ranks of the organization and before Kott could pass to sabotage actions against German troop trains, he and most of the PLAN leaders were arrested on January 14, 1940. Although savagely beaten, Kott managed to escape from the Gestapo headquarters in Szuch Avenue—the only known case of escape from it—and made his way to Lvov, where he was arrested by the NKVD and disappeared without trace in the depths of the Soviet Union. As reprisal for Kott's escape and the activities of PLAN, the Germans executed several dozen Poles and 250 Jews, most of them well known intellectuals and professional people.[34]

Such were the antecedents of the Second PLAN, which next to Major Iwański's Security Corps was to prove itself the chief ally of the Revisionist Jewish Military Organization. How far the members of PLAN, who had all been brought up on the hero-worship of Pilsudski, had moved away from their original loyalties can be judged from the fact that in the 1944 Warsaw Uprising their unit did not fight as part of the Home Army.

In theory at least, the Bund organization inside the Warsaw ghetto was in the best position to establish contacts with the Polish underground because of its close prewar links with the Polish Socialist Party (PPS). In practice, the illusions and delusions of the Bund leaders on this matter were the cause of a tragic and fatal policy.

When during Passover 1940 Luftwaffe troops organized a pogrom against the Jews and led gangs of Polish hooligans, whom they paid four zlotys for a day's work, into the Jewish districts, the Bund was the only Jewish organization to react. Its militia struck back on the fourth day of the pogrom and fought four big street battles in Solna, Krochmalna, Karmelicka and Niska Streets.[35] After the creation of the ghetto, the demand for underground activities aimed at creating a resistance organization came mostly from *Tsukunft* (The Future), the party's youth organization, but in their demands for a single Jewish resistance organization the young Bundists met with the stubborn opposition of their leaders Maurycy Orzech and Abrasza Blum.

The apparently incomprehensible attitude of the *Bund* leaders can only be understood if one is familiar with the history of the wartime Polish socialist movement. On September 26, 1939 the leaders of the PPS who had remained in Warsaw decided to disband their party for the duration of the German occupation and announced their decision in posters pasted all over the city. The decision was not accepted by the rank-and-file and rejected by the provincial organizations and the left-wing elements in the party, which before the war had been pressing against the wishes of their leaders for a People's Front against Poland's fascist rulers. This led to the creation in 1940 of a central body with the clumsy name of the Central Direction of the Movement of the Working Masses of the Towns and Villages—Freedom, Equality, Independence or WRN for short (Centralne Kierownictwo Ruchu Mas Pracujących Miast i Wsi — Wolność, Równość, Niepodległość). The leaders of WRN, Tomasz Arciszewski, Zygmunt Zaremba and Kazimierz Pużak, held that the Soviet Union threatened the Polish people as much as Hitler's Germany and therefore found themselves allied with the remnants of the OZN, which under Rydz-Śmigly and Beck had prepared Poland's catastrophe, in order to oppose Sikorski's policy of seeking an understanding with Moscow. The effect of such an alliance on the PPS leaders' attitude to Jewish demands for arms and the entire problem of Polish resistance against the Nazis can be easily understood. Unfortunately, to the Bund leaders imprisoned inside the Warsaw ghetto, who were largely unaware of what was happening in the Polish underground, this was not obvious.

The various PPS groups opposing the policies of their WRN leadership rallied around Norbert Barlicki, Stanisław Dubois, Adam Kuryłowicz, Stanisław Chudoba, Adam Próchnik, Edward Osóbka and others, who published the illegal *Barykada Wolności (Barricade of Freedom)*. The leaders of the Barricade of Freedom faction were Marxists who argued that the Soviet Union was a country where the revolution had been betrayed and whose economic system did not in essence differ from the system of state monopolies in Nazi Germany. They also believed that as a result of the war Britain and the United States would end up with similar systems, and consequently they regarded the Second World War as an imperialist war pure and simple, which would be brought to an end by revolutions in Germany and in Great Britain. As a result of the revolutions in Western Europe, there would follow revolutions elsewhere and the outcome would be the creation of the United Socialist States of Europe.[36]

The Barricade of Freedom faction made several attempts to come to an understanding with the WRN faction and recreate a single Polish Socialist Party. However, after the Nazi attack on the Soviet Union the Barricade of Freedom faction declared its support for Sikorski's policy of treating the Soviet Union as Poland's ally, while the WRN leaders adopted an even more right-wing course that allied them with Sikorski's right-wing enemies. This led to the Barricade of Freedom faction forming the *Organization of Polish Socialists* in September 1941. As the Polish Socialists became the chief allies of the Bund, it is instructive to know that at their political conference held in Warsaw in April 1942, the leaders of the Polish Socialists forecast that 1942 would see the last stage of the war and that one of the causes of Germany's collapse would be an internal revolution, which would be only one in a chain of revolutions spreading even to Britain's dominions and colonies. A year later, in April 1943, the leaders of the Polish Socialists again met in Warsaw and decided, among other things, that as a result of "the Anglo-Soviet compromise" the creation of a socialist Poland could only be ensured after Germany's defeat by the establishment of a

Maurycy Orzech "Janczyn"
(1891–1943)

Abraham Blum
(1906–1943)

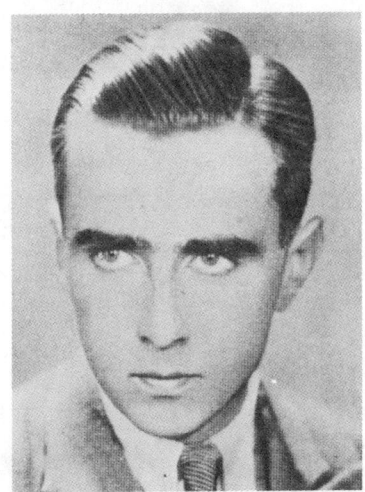
Leszek Raabe
(1913–1943)

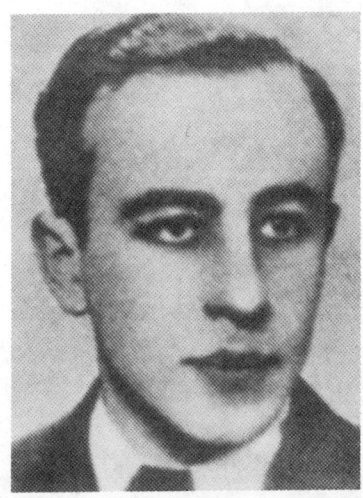
Pinkus Kartin "Andrzej Szmidt" "Piotr Karski"
(1912–1942)

Joseph Lewartowski "Finkelstein," Josyf
(1896–1942)

Mordecai Anielewicz
(1919–1943)

Isaac Zuckerman "Antek"
(b. 1914)

Mordecai Tenenbaum-Tamaroff
(1916–1943)

Schachno Efroim Sagan
(1892–1942)

Hirsh Berlinski
(1908–1944)

Joseph Kaplan
(1913–1942)

Johanan Morgenstern
(1905–1943)

Zalman Frydrych "Zygmunt"
(1911–1943)

Zofia Kossak
(1890–1968)

Dr. Adolf Abraham Berman "Borowski"
(1906–1978)

Dr. Leon Feiner "Mikolaj"
(1886–1945)

European Socialist Federation. They therefore rejected all cooperation with the Polish Workers' Party and decided to create the Polish Socialist Workers' Party (Robotnicza Partia Polskich Socjalistów or RPPS), which was to unite all left-wing non-Communist groups.[37] Nonetheless, a year later the RPPS joined the Communists. The almost complete absence of political realism displayed by the leaders of the Polish Socialists had a fatal influence on the actions of the Bund leaders.

The Bund leaders tried to maintain friendly relations with both the WRN and Polish Socialists. But they completely failed to obtain assistance in arms from the military organization of the WRN, which was one of the first to accept subordination to the orders of the Home Army Command. However, when in the autumn of 1941 the Polish Socialists created in Warsaw their own small military organization under the command of Leszek Raabe, the Bund formed an equivalent organization in the ghetto, which had to confine itself to training with dummy rifles and revolvers while waiting for promised arms.[38]

On the orders of Stalin, who distrusted both the leadership and the rank-and-file of the Polish Communist Party, the Cominform had dissolved the party in 1938. Although more than ever isolated, distrusted and hated by the overwhelming majority of Poles as a result of the Molotov-Ribbentrop pact, the former members of the Polish Communist Party and their sympathizers began to rebuild their party in 1940 by banding together in a number of clandestine organizations, of which the most important were the Sickle and Hammer, the Society of Friends of the USSR, the Freedom Struggle Organization and the Workers and Peasants' Combat Organization. All these organizations had their equivalents in the Warsaw ghetto, even though Jewish Communists were deprived of their leaders, most of whom had fled east of the Bug after September 1939.

It was not until Hitler's attack on the Soviet Union that Stalin gave his consent to the rebuilding of the Polish Communist Party. After a period of indoctrination in a school run by the Comintern, Marceli Nowotko, Paweł Finder, Andrzej Szmidt (whose real name was Pinkhas Kartin), Czesław Skoniecki, Maria Rutkiewicz and

Bolesław Mołojec* were dropped by parachute near Warsaw on December 27, 1941, and, together with a second party which was parachuted a week later, they founded the Polish Workers' Party on January 5, 1942.[39] The first directing body of the party was a triumvirate consisting of Marceli Nowotko, the Party Secretary, Paweł Finder and Bolesław Mołojec. On November 28, 1942 Nowotko was shot dead by Zygmunt Mołojec, Bolesław Mołojec's brother; a party court found Bolesław Mołojec guilty of conspiring with his brother to commit the assassination and both were sentenced to die and executed. The Jew Paweł Finder then became the party secretary and Władysław Gomułka and Franciszek Jóźwiak became his deputies. Consequently, during the Warsaw Ghetto Uprising the Polish Workers' Party had a Jew as its leader. It was after Finder's arrest by the Gestapo on November 14, 1943 that Gomułka became the party secretary.

Fully aware that Jews had always formed one of the most reliable and devoted elements in the party, the leaders of the Polish Workers' Party at once proceeded to create a party organization in the Warsaw ghetto. Joseph Lewartowski, a veteran Communist leader, Adam Meretik, whose real name was Samuel Zimmerman, and Jacob Drejer were summoned from the Bialystok ghetto for work in the Warsaw ghetto, where Lawartowski became the party plenipotentiary. In March 1942 Lewartowski succeeded in uniting the various Communist groups into one organization and Andrzej Szmidt, a former captain in the International Brigades who acted as a wireless operator for the leadership of the Polish Workers' Party, entered the ghetto and began to organize a People's Guard detachment.[40]

It was through Robb-Narbutt[40a] that the left-wing Zionists in the Warsaw ghetto established their first contacts with the Polish Workers' Party.[41] Before meeting Lewartowski, Szmidt and other representatives of the Polish Workers' Party, the only contacts Hashomer Hatzair, Dror and Hekhalutz had had with the outside Polish world were through Irena Adamowicz and a few members of the pre-war KIMB group. These contacts were later to prove of

---

* Bolesław Mołojec at one time commanded the Polish Jarosław Dąbrowski Battalion in the International Brigades.

vital importance in securing the limited assistance in arms from the Home Army. In March 1942, however, Tenenbaum-Tamarof and the other left-wing Zionist leaders began their work of creating a united Jewish fighting organization by coming together with the Communists.[42]

What brought the left-wing Zionists and the Jewish Communists together was that they both believed that the Jews imprisoned in the Warsaw ghetto and other ghettoes must join in the Europewide struggle against Nazi Germany by organizing massive resistance, and that they must make their fighting contribution to the general resistance movement not only as individuals but as a people. Moreover, the left-wing Zionists, unlike the Bund and the Revisionists, regarded the Soviet Union as the most important member of the anti-Nazi coalition and as a natural ally of the Jews. This attitude was strikingly demonstrated when at the news of the Nazi attack on Russia Mordecai Anielewicz and his Hashomer Hatzair comrades stopped working in workshops and factories contributing to the German war effort.[43] The June 7, 1942 issue of Hashomer Hatzair's *Der Oifbroi* (The Ferment) expressed this community of aims in very clear terms:

> The heroic struggle of the Red Army is inspiring all the peoples oppressed by the Nazis in their struggle for liberation.... The signal has been given by the Red Army, the army that has given the struggle against Hitler's fascism its true meaning. It has inspired the European underground with a new spirit and a new soul.... The bloody mass terror practiced by the Nazis has imposed on the Jewish masses a passivity that assumes the form of Jews going to their death like sheep to slaughter. The Jewish masses have not yet rid themselves of their distrust of their own fighting capabilities and given up the hope of salvation coming from outside. Such a state of mind must not last at a time when from the fjords of Norway to the suburbs of Paris, from the mountains of Serbia to the factories of Czechoslovakia, the liberation army is consolidating and growing. Within the limited possibilities of the ghettoes we must prepare the ground for a revolutionary Jewish deed. From Jewish pain and sufferings there must grow up the strength that together with all the revolutionary forces in Europe and the backing of the Red Army will rise to fight against Nazi slavery...

V

It was in March 1942 that the leaders of the Communists and left-wing Zionists first met in Warsaw. The Polish Workers' Party was represented by Lewartowski, Szmidt and Meretik; the left-wing Zionists sent as their representatives Mordecai Anielewicz and Joseph Kaplan of Hashomer Hatzair, Isaac Zuckerman and Mordecai Tenenbaum of Dror, Shakhno Ephraim Sagan and Hirsh Berlinski of the Left Poale Zion, and Joseph Sak and Lazar Lewin of the Right Poale Zion. The outcome of the meeting was the decision to form the Anti-Fascist Bloc, which the leaders saw as the nucleus of an organization uniting all the parties and elements in the Warsaw ghetto that were determined actively to resist the Nazis. Consequently, a few days later they made an attempt to bring in the Bund. As the Bund leaders refused to have any dealings with the Polish Workers' Party, the conference which took place in the last days of March was between Hirsh Berlinski and Meilakh Feinkind of the Left Poale Zion, Lazar Lewin and Yokhanan Morgensztern of the Right Poale Zion and Isaac Zuckerman of Dror on the one side, and Maurice Orzech and Abraham Blum of the Bund on the other.

In words remarkably reminiscent of those used by the Bundist leader Herman Kruk in his diary written in the Vilno ghetto,* Orzech stated his party's position:[44] "If it were not for the accursed ghetto conditions, we should not be sitting here at the same table. This could happen only in the ghetto. But the ghetto is not an isolated world, the destruction of the ghetto walls depends on outside political factors. The Bund is closely linked with international political factors, whose decisions are valid and binding for the Bund. Therefore the Bund cannot belong to a body whose tactics may differ from the general tactics of the party. The Bund has its own fighting groups. The other parties also have their own fighting groups. From an organizational point of view the creation of a joint organization would be harmful, for it would lead to complete deconspiration. The Bund fighting groups will not reveal to the gen-

---

* See Reuben Ainsztein, *Jewish Resistance in Nazi-occupied Eastern Europe*, p. 490.

eral military organization their forms and methods of struggle, because they are a military secret. In view of these factors the Bund will not join the common military organization."

Thus the Bund leaders still deluded themselves that there was a unity of interest and an underlying solidarity of action between Polish workers belonging to the divided Polish Socialist Party and the Jewish members of the Bund in the ghetto and, which was quite unforgivable, still refused to admit that the situation of the Jews was essentially different from that of the Poles.

In less than two months the Anti-Fascist Bloc had a combat organization of some 500 members organized in five-man units—but it was an organization without a single firearm in its possession. The chief instructors of the combat units were Szmidt, Tenenbaum, Fiszelson and Anielewicz, but Szmidt was the only one of the four to have had experience in commanding men in battle, while Anielewicz, who had been too young to serve with the Polish Army, owed his knowledge of military matters to what he had learnt in his school paramilitary training unit. At the end of May Szmidt, together with his party comrades Meretik and David Włosko, fell into the hands of the Gestapo as a result of the betrayal by Kisielew, a member of the Polish Workers' Party. In September 1942 the Gestapo arrested Joseph Kaplan and in November 1942 Tenenbaum left for Bialystok, so that Anielewicz became the natural choice for the position of commander of the Jewish Fighting Organization.

Searching for the slightest opening to join in the armed struggle against the Germans, the leaders of the Anti-Fascist Bloc eagerly seized the opportunity of joining the partisan units of the People's Guard, which was brought to them by Robb-Narbutt, one of its organizers. The first People's Guard detachment from the Polish part of Warsaw had left for the forests on May 15, 1942. At the end of August, at the height of the Great Liquidation, the first forty-strong partisan group composed of members of Hashomer Hatzair, Dror, Hanoar Hazioni and Akiba left for the Międzyrzec forests in the Biała Podlaska area. With only a few firearms and without any guerrilla experience and local allies, the group assembled in the Międzyrzec ghetto before setting out for the forests. But before they could do so, the ghetto was surrounded by Germans and Ukrainians who had come to liquidate it and most of the group were seized with the rest of the Jews. Of those who managed to reach the forests, only a few survived to join up with escaped Soviet prisoners of war and form a partisan unit. Equally tragic was the fate of another group of forty Hekhalutz members who set out for the Hrubieszów forests in the Lublin region. Some fell into the hands of the Germans on their way from Warsaw to Hrubieszów; of a unit of eighteen fighters who followed at the beginning of September, only one, Munik Sztajngold, escaped when they were ambushed in a village. The main detachment was attacked by the Germans and their henchmen and wiped out before they had had the time to establish a base and contacts with the few friendly partisan groups in the area. But a third group, composed mostly of members of the Polish Workers' Party and commanded by Gershon Alef-Bolkowiak, which left the ghetto at the end of August, was luckier. It moved from its original base to the Radom area, survived two attacks by German punitive forces and reorganized in the Mińsk Mazowiecki area.[45]

Informed by their agents of the changing mood in the ghetto, the Germans started a campaign of terror aimed at preventing the organization of an underground movement. On the night of 17 to 18 of April 1942 the Gestapo rounded up fifty-two Jews, killed them by pistol shots in the back of their heads and left their bodies lying in the streets. The victims were mostly printers, people known to have written for the underground press, trade union leaders and, to create confusion, ten members of Ganzweich's organization. The massacre was followed by the daily killings of ten to fifteen people, which went on until July 22. The victims were shot or hurled out of upper-floor windows and left in the streets to terrify the ghetto inhabitants. One of the effects of the terror was to interrupt the activities of the Anti-Fascist Bloc and the Bund because, although the victims belonged to every social group and included smugglers, merchants, workers and members of the intelligentsia, the members of the resistance groups had every reason to fear that they were known to the Gestapo. They therefore went into hiding and thus contacts between them were broken, which meant that they were unable to act collectively.

Assessed in cold, realistic terms, the Anti-Fascist Bloc from the moment of its creation until July 22, the beginning of the Great Liquidation, failed in its two most important tasks: the organization did not manage to obtain arms and it failed to convince the mass of the ghetto inhabitants that their only choice was to die fighting. Of course, the double failure was not the fault of the Anti-Fascist Bloc leaders, who did their best to overcome impossible obstacles. But to convince some 380,000 people that within the next few months they would be exterminated in gas-chambers without even possessing the knowledge of Treblinka was both practically and psychologically an impossibility for a group of anonymous people whom both the Judenrat and the two agencies of treason and subversion operated by Ganzweich, Kon and Heller described as provocateurs. As for arms, the only ally the Anti-Fascist Bloc had outside the walls was the Polish Workers' Party, which hardly had any arms itself. Nor was the Bund more successful in its attempts to acquire arms, even though it maintained contacts with the Polish Socialists and the Polish Socialist Party, which formed part of the Home Army. At the end of April 1942 the Polish Socialists promised their Jewish comrades 100 revolvers, several dozen rifles and a quantity of grenades, but did not deliver a single promised weapon.[46]

Thus, apart from the Revisionist ŻZW counting some fifty members armed with a couple of dozen pistols or revolvers, there was no *armed* resistance organization in the ghetto when on July 22, 1942 the Germans began the Great Liquidation. From the middle of July rumors, which could only have come from the Nazis and their agents outside and inside the ghetto, further divided the Jews. Most of them were to the effect that there would be a selective "resettlement" involving 20,000, 40,000 or 60,000 people and that all those without employment would be deported and used on fortification work. Tens of thousands had already been rounded up for forced labor and few of them had returned to the ghetto alive. But most of the forced laborers had been the poorest inhabitants of the ghetto or refugees from provincial ghettoes. Consequently, the majority forced themselves to believe that they would escape "resettlement" so long as they could prove that they were usefully employed. Tens of thousands of people therefore devoted all their energy and ingenuity to finding employment. "There was a massive rush to find work, to find employment in factories, in social institutions, in offices. The ladies who until then had been spending their time in the cafés suddenly transformed themselves into hard-working tailoresses, seamstresses and office workers," Edelman recalled.[47] The confusion was made worse when, reassured by the Nazi authorities on the future of the ghetto, on July 18 Czerniakow officially informed the Judenrat members and the ghetto police that the Germans had categorically denied all rumors about imminent deportations.

But on July 21 the Germans seized sixty hostages, including several Judenrat officials, and imprisoned them in the dreaded Pawiak Prison, which was situated inside the ghetto. On the following day several cars carrying SS Sturmbannführer (Major) Hermann Hoefle, the chief of staff of Einsatz Reinhard,[47a] and his assistants drove into the ghetto and stopped outside the Judenrat building. To Czerniakow and his colleagues Hoefle announced that the "unproductive" Jews of the Warsaw ghetto were being resettled in the East and ordered them and the ghetto police to help his men in their work. "After the Germans left there was a second secret meeting," Edelman recorded. "Not one of the Judenrat members posed the question whether the Jewish Council ought to carry out the orders; not one of the Judenrat members found an answer to the remark made by the secretary of the Jewish Council: 'Gentlemen, before you pass to the technical execution of the order, consider whether it should be carried out at all.'"[48]

By order of the Nazis, on July 22 the Judenrat covered the walls of the ghetto with white posters announcing that all Jews, except those employed in enterprises working for the Germans, Judenrat officials and the ghetto police, were going to be resettled and that their resettlement would be carried out by the Jewish police collaborating with the Nazi Umsiedlungsstab (Resettlement Staff). The same day 2,000 prisoners held in the Central Detention Prison in the ghetto and 4,000 beggars and paupers seized in the streets were taken to the *Umschlagplatz* (shunting yard) in Stawki Street and loaded into trains made up of cattle trucks, about a hundred to a truck, which carried them "East." This became the pattern for daily transports of 5,000 to 6,000 Jews to the gas-chambers of Treblinka that went on uninterruptedly until September 12, 1942.

On July 23 Czerniakow committed suicide. He could not have known that he had helped to send some 6,000 innocent people to the gas-chambers of Treblinka, for the first eyewitness accounts of Treblinka reached the ghetto a few days later. But he had heard enough about the fate of the Jews in Lublin, about the Chełmno death factory and the gigantic massacres east of the Bug to realize what resettlement in the East really meant. He had rejected the warnings and refused to do anything about them because he had trusted in the Nazi assurances that the Warsaw ghetto would be spared. Now he realized his responsibility for what was happening in the ghetto and could see only one way out for himself. The news of his death was received by those elements in the ghetto that rejected a fatalistic acceptance of the Nazi Final Solution as an act of desertion and moral cowardice. His duty, they believed, should have been to tell the people what awaited them and disband all the Judenrat institutions, especially the ghetto police, before taking his life.[49]

On the third day of the Great Liquidation it became clear even to those who still hoped that the "resettlement" would be confined to certain categories of ghetto dwellers that they were wrong. On the third or fourth day the leaders of the political parties and groups met to consider the situation and decide what to do. We have an account of the meeting from Hirsh Berlinski. From his report we learn that the meeting was attended by Shakhno Sagan, Maurice Orzech, Abraham Blum and Joseph Lewartowski, who respectively represented the left-wing Zionists, the Bund and the Communists. Also present were the historian Emanuel Ringelblum, a left-wing Zionist; Isaac Giterman, the head of the JOINT and a veteran of the Russian Jewish Socialist Party; Aleksander Landau, an industrialist who used his factory in Gęsia Street as a refuge for the leaders and members of the Anti-Fascist Bloc; Menakhem Kirszenbaum, the leader of the General Zionists; Dr. Isaac Schipper, the historian; Rabbi Zysie Frydman, the leader of Agudath Israel; a Jew from Lublin who also belonged to the rabbi's party, "and others." We should have liked to know who the others were, for according to Berlinski's report it was they who wanted the meeting to decide that there was only one course of action open to the Jews of Warsaw and that the course was physical resistance.

Mordecai Anielewicz was not present at the meeting, for at the time of the Great Liquidation he was visiting the ghettoes of Będzin and Sosnowiec, where he helped his Hashomer Hatzair comrades to build their resistance organizations. The representatives of Hashomer Hatzair, Hekhalutz and the Communists, as well as several Bundists representing the youth of the party, were the chief champions of immediate resistance. The views and arguments of those who wanted action were summarized by Berlinski in the following words:[50]

> It is easy to talk of self-defense, the pessimists said, but who is going to fight and where are our weapons? The rich and the smugglers will not fight, we cannot count on the Jewish ghetto police, and the Gestapo agents have sold their souls to the bloody conqueror. We must therefore rely on the poor. But the poor have sunk into apathy and despair. In order to shake the poor out of their resignation, we must have a purpose and arms. We have a purpose: to fight against annihilation. But there are no arms. With four revolvers, of which one or two are unserviceable, with crowbars or knives, axes or clubs, one cannot fight an enemy armed to his teeth. Besides, arms alone are not enough to rouse the poor to struggle.
>
> The optimists, to whom I belonged, spoke differently. We must, we argued, draw conclusions for the future from our past experiences. Even if the deportations do not mean immediate destruction, we nevertheless know that the refugees and the people from other towns and townlets resettled in the Warsaw ghetto have died out of hunger. In the labor camps even the strongest men become skeletons after a couple of weeks. Even if the deported are really settled in labor camps, 75 per cent of them are bound to die. Therefore, in one way or another, deportation means annihilation. It is therefore better to die with dignity and not like hunted animals. There is no other way out, all that remains to us is to fight. Even if we are capable of putting up a fight that will only resemble real fighting, it will still be better than a passive acceptance of slaughter.
>
> We cannot count on anybody. Neither on the Soviet Union nor even less on the Allies: they are not in a position to help us practically in our so difficult situation. The underground Polish Government could give us some concrete help, but it will not do so.
>
> We know that with the weapons which we now have it will be very difficult to lead the ghetto masses into battle. But we believe, and we are optimistic in this respect, that if we were to tell the masses the whole truth, there would rise several thousand young men and women ready to fight even if their arms consisted only of knives and axes, crowbars and clubs, sulphur and vitriol. We realize that our armament compared with that of the enemy reminds one of a fly facing an elephant. But we have no alternative—annihilation faces us in one form or another. By acting in this manner we shall show the world that we stood up to the enemy, that we did not go passively to our slaughter. Let our desperate act be a protest flung into the face of

the world, which has reacted so feebly against the crimes committed by the Nazis against hundreds of thousands of Polish Jews.

Such were the arguments of the young people who attended the meeting. Berlinski was one of the oldest among them, having been born the son of a Lodz weaver in 1908. Writing after the Warsaw Ghetto Uprising about the personality of its military commander, Ringelblum said that "... Anielewicz and the young comrades from Hashomer Hatzair and the workers' organizations paid too much attention to the views of the older generation, to the views of the wise and the prudent, who measured, weighed up and had a store of wise arguments against those who wanted to fight the Germans..."[51] He must have had that meeting in mind when he wrote these words, for the older generation of Jewish leaders found it impossible to decide that the only course of action left to the Jews of Warsaw was to provoke a contest in which the Jews, as Berlinski put it, would be "a fly fighting an elephant." But while Sagan, Lewartowski, Orzech, Blum, Ringelblum, Landau, Giterman and Kirszenbaum did not reject the idea of armed resistance but doubted whether the moment had come for it, Rabbi Frydman and Dr. Schipper rejected the idea itself. "To defend ourselves is tantamount to bringing annihilation upon the ghetto," the historian Schipper said according to Berlinski's account. "I believe that we shall be able to preserve the basic part of the ghetto. There is a war on, every people must accept sacrifices, and we too must make sacrifices in order to save the essential element of our people. If I were convinced that we shall be unable to preserve this essential element, I would draw different conclusions." The rabbi, on the other hand, argued: "I believe in God and I believe that a miracle will take place. The Lord will not allow His people to be annihilated. We must wait, we must wait for a miracle. To fight the Germans does not make sense. The Germans will wipe us out in a couple of days. I ask you, my friends who believe in the Allies, why are you gripped by despair? Do you not believe that the Allies will win and bring you freedom? And you, my friends who are counting on a revolution and the Soviet Union: do you not believe that the Red Army will bring you freedom? Trust therefore in the Red Army. Dear friends, persevere and have faith and we shall be rescued!"[52]

While the Jewish leaders were holding their meeting, the members of both the Anti-Fascist Bloc and the Bund were waiting for instructions and arms. The only outside ally the Anti-Fascist Bloc had was the Polish Workers' Party, but to repeated pleas for arms from Lewartowski the Communist leaders quite truthfully replied that they had none, for the few revolvers and grenades they had managed to acquire had gone to the partisan groups. Only the Home Army had enough arms in Warsaw to be able to help the Jews to fight back, but despite various attempts to contact the leaders of the London-controlled underground, the leaders of Hashomer Hatzair and Dror had so far failed to meet them. The Revisionist ŻZW did possess some arms, but remained in the deepest conspiracy, unknown to the Bundists and the Anti-Fascist Bloc. Thus only the Bund, because of its links with the Polish Socialists and the WRN Socialists, appeared to be in a position to initiate armed resistance. And, indeed, all the members of its Tsukunft and Skif youth organizations were mobilized on the first day of the Great Liquidation, concentrated in a number of points and told to wait for orders and arms. For three days they waited, while their party council, attended by a representative of the Polish Socialists, deliberated and sent out several desperate pleas for the arms they had been promised weeks earlier. The arms did not arrive, and after several clashes with the Jewish ghetto police the mobilized groups had to disperse in order to escape being rounded up.[53]

VI

To find out what happened to the 5,000 to 6,000 people who were being daily carried away from Warsaw, Zalman Frydrych, a Bundist, stole out of the ghetto and with the help of a Polish railwayman succeeded in following one transport. He reached Sokołów where he was informed by Polish railwaymen that the Jewish transports turned into a siding leading to Treblinka, from where the same trains returned empty. They also told him that no food was transported to Treblinka and that no civilians were allowed to travel to the Treblinka station. The following day Frydrych met in the market place of Sokołów two naked Jews, one of them a Bundist by the name of Wallach, who had escaped from Treblinka, and obtained from them an eyewitness account of what happened there. Frydrych returned to the ghetto and the Bund revealed the truth about the "resettlements" in their paper *Oif der Vakh (On Guard).*[54] But as the clandestine paper was published in only a few hundred copies which had to be distributed in great secrecy to safeguard the distributors, the truth could not have become known to many.

When other victims succeeded in escaping from Treblinka and on the eighth or tenth day of the Great Liquidation reached the ghetto, they told the Judenrat what they had witnessed, but their reports were either suppressed or described by the Judenrat officials as lies. One may therefore conclude that in the first ten days of the *Grossaktion* only a few thousand people knew about Treblinka, while a large minority sensed that something unimaginably terrible awaited the deported at the end of their journey. Later, in August, when the truth became widely known, there was the psychological difficulty of accepting it. "We ourselves," Bór-Komorowski recalled, "had, after all, been loath to believe the first reports we received of the exterminations."[55] Yet it was much easier for Poles to believe in something that happened to Jews than for the victims themselves to accept the truth about Treblinka without going mad or committing suicide. Moreover, the Nazis saw to it that their victims should still be able to reject the truth by providing them with false hope. Hoefle had brought with him from Lublin a gang of Jewish Gestapo agents who were ready to do anything to stay alive a little longer. They were installed in number 101, Żelazna Street, next to number 103 where Hoefle had his own headquarters, and there, assisted by Jewish Gestapo agents from the Warsaw ghetto, they fabricated letters, which were supposedly written by the "resettled" from labor camps in Russia and elsewhere.[56]

But in the first few days of the Great Liquidation the German and Judenrat assurances that the Jews were being deported to labor camps were widely believed. They were so widely believed that when the Jewish police put out posters promising that people volunteering for resettlement on July 31 and August 1 would each be issued with three kilograms of bread and one kilogram of marmalade and their families would not be broken up, some 20,000 of the most starved and exhausted reported to the *Umschlagplatz*.

Those people, according to Edelman, rejected what they had heard about the gas-chambers because they reasoned that the Germans would not give them bread if they intended to murder them, but they reported, above all, because "hunger, the strongest argument of all, overshadowed everything else with the image of three brown, well-baked loaves. Their taste could almost be felt, for all that one had to do to get them was a short walk from home to the Umschlagplatz, and the effect was that their eyes ceased to see what awaited them at the end of the journey, for the smell of the bread, so familiar and good, intoxicated and deprived them of the faculty to reason and understand what seemed to be so obvious."[57]

By the middle of August thousands knew of Treblinka and many more thousands, who had hoped to escape deportation because they had documents testifying that they were employed in enterprises working for the Germans, realized that their papers offered them no protection. Tens of thousands therefore went into hiding and an unknown number of individuals resisted passively or actively when rounded up. Ringelblum recorded the case of a Jew in Pańska or Twarda Street who seized an SS man by the throat and another who snatched the rifle of a Ukrainian in Nalewki Street and escaped.[58] On September 3 Samuel Braslaw of Hashomer Hatzair was shot down when with a knife in his hand he defended himself against several SS men in Gęsia Street. Many cases of individual resistance remain, of course, unrecorded, since no witnesses survived to tell about them. There were also several cases of entire houses refusing to surrender and defending themselves.[59] The Polish report *The Liquidation of Jewish Warsaw* published in November 1942[60] reveals how the mood of the people changed as they realized their fate. Thus, whereas between July 28 and 31, when the first news of Treblinka reached the ghetto, the Germans and their henchmen killed 488 Jews inside the ghetto, the figure rose to 4,517 for the whole of August and jumped to 5,961 for the period of September 6 to 12, that is, during the final stage of the liquidation when the first acts of organized resistance occurred. Although most of the murdered were old and sick people whom the murderers did not bother to transport to Treblinka, there can be no doubt that a growing percentage were resisters.

There is another aspect of Jewish behavior during the Great Liquidation that must be recalled to explain the birth of the spirit that made thousands of survivors choose nine months later to be burned alive rather than enter the railway trucks that carried them to the death factories. This was the part played by the Jewish police in the Great Liquidation, which left many Warsaw Jews ashamed of being Jews and therefore determined at all costs to redeem their national honor. There were 2,000 policemen at the beginning of the Aktion and some 10 per cent of them, as we already know, were former members of Ganzweich's organization. But the police also included a relatively high number of educated and professional people, especially lawyers, who owed their posts to the fact that being people with a university education they held the ranks of reserve second lieutenants or lieutenants in the Polish Army. At the beginning of the Aktion all the policemen were assured by the Germans that if they carried out all their orders, not only themselves and their wives and children, but also their parents and even uncles and brothers-in-law would be spared.[61] Furthermore, to make certain that they had a reliable man in charge of the police, the Gestapo released Szeryński from prison, where he was at the time on a charge of having hidden several of his fur coats with Poles. Szeryński and his deputy, Jacob Lejkin, a lawyer by profession whom Czerniakow had awarded a prize of 300 zlotys for his zeal and skill in capturing and supplying poor Jews for the labor camps,[62] excelled themselves in serving the Nazis. According to Ringelblum, Lejkin, "a little man with a small body and small head, was completely corrupted by his power. He became savage, he beat mercilessly policemen and ordinary Jews. Those who saw him during an Aktion noticed that there was no sorrow in his face. On the contrary, he looked as though he liked the resettlement operation, as though he enjoyed the whole business."[63]

Eight policemen committed suicide rather than take part in the Great Liquidation.[64] But the majority, according to Ringelblum, "carried out with the greatest eagerness the orders of the Germans. It is a fact that on most days the Jewish police supplied more victims than the quota demanded by the Germans. That was done to have a reserve for the following day. . . . Many a hideout was discovered by the Jewish police, who always wanted to prove themselves *plus catholique que le pape* and thus curry favor with the Germans. The victims who escaped the eye of the German were seized by Jewish policemen. For two hours I watched the march of victims to the trains in the *Umschlagplatz* and I saw groups exempted from deportation being forcibly driven back to the trains by the Jewish policemen. Dozens, perhaps hundreds, of Jews were sent to their deaths during those two hours by the Jewish policemen."[65] Szmerling, a former boxer, a giant with a little beard and the face of a killer who was in command of the Jewish police in the *Umschlagplatz*, did not hesitate to use his whip and took advantage of his position to extort money and jewels from wealthy victims for allowing them to escape from the point of departure for Treblinka.[66] His subordinates, acting in partnership with the Sonderdienst composed of Polish Volksdeutsche and the Ukrainian and Latvian cutthroats, demanded from 1,000 to 10,000 zlotys from their victims to allow them to escape. "There were cases when the police demanded from their victims, apart from money, also payment in kind: women had to submit to their lust."[67]

The police plumbed the depths of baseness in the final weeks of the Great Liquidation, when thousands of survivors refused to obey orders to surrender for deportation, even if it meant dying of hunger in their hideouts. Each policeman was then ordered to supply seven victims daily or share with his family the fate of other Jews. Having already sold their souls to the Nazi devil, the policemen did their best to carry out the order.[68]

This did not stop the Nazis from killing over 1,700 policemen and their families at the end of the Great Liquidation. From Ringelblum we learn how one day in September 1942 several hundred policemen were ordered to carry out a manhunt in Szczęśliwa Street. While they were away, their wives and children were driven by the Germans and their Ukrainian, Latvian and Lithuanian henchmen to the Umschlagplatz and loaded into cattle trucks. When the policemen learnt of what had happened and rushed to the Umschlagplatz, they were stopped by the rifles of the Nazi killers and could only watch, crying and wailing, their nearest and dearest, to save whom they had descended to the very depths of baseness and degradation, being carried away to Treblinka. A terrible scene, but such was the hatred and abhorrence felt by the survivors of the Great Liquidation for the policemen that Ringelblum concluded his notes on the ghetto police with these unforgiving words: "This is how the executioners of Warsaw's

Jews, the degenerate and corrupt Jewish police, perished in their majority with their families."[69]

VII

According to Hilberg, at the end of July or the beginning of August 1942, General Stefan Rowecki, the commander of the Home Army, overcame the objections of some of his officers and decided to encourage armed resistance among the Jews still in the ghetto. The reason why he acted so, to quote the Jewish-American historian, was because "He feared that after the Jews the Poles would be destroyed. He therefore felt that helping the Jews was a measure of self-protection. The Polish underground thereupon contacted the ghetto. The answer of the Jewish leaders was that perhaps 60,000 Jews would be deported, but that it was 'inconceivable that the Germans would destroy the lot.' The Jews had one request, which the Polish Home Army was glad to fulfil. They handed to the Poles an appeal 'addressed to the civilized world and to the Allied nations in particular.' The Jewish leadership demanded that the German people be threatened with reprisals."[70]

Such is the picture of Jewish behavior during the Great Liquidation painted by the Jewish-American historian. It is a picture entirely based on the version of events given by General Bór-Komorowski, who at the time was Rowecki's second-in-command, and not on the accounts of the Jewish victims. Now, there could not have been a severer critic of Jewish behavior during the Great Liquidation than Ringelblum, but his conclusions were very different:[71]

> The best proof that this passivity was a temporary state, dependent on external circumstances, was provided by the [Jewish] actions in December and April 1943.... We do not want to defend here the political and social leadership of Warsaw's Jewry—we do not deny that it did not rise to the challenge, that it allowed itself to be terrorized and that it allowed the mass murder of the Jews of Warsaw to be carried out without the victims shedding any German and Haidamak [i.e. Ukrainian] blood. But we state firmly that had the responsible Polish authorities extended moral support and helped us with arms, the

Germans would have had to pay for the sea of Jewish blood shed in July, August and September 1942.

Thus, Ringelblum's verdict on Jewish behavior is not only diametrically opposed to that of Hilberg, but contradicts the very facts that Hilberg accepts to justify his picture of Jewish helplessness and passivity—namely, the existence of a Polish offer of help which unspecified "Jewish leaders" are supposed to have rejected. Before we decide whether such an offer was really made, we must go to the source of Hilberg's version of the events in the Warsaw ghetto. The relevant passage in Bór-Komorowski's *The Secret Army* reads:[72]

> ... As early as July 29th we had learned from the reports of railroad workers that the transports were being sent to the concentration camp at Treblinka and that there the Jews disappeared without trace. There could be no further doubt this time that the deportations were but a prelude to extermination.
>
> General Rowecki, always swift in his decisions, made up his mind that we could not remain passive, and that at all costs we must help the Jews so far as it lay in our power. He called a conference, at which, however, some doubts were expressed. The argument ran: "If America and Great Britain, with powerful armies and air forces behind them and equipped with all the means of modern warfare, are not able to stop the crime and have to look impotently while the Germans perpetrate every kind of horror in the occupied countries, how can we hope to stop them?" Rowecki's opinion was that the failure to show active resistance would only encourage the Germans to further mass extermination on the same lines.
>
> We had a department in our organization which arranged protection and help for escaped Jews and the distribution of money to them which had been sent to us from London for the purpose. A certain "Wacław" was the chief of the department, and he was instructed by Rowecki to get through to the ghetto and establish contact with the Jewish leaders. He was to tell them that the Home Army was ready to come to the assistance of the Jews with supplies of arms and ammunition and to coordinate their attacks outside with Jewish resistance from within.
>
> The Jewish leaders, however, rejected the offer, arguing that if they behaved quietly the Germans might deport and murder 20,000 or 30,000, perhaps even 60,000 of them, but it was inconceivable that they should destroy the lot; while if they resisted, the Germans would

certainly do so. When Wacław reported this to Rowecki, the General decided to intensify the sabotaging of German lines of communication in such a way as to hamper and delay the deportations. . . .

Such is Bór-Komorowski's version of the events in which he played a most important role. Before we proceed any farther, we may state that apart from the fact that it may have been on July 29 that the Home Army discovered the truth about Treblinka and that following this discovery the Home Army Commander may have held a meeting of his staff to decide what should be the Home Army's reaction, the rest of Bór-Komorowski's account is patently untrue. *General Rowecki did not send Wacław to the ghetto with an offer of arms and military assistance and not a single act of sabotage of the Warsaw-Treblinka line is known to have occurred during the Great Liquidation.* The first sabotage operation against the German railway communications in the Warsaw area was staged by the Home Army on October 8, 1942, i.e., a month after the official conclusion of the Great Liquidation. The official Polish history of the Home Army tells us that on that day sabotage units of the Home Army blew up the rails of six lines radiating from the Warsaw Junction, and derailed three troop trains using the lines. It was a most successful operation, which according to the German railway authorities interrupted the movement of troop and goods trains for six to eleven hours. However, the operation had nothing to do with helping the Jews. It was ordered by Rowecki following several telegrams from Sikorski, who was being pressed by the British Chiefs of Staff to instruct the Home Army to assist the hard pressed Red Army by attacking the German lines of communication across Poland. In fact, Rowecki reported to Sikorski: "In connection with my telegrams 541 and 582 and your reply 2985 of August 5, I ordered a trial interruption of seven railway lines running from Warsaw. The task was carried out on six lines on October 8 . . ."[73]

What really happened was that in August 1942 Arye Wilner of Hashomer Hatzair, who had come to Warsaw from Vilno, was sent outside the ghetto because of his blond "Aryan" looks to seek contacts with the Home Army.* His only friends outside were a few former Polish Boy Scouts who before the war had belonged to the KIMB group and it was they who put him in touch with officers of

---

* See Reuben Ainsztein, *op. cit.* pp. 486, 489.

the Home Army. Those not only refused to help him, but saw to it that Wilner's pleas should not reach the Home Army Command.[74] Finally, Wilner met Aleksander Kamiński, who before the war had fought unsuccessfully for the right of Jews to belong to the Polish Scout movement and now held the important position of editor of *Biuletyn Informacyjny*, the official mouthpiece of the Home Army published by Colonel Rzepecki's Information and Propaganda Office. (Among Rzepecki's collaborators were also Marceli Handelsman, Assistant Professor Ludwik Widerszal, and Jerzy Makowiecki, an engineer.)* *It was already September and the Great Liquidation had either ended or was nearing its end when Kamiński introduced Wilner to Wacław*, a lawyer whose real name was Henryk Woliński and who was in charge of the Jewish Section in the Information and Propaganda Office.

The Jewish Section had been created on February 2, 1942, and as Woliński had been recommended for the post by the Jew Widerszal it can be assumed that he was known for his liberal and humanitarian views. While from Bór-Komorowski's account we learn that the Jewish Section "arranged protection and help for escaped Jews and the distribution of money to them which had been sent to us from London for the purpose," Woliński's report on the activities of the Jewish Section presents a very different picture. The duties of the Jewish Section, we learn from him, "during the first period of its existence were confined to acting as an information service. The service relied on a number of private contacts inside the Warsaw ghetto.... Characteristic of the contacts: members of the Polish intelligentsia of Jewish origin working in a number of ghetto institutions (the Judenrat, hospitals) and Bundists. During the same period the head of the Jewish Section had only indirect contacts with the Jewish nationalist circles."[75] It is clear from the whole of Woliński's report that what he had in mind by the first period was the activities of his section from the time of its creation until September 1942. Hence it follows that contrary to Hilberg's and Bór-

---

* *Ibid.*, pp. 106, 455. Handelsman, one of Poland's greatest historians, was a baptized Jew and a devout Catholic. This did not stop the Catholic fascists of the NSZ (National Armed Forces) from betraying him to the Gestapo in July 1944, and he died in the sick-quarters of the Dora-Nordhausen concentration camp probably on March 20, 1945. Makowiecki and his wife, and Dr. Widerszal were murdered by Polish fascists in June 1944 because they were Jews.

Komorowski's accounts, Wacław-Woliński did not convey any offers of an official or semi-official kind from the Home Army to "Jewish leaders" to help them resist the Germans by force of arms. Moreover, we have it from Woliński himself that the only contacts he had in the ghetto were "members of the Polish intelligentsia of Jewish origin"—that is, baptized Jews or Poles who might have had one grandparent of Jewish origin and who were all too often renegades or anti-Semites—and some Bundists. As for the majority of the Warsaw Jews, who belonged to the "nationalist circles"— Woliński's description of the Zionists—he had no contacts with them until he met Wilner in September 1942. In fact, while according to Jewish sources Wilner and Woliński met in September, according to Woliński, "It was in October 1942 that representatives of the Jewish Hekhalutz youth reached the head of the Jewish Section through the intermediary of our Boy Scout leaders."[76]

One would have expected, on the strength of General Bór-Komorowski's account, that once Wilner had met Woliński and Woliński had passed on his plea for arms and military assistance to the Home Army Command, the reply would have been swift and favorable. In fact, the opposite was the case. For General Rowecki, described by his deputy as a man of quick decisions, displayed remarkable Cuncatorian talents when dealing with the requests of the Warsaw Jews who wanted to fight. If we are to believe Bór-Komorowski, Rowecki actually overruled those Polish leaders who opposed his determination to help the Jews. It is therefore strange, to say the least, that in reply to Rowecki's messages to London, Sikorski should have deemed it necessary to answer in the following terms on September 25, 1942.[77]

> In connection with your telegrams Numbers 3262 and 3242, I make it clear: (1) In its actions with regard to Jews, the Government is guided solely by the principles of democracy, in the name of which the Allied Nations are waging this war. The Government is adhering strictly to these principles. One must bear in mind that the attitude of the Anglo-Saxon world towards anti-Semitism is uncompromising and that the condition of their unconditional backing for our interest is that we should practice tolerance and equality . . .

On September 30 Rowecki sent to Sikorski the following message:

> On the example of what is happening to the Jews, with the world

keeping silent, Poles are observing the quick mass murder of several million people.

Square [cryptonym for the National Party] and other nationalist groups, the democratic groups, Circle [cryptonym for Sikorski's Party of Labor] and the Polish Socialists demand that the Allies should retaliate. They do not plan to act themselves in Poland, unless in self-defense imposed upon them by the enemy.

Rectangle [cryptonym for the Democratic Party, whose fighting organization was PLAN] postulates action by the Allies, as well as active self-defense and partisan warfare.

Myśl Państwowa [*The State Idea*, the underground mouthpiece of former members of OZN] wants immediate action at home without waiting for instructions from the Government.

The Communist Polish Workers' Party is exploiting the state of mind of the people, criticizes the passivity of the civilian and military authorities and calls for partisan warfare in cooperation with Soviet diversion.

This threatens to develop, against our will, into large-scale fighting that would be taken over by the Communists. [My italics.]

I demand air raids, retaliations against the Germans in Allied countries, individual terror against Polish traitors and Germans.[78]

From this message it transpires that, apart from the Polish Workers' Party, no Polish party or political group was ready to assist the Jews by calling on the Polish people to engage in countrywide armed resistance against the Germans. The nearest to being ready to help the Jews was the Democratic Party, a small group of former Pilsudski worshippers to whom the romantic ideals of the nineteenth-century Polish freedom fighters were still alive. As for *Myśl Państwowa*, the author of the quoted article was not inspired by the desire to help the Jews, but by the calculation that his demand for action at home would embarrass the hated Sikorski. However, the truly significant part of Rowecki's message is his anxiety that Polish resistance groups might be carried away by emotion and attack the Germans, because such actions could develop into a large-scale uprising and thus nullify the plans worked out by London and his own staff. Afraid of this possibility, Rowecki, as he was to prove by his actions, had no intention of encouraging Jewish resistance on a large scale by helping the Jews with arms.

Such were Rowecki's and his staff's views and problems when

Woliński finally approached the Home Army Command on behalf of the Jewish resistance organization in the Warsaw ghetto. Woliński's arguments that the Jews should be helped to defend themselves and to die with honor were supported by liberal individuals in the Government Delegate's Office and in Rzepecki's Information and Propaganda Office, where one of the most active was Makowiecki, a Jew in Nazi terms. The pressure of these people increased when in October they formed in Warsaw the first *Council for Helping Jews*, which later expanded its activities to other parts of Poland.

The initiative for forming an organization devoted to the rescue of Polish Jews came from two women, Zofia Kossak-Szczucka and Wanda Krahelska-Filipowiczowa. Kossak-Szczucka, who before the war had been known to most educated Poles as the author of historical novels not devoid of anti-Semitic overtones, was the chairman of a small Catholic organization called the *Front of Polish Renaissance* (Front Odrodzenia Polski or FOP),[79] while Krahelska, a veteran of the Polish socialist movement, had been active in the Polish national liberation movement before the First World War. For their activities on behalf of the Jews Kossak-Szczucka was to find herself at Auschwitz, from where she was ransomed by her Polish friends, while Krahelska was denounced to the Gestapo by the National Armed Forces in 1944 and died in a Nazi concentration camp. Composed of Socialists, members of the Democratic Party and Catholics belonging to the FOP, as well as two Jews, Dr. Adolf Berman, a left-wing Zionist, and Dr. Leon Feiner, a Bundist, the Council for Helping Jews became the rallying point for a small number of Poles of differing political and religious beliefs, who had in common that they were unable to stand by and watch passively the extermination of three million human beings.

To the pleas and arguments of these people, who represented no organized political force in Polish society, Rowecki and the other commanders of the Home Army opposed arguments based on political and military necessity—namely, that to rise against the Germans in order to help the Jews before the time foreseen in the Polish General Staff's plans would result in terrible losses and destruction and would only help the Russians. But, in truth, their arguments were all too often only a rationalization of their own Judaeophobia and the anti-Semitic ideology that formed an integral part of the policies of the Home Army Command and the Government Delegates' Office.

For while the Council for Helping Jews came into existence as late as October 1942, when only a remnant of Polish Jewry was still alive, one of the services of the Government Delegate's Office had been helping the Nazis in their Final Solution since the creation of the underground Polish government. The agency was known as Antyk—an abbreviation for the Anti-Communist Agency—and officially its task was to combat and report on Communist activities in Polish society. This the leaders of Antyk understood in the traditional manner of Polish reaction, which was to describe Jews and Communists as being the same thing—a line also pursued by Nazi propaganda. Antyk published a bulletin, which was distributed to all the departments and organizations subordinated to the Government Delegate's Office. After the German attack on the Soviet Union the bulletin warned that the Germans' Jew-hatred "appears to be sincere, albeit not very deep; but until the outbreak of the German-Soviet war, the Germans treated the Jews with relative leniency, handling them with kid gloves." A bulletin published in August 1942, at the time of the Great Liquidation in the Warsaw ghetto, said that Poles must not save "Jewish brats" and "curly Benjamins" and that the liquidation of the ghetto was bound to weaken the Communist movement in the country and was therefore a positive development.[80] Another document issued by Antyk in the summer of 1942 said:[81]

> Whether we like it or not, Communism is attacking us. The extermination of the Jews in Europe by the Germans, which will be the final result of the German-Jewish war, represents from our point of view an undoubtedly favorable development, for it will weaken the explosive power of Communism at the moment of the German collapse—or earlier. Let us have no illusions. The liquidation of the Jews is not tantamount to the liquidation of the Commune, behind which is the Comintern and through which the Jews want to take their revenge on us.
> It is therefore absolutely essential to set in motion the propaganda, organizational and military measures of self-defense.

Part of these measures was the publication by Antyk of a list of names and addresses of Poles belonging to the Home Army whose crime was to take part in the work of the Council for Helping Jews.

This was, of course, tantamount to denouncing them and their families to the Gestapo.[82] Nevertheless, unlike the fascist National Armed Forces which felt obliged to leave the Home Army because of their hatred of Sikorski, the Antyk agents who betrayed their fellow-Poles to the Gestapo were neither silenced nor expelled by the leaders of the London-controlled underground.

It would, indeed, have required a man of exceptional political and moral stature to deal with the schizophrenic attitudes of the London-controlled underground towards Jews in a manner recommended in Sikorski's telegram. Rowecki, a professional Polish officer, was certainly not the man to carry out such a task. However, in London Sikorski was being pressed by Polish-Jewish representatives and part of the British press to do something about Polish anti-Semitism. On October 19, 1942 he therefore sent another radiogram to Rowecki, which read:[83]

> The Polish Government has protested against [Laval's] measures against Polish Jews. [Laval had delivered them with other foreign Jews to the Nazis.] Our diplomatic posts protect them as Polish citizens. Laval's government is unanimously condemned by the entire French people for its submissiveness and servility towards the Germans. The anti-Jewish action has no followers even among right-wing politicians. The Catholic circles are unequivocally against anti-Semitism. I therefore request that the principles of democracy should find the widest application in Poland. We must remember that the struggle is being waged under this slogan.

The result was that on November 11, 1942 General Rowecki finally issued an order that could be interpreted as signifying the support of the Home Army Command for the activities and aims of the Jewish Fighting Organization. According to Woliński, who transmitted the order orally to Arye Wilner and Dr. Leon Feiner, the Bund's liaison man outside the ghetto, Rowecki's order took "cognizance" of the declaration of the Jewish Coordinating Committee signed both by Wilner and Feiner, "praised the readiness to fight expressed in the declaration and recommended that the Jewish Fighting Organization be organized on the basis of five-man teams."[84]

Thus, the only practical recommendation contained in the order of the Home Army Commander was that the Jewish Fighting Organization should consist of five-man teams. The follow-up to

Rowecki's order, to quote Woliński again, was that "In December 1942, as a result of repeated pleas, the Home Army Command ordered that ten pistols with a small amount of ammunition should be supplied to the Jewish Fighting Organization. The arms were in a very poor state and only partly usable."[85]

Such, then, is the truth about the assistance which, according to Hilberg and Bór-Komorowski, the Home Army Command had offered to the Jewish leaders, who, we are told, cravenly rejected it.

And now, having disposed of the cruel and unfounded version of events presented by a Jewish historian on the basis of an *untruthful* account by the man who took over the command of the Home Army after Rowecki's arrest by the Gestapo, let us see what really happened.

Edward Fondamiński "Aleksander,"
"Stefan"
(1910–1943)

Marek Edelman
(b. 1926)

Michal Rozenfeld
(1916–1943)

Aryeh Wilner "Jurek"
(1917–1943)

Michal Klepfisz
(1913–1943)

Zachary Artsztejn
(1923–1943)

Eleazar Geller
(1919–1944)

Dawid Nowodworski
(1916–1943)

Himmler Defied

I

THE GREAT Liquidation ended officially on September 12, 1942 with the deportation of 310,322 Jews to Treblinka and the murder of 5,961 Jews inside the ghetto. On the Day of Atonement, which fell on September 21, a further 2,196 people were packed into cattle trucks and sent to the gas-chambers. When at the end of October the Germans carried out a census of the surviving Jews, 35,639 people registered, but in fact the total number of Jews was about 60,000. This total was increased by several thousand who arrived in the ghetto in November and December from labor camps in the Warsaw area and by people who managed to escape from the death trains to Treblinka, so that at the beginning of 1943 the total number of Jews in the Warsaw ghetto may have been 70,000.

The survivors of the Great Liquidation were incarcerated by the Germans in three labor camps, which were surrounded by walls. Between the three labor camps lay deserted streets and empty houses, a no-man's-land in the heart of one of Europe's capital cities where German patrols shot on sight any living person and over which wafted the sickly smell of unburied corpses. In the middle of the desolation stood the Pawiak Prison, from which parties of prisoners were regularly taken into the ghetto ruins and shot.

Thus the Warsaw ghetto consisted of three separate and isolated units:

(1) The Central Ghetto, called by the Germans Restghetto (Remnant Ghetto), which comprised Gęsia, parts of Franciszkańska, part

of Bonifraterska, Muranowska, Pokorna, Stawki and part of Smocza Street, as well as the Parysowski Square.

(2) The Brush Workshops in the quadrangle formed by Świętojerska, Wałowa, Franciszkańska and part of Nowiniarska Street.

(3) The Factories Area where Toebbens, Schultz, Roehrich and Schilling had their factories and which comprised Leszno, Karmelicka, Nowolipki, Smocza, Nowolipie and part of Żelazna Street.

The workers lived where they worked and were forbidden to communicate with the people in other workshops or factories. Their working day averaged twelve hours, but sometimes lasted nineteen. In some workshops the workers were compelled to sit for twelve hours, while in others they were forced to stand for the same number of hours. The Jewish slaves were watched by special guards, the Werkschütze, who consisted of Germans, Ukrainians, Poles and a number of Jewish ghetto policemen. For their toil they received a bowl of soup and a slice of bread, while their daily wages of three zlotys were paid by their German employers and the Judenrat to the SS, who pocketed daily a sum of 100,000 zlotys. The effect of the inhuman working conditions and extreme starvation was widespread tuberculosis, just as in the early stages of the ghetto the results of hunger and squalor had been typhus. Little better off than concentration-camp inmates, the Jewish slaves nevertheless succeeded in organizing mutual aid societies to provide extra food and medical help in several workshops.

Among the survivors there were hardly any children or old people, for in the final selection carried out on September 7 by SS officers and German industrialists, children had been the first to be sent to Treblinka. The Pole Antoni Szymanowski described the selection in his *Liquidation of the Warsaw Ghetto:*

> I saw the most harrowing sights: children being separated from their parents. One father of two children, a six-year-old girl and a baby of a few months whose mother had already been deported, was offered the chance of life, but without his children. He left them in the middle of the street and walked through the gate. The little girl's cry of "Daddy!" had to be heard to be believed. I shall never forget it. Another woman, who was allowed to go, tried to take her little boy with her. A German snatched him away and in full view of everyone began whipping, kicking and slapping her face and head. By the time he had

stopped and she came to, the child was gone ... I shall never forget them. An old Jew of about eighty knelt down before an SS man, a stripling barely out of his teens, and begged him to spare the life of the boy with him, probably his grandson. The German just laughed. I shall never forget that.

When the Great Liquidation was over, the Germans learnt that several hundred children, whose parents had been murdered at Treblinka, still survived in the ghetto, and so one day an SS officer called on the Judenrat and told its officials that the children ought to be cared for in orphanages, which the German authorities would supply with food. As usual, the Judenrat officials complied and when the orphans were assembled in the orphanages, the Nazis descended on them, packed the children into lorries and carried them off to Treblinka.[1]

The result was that while at the beginning of 1942 children up to the age of fourteen had formed 26 to 27 per cent of the ghetto population, in November 1942 registered children constituted only 2 to 3 per cent. As for older people, the number of registered Jews above the age of fifty was 701. Furthermore, while at the beginning of 1942 there had been 134 women for every 100 men, in October 1942 the ratio was 79 women to 100 men.[2] Thus, the ghetto now contained thousands of people who were no longer inhibited in their actions by the thought of their effect on the fate of their families.

The thoughts and feelings of the survivors have been recorded by Ringelblum. By October 1942, he tells us,

> the majority of Jews understood what a terrible mistake had been committed by not resisting the SS. Now people reasoned that if on the day the resettlement Aktion had been announced everybody had risen; if everybody had attacked the Germans with knives, clubs, shovels, choppers; if we had received the Germans, Ukrainians, Latvians and the Jewish ghetto police with acid, molten pitch, boiling water and so on—to put it in a nutshell, if men, women and children, the young and the old, had risen in a single people's levy, there would not have been 350,000 murdered at Treblinka, but only 50,000 shot dead in the streets of Warsaw. Men tore the hair out of their heads at the thought that they had allowed their nearest and dearest to be hauled away with impunity; children reproached themselves aloud that they had allowed their parents to be carted away. People swore

aloud: "Never again will the German remove us from here with impunity. We shall perish but the cruel invader will pay with his blood for our blood. We must not think of saving our own lives, for each of us carries his sentence of death in his pocket, but we must think of dying with honor, of dying in battle."

And Ringelblum concluded: "The oath sworn over the heads of the dearest victims was kept. The ghetto began to arm itself."[3]

That Ringelblum faithfully recorded the thoughts and behavior of his fellow-survivors is confirmed by Perle, another chronicler of the Great Liquidation, who wrote in October 1942: "We could have defended ourselves and resisted the slaughter. If all the Jews had left their houses, if all the Jews had broken through the walls, if they had invaded all the streets of Warsaw, both the Jewish and non-Jewish streets, shouting, with axes, stones and choppers in their hands, then 10,000, 20,000 of them would have been shot down—but 300,000 could not have been gunned down at once. We should have died with honor. Those who survived would have scattered all over the country, in all the townlets and in all the villages. The Nazi murderer would not have found it so easy to exterminate us."[4]

During the Great Liquidation the Anti-Fascist Bloc and the Bund's fighting organization, having failed to convince the older generation of Jewish leaders that the only course of action was hopeless revolt, had concentrated most of their efforts on saving their own members. In this the Bund was less successful than the left-wing Zionists: of its 500 fighters only a handful escaped.[5] During the same period the Anti-Fascist Bloc, as we already know, dispatched three partisan groups and made repeated and unsuccessful attempts to contact the Home Army and obtain arms from it.

Armed resistance began when on August 15 or a few days earlier the first revolver reached the leaders of the Anti-Fascist Bloc. The weapon was smuggled into the ghetto by Henryk Kotlicki, a Jew who was a military instructor to one of the district cells of the Polish Workers' Party in Warsaw and who had acted since April 1942 as a liaison man with the party organization inside the ghetto. The revolver was one of the two owned by his cell.[6] On August 17 the Anti-Fascist Bloc pasted a number of posters on ghetto houses and walls charging the officers and members of the ghetto police with the crime of collaboration in the annihilation of Warsaw's Jewry and on August 25 Israel Kanał, a member of the Akiba Organization, managed to penetrate into Szeryński's home. He fired Kotlicki's revolver at the man who had become the symbol of the hated ghetto police and wounded him in the shoulder. A few months later Szeryński committed suicide in the hospital where he was recovering from his wound.

The importance of the attempt on Szeryński's life cannot be overstressed. In the Vilno ghetto the FPO had failed to deal with the Jewish collaborators and traitors and consequently failed to establish its authority among the mass of ghetto inhabitants, so that in the end it was unable to stage the planned revolt. The resistance organizations in the Warsaw ghetto—both the Jewish Fighting Organization and the Jewish Military Union—had no doubt about their priorities: both concentrated on the elimination of Jewish traitors as a first step to the planned battle against the Germans and consequently before the end of 1942 they replaced the Judenrat as the leading authority inside the ghetto.

The effect of the attempt on Szeryński's life was unmistakable, but the Anti-Fascist Bloc was unable to exploit it for lack of arms. A consignment of nine revolvers and pistols and five grenades sent by the Polish Workers' Party before the end of August did not reach it because Regina (Malka) Justman, who was to smuggle the weapons into the ghetto, fell into the hands of the Germans.[7] But the acts of individual and collective resistance were no doubt inspired by the news of the attempt. An anonymous chronicler registered two acts of physical resistance in Pańska and Twarda Streets[8] and Ringelblum, as previously mentioned, recorded the case of a Jew who flung himself on a German and tried to throttle him and of another Jew who wrenched a rifle from the hands of a Ukrainian and ran away with it. Moreover, in Dzika and Wołyńska Streets groups of Jews attacked the ghetto police and the Germans and their henchmen had to make increased use of their firearms to round up their victims.[9] On September 16th the sporadic and individual acts of resistance were replaced by an organized act of sabotage: members of Hashomer Hatzair and Dror set on fire several warehouses containing raw materials used in the factories working for the German war machine.

At the end of October 1942 the groups which had first formed the Anti-Fascist Bloc—Hashomer Hatzair, Dror, Gordonia, Akiba, Poale Zion and the Communists—held a conference and decided to form the Jewish Fighting Organization (Żydowska Organizacja Bojowa or ŻOB) and a joint political representation to be known as the Jewish National Committee (Żydowski Komitet Narodowy or ŻKN). Also about the middle of October, under the pressure of their rank-and-file, Orzech and Blum gave way and agreed to the Bund joining the ŻOB. But it was not until November that the Bund's combat organization became officially part of the Jewish Fighting Organization. Even then the Bund leaders refused to join the Jewish National Committee and so on December 2 a compromise solution was found in the creation of the Jewish Coordinating Committee (Żydowski Komitet Koordynacyjny or ŻKK), on which Bund representatives agreed to serve together with those of the ŻKN. At the same meeting the ŻKK approved the statute of the ŻOB, which stated that "The Coordinating Committee is formed in order to organize the defense of the Jewish population of Warsaw against annihilation and in order to protect the Jewish population against the traitors and agents collaborating with the Germans. . . . The Coordinating Committee calls into being the Fighting Organization, defines the guiding lines of its activities and controls them. Each party is represented on the Coordinating Committee by a single delegate."

The statute defined the tasks of the ŻOB as follows: "(1) Resistance in case of another deportation under the slogan: 'We will not surrender a single Jew.' (2) Terrorist actions against the Jewish police, the Jewish communal authorities and the Werkschütze [factory police]. (3) An active struggle against the workshop managers, foremen and known and secret Gestapo agents in the name of the defense of the Jewish masses." The ŻOB was to consist of six-man teams organized in each workshop. Where there was more than one team in a workshop, the overall command over the teams was exerted by a commander assisted by two deputies. The teams were to be formed by people belonging to the same political party, but whenever this was impossible, by people belonging to different parties or without political affiliations. The choice of commanders was not to be decided on political grounds, but only by military and other relevant qualifications. The entire Jewish Fighting Organization was to be commanded by one man assisted by a staff of five.

The commander was to take part in the meetings of the Jewish Coordinating Committee to ensure close collaboration between the political and military leaderships.

The Coordinating Committee consisted of Yokhanan Morgensztern of the Right-Wing Poale Zion, Abraham Blum of the Bund and Edward Fondamiński, who after Lewartowski's death in the Great Liquidation became the secretary of the Polish Workers' Party organization in the ghetto. Mordecai Anielewicz of Hashomer Hatzair was elected as commander and his five-man staff consisted of Hirsh Berlinski of the Left-Wing Poale Zion, Isaac Zuckerman of Dror, Marek Edelman of the Bund and Michał Rojzenfeld of the Polish Workers' Party. In its contacts with the Home Army and the Government Delegate's Office, the Jewish Coordinating Committee was represented by the Bundist Dr. Leon Feiner and the left-wing Zionist Dr. Adolf Berman, while the ŻOB was represented by Arye Wilner of Hashomer Hatzair. Wilner was arrested by the Gestapo on March 6, 1943, while he was staying in the flat of a Polish friend of the KIMB group, and after days of torture at the Gestapo headquarters, which failed to make him talk, he was transferred to the Pawiak Prison. There, afraid that he might not stand up to further tortures, he joined a group of prisoners under sentence to death in the belief that they were being taken to their execution. Instead, the prisoners were transported to a labor camp at Rembertów and from there he fled with the help of his Polish friends and returned to the ghetto to fight and die in the revolt.[10] His place as liaison man with the Home Army was ultimately taken by Isaac Zuckerman.

Parallel to the Jewish Fighting Organization, the Revisionists built up their own Jewish Military Union. When in 1941 the Germans had begun to round up tens of thousands of Jews for labor camps, the Revisionist organization sent a number of youths belonging to the Betar organization to the Hrubieszów District in the Lublin region to work as agricultural laborers on Polish estates and peasant farms,[11] thus hoping to save them from the Nazis and at the same time prepare them for their future life in Israel. When the total extermination process began in the Lublin region, some of the Betarim joined the partisans but most made their way back to Warsaw, where they helped to expand the nucleus of forty fighters, which the ŻZW had numbered before the Great Liquidation, to a force of 150 men in October 1942.

Under the command of David Apfelbaum, Paul Frenkel and Leon Rodal, the ŻZW with its large number of members who had held commissioned and non-commissioned ranks in the Polish Army reserves became a well organized fighting force. Moreover, thanks to the arms supplied by Captain Iwański's Security Corps and Captain Ketling of PLAN, the ŻZW could rightly claim to be an incomparably more effective fighting force than the ŻOB was at the time, even though the Jewish Fighting Organization had a much larger membership. Therefore, when Tsivya Lubetkin of Dror and Mordecai Anielewicz met Dr. Michał Strykowski, Dr. Wdowiński and Leon Rodal, the political leaders of the Revisionist organization in the ghetto, to discuss the fusion of both fighting organizations, the Revisionists demanded that one of their own men should be given the command of the united organization in view of his military background and the strength of the ŻZW. Lubetkin and Anielewicz rejected the Revisionists' conditions and countered with the demand that the members of the ŻZW should join the ŻOB individually and not as a group. After two meetings the two parties failed to agree, but nonetheless this did not prevent the two fighting organizations from collaborating.[12]

At this stage it will be appropriate to learn more about Mordecai Anielewicz. He was born in 1919 in the poor Solec quarter of Warsaw, where his father, a native of Galicia, was a small shopkeeper. Both his father and his mother, who was born at Wyszków on the Bug, believed in education and devoted their lives to ensuring that their children should receive it. Mordecai entered the Laor lycée, a privately owned establishment in which the language of instruction was Hebrew, and helped his parents to pay his fees by delivering orders every morning to their customers before setting out for his classes. His best subjects were Polish and history and his worst was mathematics. But on the whole he did so well as to be for two years running the top student in his class and thus earn a grant awarded by the parents' committee, which took care of his school fees.

In 1934 he joined the right-wing Betar organization, no doubt attracted by its love of uniforms and cult of military virtues that was deeply influenced by Polish militarism. However, within a year he found the nationalistic and rightist beliefs of his Betar comrades not to his liking and joined the opposite extreme in the Zionist movement, the Marxist Hashomer Hatzair. But he retained his interest in military matters and became the commander of the school paramilitary unit, although many of his new comrades were convinced pacifists. In the ghetto he was to tell the leaders of the Jewish Military Union: "It is fortunate that I was once a Betari and carried away from there a certain spirit which I am now able to inplant amongst the Jewish pacifists."[13]

In 1937 he became a member of the leadership of the Warsaw Hashomer Hatzair organization and in 1939 a member of the national leadership. His devotion to organization work had an effect on his studies, for in the spring of 1938, after passing his matriculation examinations in Polish literature, history, physics and mathematics, he failed in Latin when he was told to translate one of Horace's odes. According to his school mate H. Lajtajzen, it was the general view that "Aniołek" (The Little Angel), as Anielewicz was fondly called by fellow-students, had been unjustly failed by the headmaster, Dr. Simon Tenenbaum, a former officer in Piłsudski's Legions. Dr. Tenenbaum, who taught natural sciences and was a great believer in assimilation, owed his position as head of a Hebrew school to the fact that as a veteran of the Legions he had enough pull with the Polish authorities to ensure for the school the right of matriculating its students. Contrary to school regulations, which sternly forbade the wearing of party uniforms, Anielewicz turned up at the matriculation examinations dressed in his Hashomer Hatzair shirt and this incensed the headmaster to such an extent that he apparently made use of his casting vote to fail the future commander of the ghetto revolt.

After Poland's collapse in September 1939 Anielewicz fled to the Soviet part, where with other left-wing Zionists he began to build a network of underground roads to Palestine for trained members of the movement. In 1940 he found himself in Vilno doing the same work and from there he made his way back to Warsaw, where he became the leader of the Hashomer Hatzair organization. In May 1942, after the creation of the Anti-Fascist Bloc in the Warsaw ghetto, he set out on several missions to other Polish ghettoes to carry there the idea of armed resistance that had first been born in Vilno. He was at Będzin and Sosnowiec at the time of the Great Liquidation and when he returned to Warsaw he learnt that his mother and sister had been carted away to Treblinka. During the ghetto revolt he was to demonstrate qualities of leadership that made Polish anti-Semites claim that the rising was being led by parachuted Jewish Red Army officers. He became the very embodiment of the ghetto revolt because he was in many ways typical of his generation of Polish Jews.

II

The short period from October to the end of 1942 was spent by both the ŻOB and the ŻZW on two chief tasks: (1) organization, training and the acquisition of arms, and (2) elimination of traitors and collaborators. The second task was inseparably linked with the process of establishing the two fighting organizations as the dominating and guiding authority in the ghetto.

On October 29 three members of Hashomer Hatzair, Elijah Różański, Mordecai Growas and Emilia Landau, the daughter of the factory-owner Aleksander Landau who acted as patron of left-wing Zionists, killed Jacob Lejkin, Szeryński's deputy. On the following day the ŻOB announced in posters displayed in the three ghettoes that it regarded as guilty men the following groups: the members of the Judenrat for having signed the Nazi deportation order and collaborated with the Germans in carrying it out; managers and officials responsible for the exploitation of the people employed in the workshops; and those Werkschütze who were torturing the workers and hunting the "illegal" inhabitants of the ghetto. In fulfillment of the threat contained in the posters, the ŻOB killed thirteen Jewish policemen who had played a particularly foul part in the Great Liquidation, but failed to kill Szmerling, who owed his survival to the fact that he was in hospital with a broken leg and guarded day and night. Furthermore, on November 29 David Szulman, covered by Ber Brojdo and Sarah Granatsztejn, all three Dror members, killed Israel First, the head of the Economic Section in the Judenrat, who had acted as liaison man between the SS Security Office and the Judenrat and had become notorious as a willing collaborator.[14]

These first acts of armed resistance were made possible by the supply of a few pistols or revolvers from outside. For unlike Vilno or Bialystok, where large numbers of Jews were employed by the German armed forces and were therefore able to steal arms and ammunition from German armories, ammunition dumps and barracks, the fighters of the Warsaw ghetto, living in what was virtually a concentration camp, had no such means of arming themselves. It is true that Jews employed at the Eastern Railway Station, including members of the ŻZW, succeeded in stealing a few pistols or revolvers from German military trains,[15] but this hardly altered the fact that the fighters of the Warsaw ghetto were almost completely dependent for their firearms on the outside help of Poles.

The determination of Warsaw Jews to obtain arms whatever the risk involved is illustrated by the experiences of Henryk (Mordecai Khaim) Zylberberg, who commanded one of the ŻOB units during the ghetto uprising. Thirty-nine-year-old Zylberberg, his thirty-seven-year-old wife and seven-year-old daughter Michaela were deported from Golina near Kolin to Warsaw in December 1939. In 1941 Zylberberg was working as a house porter in Smocza Street and it was then that he came to know Corporal Kneibel, a German gendarme, who made it clear to him that he did not give a damn for the Führer and Vaterland and was prepared to sell food to Jews so long as he was paid in gold and diamonds. To save his daughter from a hunger death, Zylberberg gave Kneibel his wife's jewelry and received for it a few loaves of bread and a few white rolls as a special treat for his child. Then came the Great Liquidation and on August 15, 1942 the inhabitants of the house where Zylberberg lived were rounded up. "The Nazis drew up in a line across the street," Zylberberg recalled twenty-seven years later, "separating the men from the women and children. Then a second cordon of Nazis separated the children from the women. Michaela gripped her mother's hand and screamed 'Mummy, mummy!' I saw Kneibel seize her by the arm and drag her away. She would not let go of her mother. In the end he dragged her behind the line, got hold of her waist and before my eyes smashed her little head against the wall of the house."[16] At the beginning of July two of the inhabitants in his house, who were members of the Polish Workers' Party organization in the ghetto, had introduced Zylberberg and over a dozen other people in the house into the activities of the Anti-Fascist Bloc. Thus Zylberberg became a member of the Jewish Fighting Organization when it was finally created, and acting on behalf of the ŻOB he purchased from the same Kneibel in November and later several Browning pistols for bracelets and rings supplied by the organization.[17]

After supplying the ghetto fighters with their first revolver in the middle of September, the People's Guard prepared a consignment of nine revolvers and five grenades which, as we already know, did not reach the Jews because Malka (Regina) Justman fell into the hands of the Gestapo. However, in October and November the Jewish Fighting Organization received a few more revolvers and pistols from the People's Guard. The fact that among the People's Guardsmen who smuggled the arms into the ghetto were the legendary Niuta Tejtelbaum, Wyszyński, a former member of Hashomer Hatzair who joined the Communists, and Mieczysław Heyman, also a Jew, explains why the Communists, despite their very limited resources at the time, did so much in this field. How limited their resources were can be judged from the report of the Command of the Warsaw Area People's Guard of December 27, 1942, which put the amount of arms in its possession at thirteen pistols and seventeen grenades, and that of January 1, 1943, which gave the figures as twenty-four pistols and eighteen grenades.[18]

At the same time the Bund renewed its efforts to obtain arms from the WRN Socialists and the Polish Socialists. But despite the good friends they had in the military organizations of the two Socialist parties, the Bundists again failed to obtain more than a few pistols and grenades. Matters improved when in the winter of 1943 the Bund delegated Michał Klepfisz, a brilliantly inventive engineer who was the chief arms expert in the ghetto, to the "Aryan" side with the mission of collaborating directly with the leaders of the Polish Socialists' People's Militia and Leszek Raabe's Socialist Fighting Organization (Socjalistyczna Organizacja Bojowa or SOB). The Socialist Fighting Organization was formally part of the Home Army, but as Leszek Raabe had until the end of 1942 been in command of the Polish Socialists' People's Militia and had joined with his group the WRN Socialists only at the beginning of 1943, he continued to help his Bund comrades. The outcome of Klepfisz's mission was that with the help of his Polish comrades he managed to buy a number of pistols and grenades and also 2,000 liters of petrol for the production of Molotov cocktails inside the ghetto.

Since October the Jewish Fighting Organization had also been producing its own arms and repairing the frequently unserviceable revolvers and pistols acquired from outside. The first weapons produced by the ŻOB appear to have been a primitive form of grenade which consisted of bulbs filled with a mixture of sulphur and dynamite. In this field too Mordecai Tenenbaum had been one of the pioneers. However, it was some time after his departure for Bialystok in November 1942 that the production of arms inside the ghetto got into full stride. Under the guidance of Klepfisz and Fondamiński, who was also an engineer, and with the help of instructions received from the People's Guard and the Home Army in the first months of 1943, the ŻOB produced a large number of Molotov cocktails and a quantity of electrically detonated mines. Because of the lack of firearms, ammunition and handgrenades, the Molotov cocktails became the chief weapon of the ŻOB fighters, and were therefore manufactured on a very large scale. How large was the amount produced became apparent in April 1964, when in the course of building work carried out in what had been Miła Street, Polish workmen uncovered a bunker containing about 100,000 detonators for Molotov cocktails consisting of glass tubes filled with an explosive.

Denied weapons by the Home Army, which at the time was the only underground organization in Warsaw and the whole of the General-Government to possess big stocks of arms, the ŻOB had to find large sums of money for their purchase. The ŻZW also acquired many of its arms for money, but was fortunate in having the wholehearted assistance of Iwański's and Ketling's groups, who did their best to buy for their Jewish friends the most effective weapons, which mostly came from German and Italian soldiers. The necessary funds were at first obtained both by the ŻOB and the ŻZW from voluntary gifts in money, jewels and goods made by members of the two organizations and sympathizers. Large contributions were made by Landau and Abraham Gepner, a factory-owner and Judenrat member, who contributed both to the ŻOB and the ŻZW. However, the voluntary contributions were not enough to provide the large sums of money needed for the purchase of arms and from December 1942 both the ŻOB and the ŻZW began to depend increasingly on expropriations and confiscations of money, jewels and goods from smugglers, speculators, police officers and factory owners. Moreover, in the night of January 29, 1943 a ZOB group confiscated 100,000 zlotys from Ephraim Melamud, the treasurer of the Judenrat, and in February it took a similar sum from the Ghetto Bank. The ŻOB also imposed a contribution on the Supply Department of the Judenrat and thus obtained a sum of 710,000 zlotys. When Maksymilian Lichtenbaum, the Chairman of the Judenrat who was known for his hostility to the underground organizations, refused to pay a contribution of 50,000 zlotys, the ŻOB took his son as a hostage and released him only after his father had paid up. According to Marek Edelman, the ŻOB thus collected about 10,000,000 zlotys in the last three months before the uprising.[19] The ŻZW was no less efficient in extracting funds, for Ringelblum witnessed its leaders concluding with a Polish officer a transaction for the purchase of arms worth 250,000 zlotys.[20]

Impressive as the sums collected sound, in actual fact their purchasing power was very small. For while the Home Army paid in 1943 3,000 zlotys for a pistol and one clip of ammunition, the Jews paid for the same 10,000 to 20,000 zlotys; while the price of a rifle to the Home Army was 4,000 zlotys, to the Jews it was 20,000 to 25,000; while the Home Army paid 100 zlotys for a grenade, the Jews had to pay 1,000 to 1,500 zlotys; and while the Home Army could purchase a heavy machine gun for 12,000, the same weapon cost the Jews 40,000 zlotys. As for light machine guns and submachine guns, the Home Army paid for them 7,000 apiece, which means that the price of the same weapon to the Jews would have been at least four times as much. On top of that came the exorbitant price of ammunition. Whereas the Home Army paid for a round between two and five zlotys, the Jews had to pay between 80 and 120, the sellers taking full advantage of the fact that the weapons in Jewish possession were useless without ammunition.[21]

The acquisition of firearms thus remained the chief problem facing both the ŻOB and the ŻZW. One might have expected that the ŻOB, once it had been officially recognized by General Rowecki, would have been the more successful of the two in providing its fighters with rifles, grenades, machine guns and ammunition, but it was not so. For after receiving from the Home Army in December 1942 ten pistols, only some of which worked, the Jewish Fighting Organization waited in vain for more weapons. On December 2, 1942, probably on the day when the first consignment was delivered or a day later, Woliński met Wilner and Feiner who begged him to pass on to the Home Army Command the pleas of the ŻOB leaders for the immediate delivery of more arms, because they expected that the final liquidation of the ghetto might be resumed at any moment. On the following day Woliński wrote a memorandum, in which he recommended that the Home Army should supply more arms "because the ten pieces received are not sufficient for the organization of collective armed resistance or any other action of a collective nature . . ." and also that the Home Army should "facilitate and organize the purchase of arms. . . . (As I see it: the purchases should be carried out by us with a view to keeping control over them.)" He concluded his short memorandum with the words: "As regards Point 1, I wish the arms supplied could reach at least the figure of *kilkanaście* pieces mentioned several times."[22] The untranslatable word *kilkanaście* means between eleven and twenty.

Because of the implacable hostility of the London-oriented underground and the Home Army to any dealings with Communists, the fact that the Polish Workers' Party in the ghetto belonged to the Jewish Fighting Organization was not revealed to the Polish leaders. Jewish documents, including those which were sent through Woliński to London, did not mention the fact, while a few referred to the Jewish Communists as "members of the left-wing unions." The Communists formed only a small percentage of the ŻOB members—they had four or five combat units as compared with fourteen Zionist and four Bundist ones—but this did not stop General Rowecki from sending the following radio message to Sikorski on January 2, 1943:[23]

> Now, when it is too late, Jews from various little Communist groups are turning to us for arms, as though we had storehouses full of them. As a test I have given them a few pistols. I have no certitude that they will use them. I will not give them any more arms, for as you know we ourselves have not got them. I am waiting for deliveries. Let me know what means of contact our Jews have in London.

The closing sentence of Rowecki's radiogram is highly significant. Pressed by the Council for Helping Jews to do something to assist the Jews and embarrassed by Sikorski's instructions to produce proof to Britain and the United States that anti-Semitism was no longer the ideology of the Polish establishment, Rowecki was principally concerned lest the surviving Jews might have found a way of letting their own representatives and friends in London know what was really happening in Poland. In fact, neither the Jews in Poland nor their fellow-Jews in London or elsewhere found a way of establishing such communications and remained completely dependent on the Home Army, so that reports from the Warsaw ghetto either did not reach the Jewish representatives in London or reached them with such delays that the actions they called for no longer had any justification.

However, the illwill and dishonesty of Rowecki's message is, above all, transparent in his claim that he had no arms to spare. Whether this was so we can find out by consulting the official history of the Polish Armed Forces in the Second World War, published in London by a commission of the Polish General Staff under the auspices of the Sikorski Institute. In the third volume of the work, which is the history of the Home Army, we read that the Home Army was organized in seven territorial commands, each with its own stocks of arms.[24] The Warsaw Command possessed the following stocks of arms concealed since the September 1939 Campaign: 135 heavy machine guns with 16,900 rounds of ammunition; 190 light machine guns with 54,000 rounds; 6,045 rifles with 794,000 rounds; 1,070 pistols and revolvers with 8,708 rounds; 7,561 grenades; seven small anti-tank guns with 2,147 rounds.

The other six commands had rather similar amounts of arms and ammunition. It is true that by the end of 1942 a certain percentage of the arms and ammunition had become unserviceable due to the conditions in which they had had to be hidden, but in the case of the Warsaw Command they were more than replaced by purchases and airdrops from Britain. As regards supplies from Britain, from February 15, 1941 to April 30, 1942 ten planes flown by Polish crews and two planes flown by British crews dropped nineteen containers, five of which were lost. During the period August 1, 1942 to April 30, 1943 forty-nine planes flown by Polish crews and sixteen aircraft flown by British crews dropped 241 containers, of which forty-two were lost. It is not clear what amounts of arms were in the containers carried during the first period, but those used during the second period were of two types: MD and OW. Each MD container was filled with 509 pounds of explosive, 10 Sten guns plus 3,000 rounds of ammunition, 27 045 mm. revolvers plus 775 rounds of ammunition, 20 Mills bombs, 8 anti-tank grenades, 15 anti-tank detonators and 13 charges for blowing up trains. As for the OW containers, each carried 2 Brens plus 2,520 rounds of ammunition, 18 Stens plus 9,400 rounds of ammunition, 27 045 mm. revolvers plus 575 rounds of ammunition, 40 Mills bombs, 76 anti-tank grenades, 27 anti-tank detonators, and 206 pounds of explosives.[25]

How many serviceable arms Rowecki had in Warsaw when he sent his radiogram to Sikorski we do not know. But a year later, on July 7, 1944, his successor Bór-Komorowski was able to send 900 submachine guns to Home Army partisan units east of the Bug[26] and still have enough infantry arms left to order a rising against the Germans in Warsaw. It is true that during the Warsaw Uprising many of the insurgents never obtained their arms, but this was principally due to faulty planning, bad logistics and German counter-actions and not to lack of weapons. Thus, in 1947 one of the Home Army storekeepers revealed that he had had 678 submachine guns and 60,000 rounds of ammunition hidden in Leszno Street, which had never reached the hands of the insurgents.[27]

But let us return to the desperate appeals for arms made by the representatives of the ŻOB as well as by Woliński and other Polish friends on the Council for Helping Jews. These pleas were made not only to the Home Army Command, but also to the Government Delegate. The Government Delegate's Office had regarded the problems of its Jewish citizens as of so little interest as not even to have a single full-time official to deal with them. However, under the impact of events and to deal with the organized pressure of the Council for Helping Jews, it decided in January 1943 to establish a Jewish Section in its Department of the Interior. As head of the Section the Government Delegate's Office appointed Witold Bieńkowski, and as his deputy Władysław Bartoszewski,[26] both members of the Catholic Front for Polish Renaissance and active participants in the work of the Council for Helping Jews. The interventions of the Jewish representatives and their Polish friends had the effect that despite his radiogram to London, and probably after Himmler's and Globocnik's tour of the ghetto on January 9, Rowecki relented and ordered that the ŻOB be supplied with ten more pistols and instructions on how to carry out diversionary actions and how to make Molotov cocktails.[29]

This was the length to which the commander of the Home Army was ready to go in order to help the Jews of Warsaw, even though rumors of the impending final liquidation of the ghetto had been rife among the Germans in Warsaw already in December 1942. Nor was his attitude affected by the fact that after Himmler's and Globocnik's visit the fear began to be expressed in some Polish quarters that the final liquidation of the ghetto would be followed by similar actions of mass annihilation against the Poles.

III

The rumors about the impending liquidation of the remnant of Warsaw's Jews were quite justified. When Himmler had given the order for the Great Liquidation of the Warsaw ghetto in the summer of 1942, he had satisfied not only his own murderous obsession but Hitler's express wish to see the largest concentration of Jews in occupied Europe exterminated. Himmler's original decision had been to liquidate completely the Warsaw ghetto, but he had met with strong objections from Lieutenant-General, Schindler, the Wehrmacht's Armaments Inspector-General for the General-Government and Max Frauendorfer, the head of the Labor Department in Governor-General Hans Frank's government. Both had the support of Frank himself when they pointed out in June 1942 that of the 1,000,000 people employed in the General-Government in industries working for the German armed forces, 300,000 were Jews, including 100,000 Jewish specialists, who could not be replaced because Polish specialists were nonexistent or already employed in Germany. After intervening with the SS leaders in the General-Government on behalf of German industrialists who wanted to keep their Jewish workers and failing to stop their extermination, Schindler finally addressed a memorandum to the High Command of the Wehrmacht on September 18, 1942. In this he argued that "The immediate removal of Jews would have the consequence of considerably lowering the war potential of the Reich" and that the drop in production of the war industries in the General-Government would be from 25 to 100 per cent, while in the motorcar repair workshops it would amount to 25 per cent.[30]

However, acting in accordance with Hitler's wishes and after conferring with Globocnik in Lublin, on July 19, 1942 Himmler had instructed SS Obergruppenführer (General) Krueger, the State Secretary for Security in the General-Government, that the General-Government must be cleared of all Jews by December 31, 1942. After that date the only surviving Jews would be those selected to work for the needs of the Wehrmacht in *Sammellagern* (collection camps) in Warsaw, Cracow, Częstochowa, Radom and Lublin.[31] The objections of men like Frauendorfer and Schindler therefore had little effect on the speed of the extermination of the Jews of the General-Government. However, the conflict between the growing needs for manpower and the policies of immediate and total genocide flowing from Hitler himself led to Speer and Himmler arguing their cases before Hitler on September 20–22, 1942. Speer wanted all slave labor to be employed in the war industries under his control, while Himmler argued that Jews and others destined for extermination could work for the war effort in enterprises set up inside the concentration camps. Hitler saw no reason for halting the extermination of the Jews, but agreed that Himmler should not build any more armaments works inside the concentration camps and should instead supply concentration-camp labor to existing works and factories and be paid 3 to 5 percent of the global production of his prisoners for equipping his own SS division.[32]

It was the intervention of Lieutenant-General Schindler speaking in the name of the German industrialists, who were making millions out of the exploitation of Jewish labor in the Warsaw ghetto, as well as the influence of some local SS officials who saw in the preservation of a rump ghetto a source of personal enrichment and a guarantee of safe employment far from the Russian front line, that were responsible for the survival of the 60,000 Jews after the Great Liquidation. Himmler was persuaded not to order the total annihilation of the Warsaw Jews in the summer of 1942, but his orders to leave only a minimum of Jews were so strict that despite the repeated attempts by Colonel Fretter, the Wehrmacht's Armaments Inspector for the Warsaw Distrikt, to preserve at least part of the armaments workers in the ghetto, all he achieved was to slow down their dispatch to Treblinka.[33] In a letter addressed to SS Obergruppenführer Oswald Pohl, the head of the SS Chief Economic Administration, SS Obergruppenführer Friedrich

Krueger, SS Gruppenführer (Lieutenant-General) Odilo Globocnik, the man in charge of the extermination program in Poland, and General Eduard Wagner, the Quartermaster-General of the Land Forces on the Russian front, Himmler had explained at the time that although he agreed to leaving some Jewish skilled workers for the needs of the armaments industries, "One day even these Jews must disappear, in accordance with the Führer's wish."[34]

Unable to accept the survival of a Jewish ghetto in Warsaw, Himmler toured it with Krueger on October 14, 1942 to see for himself how far the objections of Fretter and the local industrialists were justified.[35] The result of his tour was to order Krueger to make preparations for liquidating it by speeding up the transfer of factories to concentration camps. At the same time, to lull the watchfulness of the Jews, Heinz Auerswald, the Nazi commissar for the ghetto, proclaimed an "amnesty" for Jews who returned to the ghetto by November 31, 1942, and advised the Judenrat to open cafés, cinemas and a theater in the ghetto.[36] Dissatisfied with the delays in liquidating the ghetto in Warsaw, Himmler wrote to Pohl on January 1, 1943 ordering him to remove without any further delay the machines and raw materials from the ghetto, which, of course, meant also the removal of the ghetto inhabitants. Pohl at once sent three experts to the ghetto with instructions that by January 7 all the machines must be dismounted and collected in a number of points inside the ghetto, the best picked out for use in SS-run labor camps and the remainder given to the Armaments Inspectorate or sold as scrap. But Colonel Fretter and the German industrialists once again protested that the ghetto workshops and factories were in the middle of carrying out essential orders for the Wehrmacht and obtained a postponement of Himmler's liquidation order.

Thereupon Himmler decided to see for himself. "I did not know I was going and I did not inform you," he told Krueger on his arrival in Warsaw.[37] On January 9 he was driven at great speed through the deserted streets of the ghetto, his vehicle preceded by two armored cars and followed by two more.[38] Two days later he wrote a confidential letter to Krueger, in which he informed him that of the 40,000 Jews in the ghetto, 24,000 were in no way armaments workers but tailors and furriers working for German entrepreneurs who concealed the true nature of their work because of the immense profits they derived from cheap Jewish labor. The worst of them was Toebbens, a man who had had no property three years earlier, and who ought to be called up and sent to the front line as soon as possible. In the meantime, Himmler informed Krueger, he had ordered the Chief Security Office to go through Toebbens's books "with a microscope."

The letter went on to instruct Krueger that the ghetto must be liquidated by February 15. To achieve this, 8,000 Jews were to be sent at once to Treblinka and 16,000 transported to the Lublin camps. All the smaller workshops producing aircraft and machine parts were to be closed at once, while the clothing, fur and leather factories were to be moved to a camp in the General-Government and manned exclusively by Jews.[39]

Krueger entrusted the task of carrying out Himmler's orders to SS Oberführer (Brigadier-General) and Police Colonel Dr. Ferdinand von Sammern-Frankenegg, a lawyer by profession, who had been appointed SS and Police Chief of the Warsaw Distrikt shortly before the Great Liquidation. His plan was to invade the ghetto on January 18 and round up the 8,000 Jews for Treblinka and the 16,000 for the Lublin labor camps. Aware of the existence of a Jewish resistance organization, he planned the operation on military lines and took every precaution to secure the element of surprise—so much so that the Germans on guard duties inside the ghetto were themselves taken by surprise when Sammern-Frankenegg's force entered the ghetto at half past seven in the morning of January 18.

The force, which was supported by armored cars, field guns and abundantly equipped with heavy and light machine guns, consisted, according to Polish reports,[40] of 200 Germans, 800 Latvians and Lithuanians, as well as of units of Polish police. As soon as Sammern-Frankenegg, accompanied by SS Obersturmführer (Lieutenant) Brandt, the chief of the Jewish Section in the Warsaw SS Chief Security Office, and SS Hauptsturmführer (Captain) Theodor von Eupen-Malmedy, the commandant of Treblinka, had set up his operational headquarters in Muranów Square, the managers of the factories were ordered to tell their workers to report in the Stawki railway yard for transportation to labor camps in the Lublin region. However, only a handful of the workers complied.

The ŻOB had not expected the attack on the ghetto, but its own activities and those of the ŻZW had prepared the ghetto inhabitants for such an eventuality. Although so far the ŻOB had succeeded in acquiring only a few dozen pistols and revolvers and a few grenades, its organized membership was considerable, for according to Edelman the Jewish Fighting Organization had fifty combat groups.[41] These varied in strength from twenty to thirty fighters, so that each represented the equivalent of a platoon. If we put their average strength at twenty-five, we obtain a figure of 1,250 fighters, to which should be added the members of the Jewish Military Union. Thus, even though only a fraction of the combat groups was able to take part in the fighting, the very presence of such a number of determined and organized men and women was bound to have a profound effect on the behavior of the mass of people. The new spirit of the ghetto had been expressed only a few days earlier by a worker in Hallmann's Carpentry Workshops: he dealt with a particularly brutal Werkschutz by throwing sulphuric acid over him. The Germans arrested one of the workers, a ŻOB member by the name of Zandman, after discovering a bottle filled with sulphuric acid in his possession. But the same day Anielewicz and a group of fighters attacked the guardhouse and freed their comrade.[42]

The reaction of the Jewish fighters to the invasion of the ghetto was quick, but the command of the Jewish Fighting Organization did not manage to overcome the effects of the element of surprise achieved by the Nazis. Because few of the fighters lived in barrack conditions, with their arms at hand, only five combat groups were actually able to take part in the fighting as organized units.

The first to fight back were the workers in the Ostbaustelle Carpentry Workshop in Gęsia Street, which formed the southern limit of the Central Ghetto. The fight began when Emilia Landau threw a grenade at the Nazis. Several Germans were killed, but Emilia also lost her life. The Germans managed to round up a large number of workers whom they drove through Zamenhof Street towards the railway yard. Among the workers was a Hashomer Hatzair combat group commanded by Anielewicz, whose arms consisted of five revolvers, five grenades, Molotov cocktails, crowbars and clubs. When the column reached the corner of Niska Street, the ŻOB fighters attacked the SS men. Anielewicz killed several Nazis with his two grenades and disarmed a gendarme, capturing his rifle and

Lüger. In the end he found himself surrounded by several gendarmes and was only saved by Sukiennik, one of his comrades. The Nazis bolted, leaving behind their caps, helmets and some arms and the column of Jews scattered in search of shelter.[43]

Twenty minutes later the Germans returned. Part of Anielewicz's combat group retreated and barricaded themselves in a house in Niska Street, where they defended themselves to the last bullet. When the Nazis broke into the house, the Jews set the staircase on fire. Only a few of the group managed to get away alive. An equally determined resistance was put up in a house at the corner of Niska and Zamenhof Streets by a combat group led by the porter Moses Czempel. Czempel used his last bullet to kill himself in order not to fall into the enemy's hands.[44]

In these head-on clashes with an enemy armed with an abundance of submachine guns, rifles and grenades, the Jews with their few revolvers and pistols and a few rounds of ammunition suffered very heavy losses. But they learnt quickly. Without any battle experience behind them, they soon found a way of applying partisan tactics to street fighting. Groups commanded by the Dror members Zachary Artsztejn, Isaac Zuckerman and Tsivya Lubetkin lay in wait for the Nazis in several houses in Zamenhof, Miła, Muranowska and Franciszkańska Streets. Their groups had scarcely any firearms—one unit had only four pistols and three grenades—and so they allowed the Germans and their henchmen to enter the houses and only then attacked them with Molotov cocktails, crowbars and grenades. They carried on with their partisan tactics through January 18 and 19.[45]

In the Factories Area the brunt of the fighting was borne by three combat groups commanded by Benjamin Lejbgot, a Communist, Bronisław Jaworski, also a Communist, and the Zionist Israel Kanal, whom we met before. The three groups had only two pistols and one grenade: their armament consisted of electric bulbs filled with sulphur and dynamite. At number 78, Leszno Street the three combat groups put up a sufficiently strong resistance to force the Germans to retreat, but Lejbgot and many other ŻOB members fell in battle.[46]

Apart from the ŻOB combat groups, entire houses defended themselves and had to be shelled and stormed before the survivors could be rounded up by the Nazis. Nor did resistance cease when the captured Jews were herded into the Umschlagplatz. A combat group who were captured before they could reach their arms refused to enter the cattle truck and were joined by the other Jews in the railway yard. Altogether, sixty Jews were shot down by Eupen-Malmedy and his men, before the others could be driven into the trucks.[47]

On the third day of the Aktion the Germans and their henchmen no longer dared to pursue Jews into houses and cellars and confined themselves to capturing those whom they found in the streets. On January 22 Sammern-Frankenegg withdrew his force from the ghetto, having killed about 1,000 Jews and removed 5,500. Thus, for the first time in the history of the Third Reich, Himmler's orders were thwarted by the armed resistance of captive Jews.

The Jews killed at least twenty and wounded at least forty Germans and their henchmen. According to some Polish reports, the losses inflicted by Jews were much higher and even Bór-Komorowski, who had no reason to extol Jewish military achievements, recalled: "We learned from a telephone call which we tapped that a German detachment of sixty men lost half its strength, including twenty killed."[48] Hilberg, however, even though he relies on Bór-Komorowski's description of Jewish behavior during the Great Liquidation, ignores both Bór-Komorowski's and Jewish estimates and prefers those of the Nazis, so that the January resistance is reduced by him to a "fracas" in which "one German police captain was severely wounded in the abdomen."[49]

The losses of the Jewish Fighting Organization were, however, shattering: four-fifths of its members were captured or killed.[50] They were so severe that, as we shall see, the ŻOB never managed to rebuild its strength to the fifty combat groups it had on January 18. The cruel losses were, above all, due to the fact that the Jewish fighters had had no firearms, ammunition or grenades, so that armed with home-made bombs, crowbars, knives and clubs they had had to fight professional killers armed with rifles, submachine guns and grenades and supported by machine guns and artillery. The leaders of the ŻOB accepted the absence of arms as an "objective fact" and concentrated on learning all the lessons that could be learnt. They found that their command chain had not proved equal to the task because of lack of coordination and communications, so that the leaders of combat groups did not know where to find the ŻOB commander and his staff. They also realized that if all the fighters had lived in barrack conditions with their weapons at hand, as was the case with the Hashomer Hatzair, Dror, Akiba and Gordonia people who lived in kibbutzim, not five but many more combat groups would have been able to take part in the fighting. They also found that the supply service had been so bad that most of the fighters had gone hungry throughout the fighting. Anielewicz and his staff therefore decided that all the ŻOB members must live in barrack conditions under strict military discipline, and that to prevent again being taken by surprise the ghetto gates must be watched by ŻOB units day and night.

IV

The importance of the January events as a turning point in the history of the Warsaw ghetto was summed up by Anielewicz in the following words: "Beginning with January 18 the Jews of Warsaw have been in a state of permanent struggle against the Germans and their henchmen. Those who deny or doubt it are nothing but malicious anti-Semites."[51]

The effect on Poles of Jews staging the first act of collective armed resistance in a Polish city since the fall of Warsaw in 1939 was also far-reaching. The success of the Jewish fighters was exaggerated by ordinary Polish people, who have never lacked in imagination, into ranged battles of Jews armed with petrol bombs against German tanks and Jewish victories resulting in the deaths of several hundred Nazis. As at the time of the ghetto fighting the Red Air Force had carried out bombing raids on a number of targets in Warsaw, the successes of the Jews were explained by some Poles as due to the aid they had received from Soviet parachutists. *Gwardzista (Guardsman)*, the mouthpiece of the Communist People's Guard, expressed the new mood by drawing the conclusion that "The Jews have roused themselves from their passivity, thus setting an example of resistance worthy of imitation."[52]

Biuletyn Informacyjny, the mouthpiece of the Home Army edited by Kamiński, in its No. 8 issue of February 25, 1943 was equally positive in its assessment of the events: "The echoes of the firings and explosions, which reverberated through the Warsaw ghetto in January, have been heard all over Poland. Polish society has received with respect this proof of determination and virile will to resist. The Germans do not conceal their amazement and still find it hard to accept it." The Germans, aware that the effect of the ghetto fighting on the Poles was to encourage those who had been calling for armed resistance, proceeded to carry out arrests on January 19–21 in the "Aryan" part of Warsaw on a scale hitherto unknown and placed all their security forces and the garrison in a state of alert.[53] The new mood also became a cause of great concern to the Home Army Command, whose nightmare was a countrywide rising on the Yugoslav model.

The Jewish resistance leaders had no illusions about the effect of their success on the Nazis. They expected them to react by preparing with the usual German thoroughness and then strike with overwhelming force against the remnant of Warsaw's Jewry. They therefore proceeded with even more energy and determination to arm and organize themselves and to prepare the ghetto for the ultimate battle by destroying the traitors and enemy agents in their midst.

The most common argument put forward by the Home Army leaders to justify their refusal to supply the Jews with arms had been to sneer at the Jewish willingness or ability to use them. The events of January gave the lie to this particular argument and aided Woliński and the members of the Council for Helping Jews in their efforts to obtain more arms for the ŻOB. But their task was not an easy one. When on January 29 they met Witold Bieńkowski, the head of the Jewish Section in the Government Delegate's Department for the Interior, and demanded more arms for the Jews, he told them "that armed assistance is impossible at present because of London's ban."[54] After more pleas and arguments they obtained from the Home Army a consignment of forty-nine or fifty pistols, and fifty grenades, which, according to Marek Edelman, reached the ŻOB at the end of January, but more likely, to conclude from Woliński's previously quoted report, in February.[55] Woliński also recorded in his report that the Home Army officers, who guided by Arye Wilner transported the arms to the ghetto, "unnecessarily declared in his presence their antipathy towards, and distrust of, Jews . . ."[56] or, to put it in simple language, made it clear to him that they carried out the order against their convictions and inclinations.

At about the same time, in February, Woliński had three meetings with Colonel Antoni Chruściel, whose *noms de guerre* were Monter or Konar and who held the crucial post of commander of the Home Army Warsaw Region Command. According to Woliński, Chruściel "agreed to assist the Warsaw ghetto with material help and instructions and also mentioned the possibility of our units helping from outside." Woliński then introduced Wilner to Chruściel's chief-of-staff, Major Stanisław Weber, and, to quote Woliński again, "A joint plan of battle inside the ghetto was worked out and it provided for the assistance of our units."[57]

In the middle of these talks, on March 6, the Gestapo arrested Wilner but, as we already know, failed to make him talk despite the most brutal tortures. Thus Wilner's arrest interrupted the contacts between the ŻOB Command and the Home Army at a most crucial moment. Isaac Zuckerman was sent out of the ghetto on April 13 to act as the new liaison man, but found it very difficult to re-establish Wilner's contacts, for the Poles feared that Wilner had broken down and told the Gestapo what he knew. Meanwhile the following letter from Anielewicz, written by the ŻOB commander on March 13, had reached the Home Army Command and the Government Delegate's Office:[58]

> Dear Sirs,
> The situation is deteriorating hourly. Fifteen hundred people employed at Schultz's are to leave today. We are expecting a round-up on the territory of the ghetto and workshops. The brushworkers chapter, [i.e., the January fighting], which ended with our indisputable victory, has convinced the Germans once and for all that they must return to the methods of blockades and superior force. The next few days may see the end of Warsaw Jewry.
> Are we prepared? Materially, very badly. Of the 49 pieces allocated to us, only 36 are serviceable, and this because of lack of ammunition. Our stock has got worse after the numerous actions carried out during the last few weeks, in which we used up a great deal of ammunition. At present we have over ten rounds per machine [i.e., pistol]. This is a catastrophic situation.
> Please tell the authorities in our name that if there is no immediate large-scale assistance, we shall consider it as due to the indifference of

the Government Delegate's Office and the [Home Army] authorities to the fate of Warsaw's Jews. To allocate machines without ammunition creates the impression of a cynical game with our fate and confirms the supposition that the venom of anti-Semitism is continuing to poison Poland's ruling circles, despite the so cruel and tragic experiences of the last three years.

We have no need to convince anybody of our readiness and ability to fight. Beginning with January 18, the Jews of Warsaw have been in a state of permanent struggle against the Germans and their henchmen. Those who deny or doubt it are nothing but malicious anti-Semites.

But from the [Home Army] authorities and the Government Delegate's Office we expect not only "understanding" for our cause, but that they shall treat the murder of millions of Jews who are Polish citizens as the chief problem of the present. How we regret that we have no possibilities of direct contact with the governments of the Allied States, with the Polish Government and Jewish organizations abroad, so as to be able to inform them of our situation and the attitudes of the authorities and the Polish people.

Dear Sirs, I beg you to take at once the necessary steps with the Military Authorities and the Government Delegate's Office. Please read this letter to them and demand categorically the immediate delivery of at least 100 grenades, 50 pistols, 10 rifles, a few thousand rounds of ammunition of all calibers. I am prepared to supply within the next two days the plans of our positions, including layout sketches so that there should be no doubt about the need for supplying arms.

We have no definite information from Jewish sources on the amount of arms the ŻOB received from the Home Army following Anielewicz's letter. We therefore have to rely on the figures in the previously quoted third volume of the official history of the Home Army, which are those of the total amount of arms supplied to the Jews. On pages 326–7 we read that the Home Army supplied the Jewish Fighting Organization with the following arms: "First Consignment: 70 pistols, each with two magazines and ammunition; 500 defensive hand grenades; 15 kilograms of plastic explosives with detonators; material for making Molotov cocktails. Second Consignment: one light machine gun; one submachine gun; 20 pistols with magazines and ammunition; 100 offensive grenades and various sabotage materials, such as time bombs and time fuses." The reliability of even these pathetic figures may be doubted on the strength of Anielewicz's letter, who would not have complained that thirty-six pistols could not be used for lack of ammunition if the pistols had truly been accompanied by two magazines and ammunition. Furthermore, it should be pointed out that not a single rifle was supplied by the Home Army and this weakened greatly the combat ability of the ŻOB, for on the fourth day of the uprising Anielewicz wrote to Zuckerman that pistols and revolvers "are of no importance. We use them rarely. We badly need grenades, rifles, machine guns, explosives."[59]

The amounts of arms supplied by the Home Army to the ŻOB were thus less than was transported in two containers flown from Britain. The excuses given by Rowecki, Bór-Komorowski and others have been that the Home Army's stocks of arms were too low to make it possible for the Home Army Command to supply the Jews with more arms. But we already know that this was not so in view of the official figures on the amounts of arms held in the Warsaw region alone. Moreover, the amount and quality of arms supplied by the small Security Corps unit under Iwański's command prove how much could be done by people who truly wanted to help. Thus his unit supplied the Jewish Military Union with 2 heavy machine guns, 30 rifles and about 60 pistols.[60] And even the tiny PLAN unit managed to supply the ŻZW with a number of pistols, rifles and ammunition and is known to have delivered on one occasion a case of 60 grenades.[61] The failure of the Home Army to supply the ŻOB with an amount of arms at least proportionate to that delivered by Iwański or Ketling therefore had nothing to do with the stocks available or difficulties of delivery. On the contrary, as many of the Polish policemen guarding the ghetto were members of the Home Army, the latter had fewer difficulties than the Security Corps or the PLAN in getting their supplies across the ghetto walls. That reasons other than lack of arms were responsible for the actions of the Home Army was obvious to Jews and Poles. At a meeting of the Warsaw Council for Helping Jews in August 1943 Bieńkowski admitted: "The refusal to supply the Jews with arms was to stop the excessive distribution of arms, which might have reached the wild gangs of a Communist nature."[62] Ringelblum, who obviously had none of Bieńkowski's sources of information, guessed as much when he wrote several months after the uprising:[63]

> As regards supplying arms to the ghetto, the military circles adopted a negative attitude which remains unchanged. Their attitude was explained as being due to the lack of trust of the official circles in the loyalty of the Jews—they fear that the arms might be used against Poland. I do not know how much truth there is in these rumors, but how is one to explain the consistent refusal to supply arms to the ghetto? In prettily worded resolutions it was preached that the duty of the military authorities was to help the ghetto fight the Germans, but in practice the resolutions remained scraps of paper.

Furthermore, the efforts of the liberal elements in the Home Army Command to help the Jews were sabotaged by the anti-Semites, at least one of whom was a German agent. Thus, Zuckerman in the course of his attempts to obtain arms from the Home Army met a Major Janiszewski, who told him that if he learnt that the ŻOB had members belonging to the Polish Workers' Party, he would lead his own detachment against the ghetto. Present during the meeting was another Home Army officer by the name of Hajduk, who, according to Zuckerman, had tears in his eyes when he heard his superior express his hardly disguised hatred of Jews. In 1944 the Home Army discovered that Janiszewski was a German agent and Hajduk was ordered to kill him, which he did.[64]

As promised by Anielewicz in his letter, Zuckerman supplied Weber with the battle plan of the Jewish Fighting Organization, which in due course reached Chruściel. Once again, in the final week of March and at the beginning of April, Zuckerman and Chruściel's chief-of-staff discussed the question of how the Home Army could help the ghetto fighters. Zuckerman proposed that those of the Jewish fighters who survived the battle in the ghetto should be helped to escape and be allowed to join the Home Army units in the Warsaw region. Chruściel told Woliński that this was impossible and offered to help the Jews make their way to Volhynia where they could join the Home Army's partisan units. The Jews rejected Chruściel's offer on the self-evident grounds that it would be impossible for them to reach Volhynia. Finally, Zuckerman was informed that special Home Army units would help the fighting Jews by breaching the northern wall of the ghetto to help them escape. According to Chruściel, the plan worked out by his staff was "simple. It was to open the walls of the ghetto in order to facilitate the escape of those who wanted to escape and were capable of fleeing. For this purpose we had to make several breaches in the wall from the side of the Powązki Cemetery and Stawki Street in order to allow them to flee in the direction of the Kampinos forests. To mislead the Germans, they were to be previously attacked all along the ghetto walls. Those of the Jews who were incapable of long marches but wanted to save themselves, we were to bring out through the sewers."[65]

Such were, in the colonel's own words, the promises of assistance made by the Home Army to the Jewish Fighting Organization. As we shall see, they were not kept.

While the desperate search for arms was taking place, the ŻOB and the ŻZW were successfully defeating the Nazis' attempts to liquidate the ghetto by "peaceful" means. For as Himmler's final date for the liquidation of the ghetto was February 15, Globocnik, to whom the machinery and workers were to be transferred from the ghetto, stepped in and tried to achieve by other means what Sammern-Frankenegg had failed to accomplish by the use of force. On January 31 he concluded an agreement with Toebbens to the effect that from February 1 all the enterprises in the Warsaw ghetto became the property of the SS and were to be run by them. Furthermore, the agreement stipulated, all the required machines and raw materials, as well as 10,000 Jewish workers, were to be transferred from the ghetto to the Poniatowa Concentration Camp in the Lublin region, where they would be under the supervision of the Warsaw Armaments Inspectorate. As for Toebbens, having ceased to be a factory-owner, he was to become the production manager of the new industrial complex.

On February 2 Sammern-Frankenegg informed Himmler of Globocnik's deal with Toebbens and that the gradual transfer of men and machines from the ghetto to the concentration camps in the Lublin region would begin on the following day. In giving his assurances the SS and police commander of the Warsaw Distrikt no longer relied on the use of force but counted on Schultz, whose fur factory was to be moved to the Trawniki Concentration Camp, and on Toebbens, the owner of the largest factory producing military uniforms, to persuade the Jews to leave the ghetto. To convince the Jews that the alcoholic Schultz had the authority to make promises, he was given the title of resettlement commissar, and when he proved unequal to his task the title was transferred to Toebbens.[66]

Both Toebbens and Schultz addressed their workers and assured them that they and their families would find decent working conditions, food and security from Aktionen in the two labor camps. To prove to the Jews that they were not lying, they sent several Jewish managers to Trawniki and Poniatowa and those returned with glowing accounts of conditions there. And, as further proof, at the beginning of February they brought from the Lublin camps twelve Jewish foremen to act as recruiting agents. The ŻOB and ŻZW reacted by shooting dead one of the foremen and giving such a beating to the others that they had to be removed at once by their Nazi masters to where they had come from.[67]

It was also during the same period that Stach and Salek, two members of the ŻOB in the Factories Area, were arrested whilst crossing the no-man's land which separated the ghettoes. The German who had arrested them was the SS man Klostermayer, one of the NCOs in the Befehlstelle, the SD headquarters inside the ghetto at 103, Żelazna Street. On learning of the arrest, their comrades led by Bronek penetrated inside the Befehlstelle, terrorized the SS men and freed the two prisoners. Shortly afterwards Bronek himself was arrested and imprisoned in the police post at the corner of Nowolipki and Smocza Streets. After consulting the ŻOB Command, in the afternoon of the same day Hirsh Kawe and Motl Goldsztejn with a group of fighters from the Factories Area invaded the police post, overpowered the policemen and released Bronek and all the other prisoners. As soon as the fighters left, the police telephoned the SS men at the Befehlstelle, but in the winter darkness the Nazis preferred to stay in their fortified headquarters.[68]

At the same time both the ŻOB and the ŻZW took ruthless measures to clear the ghetto of Jewish and Polish gangsters. The Jewish gangs were formed by men who lived in the ghetto "illegally" and were therefore not entitled to any food rations; to find the money for the purchase of food, they carried out robberies pretending to be members of the underground organizations. As for the Poles, they made their way into the ghetto through the sewers and combined robberies with rape and physical assaults on Jews. After one of the Polish gangs had been wiped out by the ŻZW, their visits to the ghetto ceased. At the same time both organizations continued their actions against the Germans and their henchmen. Thus, two

ŻOB members settled accounts with two German factory guards, nicknamed Pat and Patachon, after two Danish film comedians of the 1920s, who excelled in their brutal treatment of Jewish workers. They killed Pat; Patachon escaped, but did not reappear in the ghetto. On February 11 members of the ŻZW killed an SS man in Nalewki Street and on February 18 they shot dead two gendarmes. On February 21 the ŻOB and the ŻZW combined to deal with the Jewish agents of the Gestapo who were trying to persuade the brush workers to volunteer for resettlement, and the ŻZW killed four and wounded one. The badly wounded man, Skosowski, managed to escape, but survivors of the ŻZW tracked him down in November 1943 and shot him dead in a Polish bar.[69]

In their campaign against the traitors, the Jewish resistance organizations were helped by the Security Corps, whose men obtained the names of the Jewish agents and passed them on to the ŻZW. In each case they supplied both the number of the Gestapo card and the number of the pistol issued by the Gestapo to their Jewish agent. Among the agents thus revealed to the ŻZW and subsequently, the ŻOB, was Dr. Nossig, who after the January events had prepared for the Gestapo a six-page memorandum on the Jewish resistance movement and a chart of the system of bunkers and underground passages in the ghetto. He was executed on February 22 in his home at 42, Muranowska Street by three ŻOB fighters.[70]

On the 26th it was the turn of Brzeziński, a Jewish police officer who had distinguished himself by his zeal in loading Jews into the "resettlement" trains and had informed the Gestapo on the activities of the ŻOB and the ŻZW. His execution was followed by the shooting of Jerzy Firstenberg, another ghetto police officer, and the Gestapo agents Pinie and Prużański and his son. Another Gestapo agent by the name of Singer had vitriol poured over his face. Two degenerates known as Elias the Ape and Nosak, who had betrayed to the Nazis the hiding places of Jews during the January Aktion, also received their deserts. In an announcement issued on March 3 the ŻOB Command justified the executions in the following words:[71]

> The passive and active resistance of the Jewish masses during the memorable days of January 18–22, 1943 took the Nazi gangsters by

surprise and convinced them that the Jews would no longer go to their slaughter like sheep. A break in the deportations has been imposed on the German thugs. The bloody invader has realized that he cannot destroy the remnants of Warsaw's Jews by his previous methods. But, unfortunately, the basest outcasts in the Jewish social body have rushed to his succor! With their assistance the invader wants to discover and destroy the centers of armed resistance. It is they who supply him with information about our hideouts. It is their degenerate brains that are suggesting to the Nazi beasts plans for the liquidation of Warsaw's Jews by means of Poniatowa or Lublin . . .

To deal with the Jewish resistance organizations, SS Obersturmführer Brandt sent Ganzweich back into the ghetto, where he revived the Żagiew *(Firebrand)* organization. The aims of the organization became quite clear when it issued an appeal calling on all the inhabitants of the ghetto to gather outside the Judenrat in Zamenhof Street and there begin an uprising. Had the Jews followed the appeal, it would have been very easy for the Germans to surround them and drive them to the railway yards. Of the sixty members of Żagiew, the ŻZW and the ŻOB liquidated fifty-nine, including the editor of their paper, Adam Szajn,[72] but failed to capture Ganzweich.

When by February 15 Sammern-Frankenegg failed to liquidate the ghetto, Himmler wrote on February 16 to Krueger ordering him to establish a concentration camp on the territory of the ghetto and to move the factories and the Jews inside it. After having done this, the machines and the inmates were to be transferred to the camps in the Lublin region in such a manner as not to cause any interruption in the output of the factories and workshops. That was to be followed by the total destruction of the ghetto. "The destruction of the ghetto," Himmler wrote, "is essential because otherwise we shall never pacify Warsaw, and as long as the ghetto exists it will be impossible to wipe out the criminal elements. . . . In any case, what must be accomplished is that the area at present occupied by over five-hundred thousand subhumans and forever unsuitable for Germans should disappear and that Warsaw, the city with a million inhabitants which continues to be a dangerous center of disintegration and diversion, be reduced in size."[73]

But aware of the growing power of the Jewish resistance organization, Krueger did not even attempt to carry out Himmler's order to establish a concentration camp as a first step to the liquidation of the ghetto. Instead he allowed Sammern-Frankenegg to go on with his attempts to remove the factories and workers by means of psychological warfare. However, by the middle of March it became obvious to the Nazi chiefs that the usual ruses and duplicity would not succeed. The influence of the ŻOB and the ŻZW on the mass of the workers was such that when at the end of February the Germans tried to evacuate Hallmann's furniture factory, only 25 of the 1,000 workers reported for "resettlement." Moreover, when night fell, two groups of ŻOB men set fire to the workshops, destroying a great quantity of furniture that was due to be delivered to the Wehrmacht, much of the machinery and huge stocks of timber. Unwilling to admit that Jews had carried out this massive act of sabotage, the Germans on the following day issued a statement accusing parachutists of being responsible for it.[74]

A few days later, at the beginning of March, Toebbens called on the 1,600 workers employed in the Toebbens and Schultz factories to report for resettlement. Only 280 reported, but even of those a number escaped when they were lined up prior to being marched off to the railway yard. The factory guards seized the escaping men and locked them up in their guardhouse, but the ŻOB sent a combat group who freed them, whilst the thirty factory guards looked on, afraid to intervene. On March 6 the Jewish fighters set on fire the SS warehouses in Nalewki Street and a few days later, when the machines from the brush workshops were moved to the railway yards, they placed petrol bombs with delayed-action detonators inside them which set the train on fire. As for the 4,000 brushworkers, only twenty reported and those the Nazis marched through the "Aryan" part of the city to avoid having them forcibly rescued by the Jewish fighters.[75]

In the second week of March the factory guards and the soldiers who guarded the Wehrmacht workshops and factories in the ghetto went on the rampage and carried out a series of organized robberies and shootings. In retaliation, on March 13 a Jewish combat group attacked a group of factory guards as they were carrying out a robbery in Miła Street, killed two and captured one. An SA*

---

* Sturmabteilung—auxiliary police unit made up of Nazi party members. The original Stormtroopers or Brown Shirts commanded by Ernst Roehm until his murder, on Hitler's orders, in the blood bath of June 30, 1934.

unit came to the rescue of the factory guards and in the ensuing exchange of fire one of the Germans was badly wounded while the Jews had no casualties. Other groups of Jews attacked the Ukrainian factory guards and disarmed them. When the SA captured an armed Jewish fighter, his comrades killed two of the captors and rescued him. The same day a group of porters killed a Luftwaffe officer, who had come into the ghetto on a robbing expedition, in Muranowska Street, while in Leszno Street Jewish fighters killed two Germans and a Polish policeman, losing only one man in the fight.[76]

At nine in the morning the SA withdrew from the ghetto and at two in the afternoon Brandt appeared with a large force of Nazi cutthroats. For two hours his men hunted for victims in the section of Miła Street between Zamenhof and Nalewki Streets, killing about 200 people, including fourteen children, and then withdrew. The effect of the slaughter was to make Toebbens' efforts to find Jewish volunteers for "resettlement" even more futile. In fact, on March 20 he appealed in posters to the Jews not to listen to the "Command of the Fighting Organization" and to volunteer for work at Trawniki "because there exists the possibility of living and surviving the war." When there was no response to his appeal, he asked the Judenrat to arrange a meeting between himself and the leaders of the ŻOB. The ŻOB leaders ignored his invitation.[77]

The massacre of March 13 had also failed to impress the ŻOB and the ŻZW in other ways. This was demonstrated when in the last days of March or on one of the first days of April a detachment of Polish police attacked in Nalewki Street a ŻOB group commanded by Zachariah Artsztejn, who were transporting money and weapons. The police got hold of the money and the arms and barricaded themselves in the Judenrat bank. Artsztejn surrounded the house, cut off the telephone lines and warned the Poles that unless they surrendered the money and the arms they would all be killed. The policemen complied.[78]

It was about the same time, at the beginning of April, that Anielewicz made a few notes on the state of mind of the people in the ghetto and recorded his conversations with two ordinary persons who did not belong to the ŻOB or the ŻZW. The first man replied when Anielewicz asked him what he would do when the Germans came to cart him away to his death: ". . . 'I would gather my companions, we would get hold of axes, iron bars, hammers and go into the cellars or barricade ourselves in our homes. Let them come for us! Let them fire their machine guns! What harm can they do me if they can't see me? But let one of them put his head into my room and he'll be mine. I'll get ten of them with my axe. I may be the eleventh, but at least it'll be worth dying for. No, they won't get us as they did last time! And as for them, our Jewish policemen, look what I've got ready for them'—and he showed me a long, strong, well sharpened knife . . ."

The other man told Anielewicz: ". . . No, they will not find it so easy. We shall lock ourselves in our houses, we shall barricade the gates, we shall arm ourselves with axes and then let them capture us. Let them throw grenades and bombs, let them use mines and dynamite. That's how they'll have to take us. We will not go into the streets to be marched off to the trains. And if one of them dares to go into our houses, he will not emerge alive. If they find me in my hideout, I will fight on. Either them or me. If I have to die, I shall die like a man and not like a sheep in a flock . . ."[79]

Gen. Stroop and his subordinates

Shelling of Muranów Square

Stroop in Jail

The Uprising

I

INFORMED of what was happening in the Warsaw ghetto, Himmler ordered Krueger to delay no longer with its total liquidation. Krueger charged Dr. Ferdinand von Sammern-Frankenegg with the task and the commander of the SS and the police in the Warsaw Distrikt worked out a plan that was based on the use of as little force as possible in order to safeguard the factories, machinery and raw materials inside the ghetto from destruction. After surrounding the ghetto walls with machine-gun positions and stopping the movement of trams in the "Aryan" streets bordering the ghetto walls, Sammern-Frankenegg planned to move into the ghetto with a strong force, establish himself with his men in Zamenhof Street and from there send small detachments into the other streets with orders to round up the inhabitants. He expected that the show of force combined with the activities of Toebbens and other German industrialists would be enough to make the Jewish workers report for "resettlement" and that the entire operation, due to begin on April 19, would take three days to complete.[1]

Not entirely convinced, after Sammern-Frankenegg's failure in January, that the plan would succeed, Krueger decided to send to Warsaw an expert in partisan warfare. The man he chose for the job was SS Brigadeführer (Major-General) Juergen Stroop, who on receiving his order in Lvov on the morning of April 17 arrived in Warsaw in the evening of the same day. Born in 1895, the son of a German policeman, Stroop had followed in his father's footsteps in his choice of a career. In 1932 he joined the National Socialist Party and in 1934 he reached the rank of a sergeant in the SS. But in

1939 he already held the rank of SS Oberführer (Brigadier-General) and Colonel of the Police in the Sudetenland. After the conquest of Poland in September 1939, Stroop was moved to Poznań, where as chief of the German Selbstschutz (Self-Defense) he distinguished himself by his terrorist activities against the local Poles, and after Germany's attack on the Soviet Union he further extended his experience in the methods of mass terror by fighting the rising partisan movement in the Ukraine. Promoted to SS Brigadeführer, he was posted for a time to Berlin where he organized special subversion and terrorist units for operations in the Caucasus. In March 1943 he was back in the East, having been posted as an expert on combating partisan activities to SS Brigadeführer Katzmann, the SS and Police Leader of the Galician Distrikt.[2]

Unlike what happened in other ghettoes, the Jewish fighters in the Warsaw ghetto knew from their intelligence sources outside of the impending operation and did all that was in their power to be ready for battle. The Polish and Jewish intelligence sources outside the ghetto were able to discover what was being prepared by the Germans because not only the special extermination force, but the entire German garrison in Warsaw had been alerted to deal with a possible general uprising in the conquered but defiant city. Furthermore, the Polish friends of the ŻZW had their agents in the Polish police, which had been mobilized to take part in the liquidation of the ghetto, and from them they were able to obtain detailed information on the plans of the Nazis. According to Dr. Ryszard Walewski, one of the leaders of the Jewish Military Union, his organization learnt of the impending operation about midday on April 18 and at once passed the information to the ŻOB Command. A few hours later the liaison man of the ŻZW on the "Aryan" side telephoned Walewski and told him that he was trying to obtain the detailed plan of the German operation and that he would bring it as soon as he had it. Dr. Walewski waited for the man in Muranów Square until late in the evening of April 18 when he received news of his appointment as chief liaison officer between the Jewish Fighting Organization and the Jewish Military Union.[3]

It was while Dr. Walewski was waiting for the man from the "Aryan" side that he learnt of the decision to unite the two Jewish fighting organizations. The news was conveyed to him by Elias

Gutkowski, a member of the Right-Wing Poale Zion, who acted as the liaison man of the ŻOB in its contacts with the ŻZW. Gutkowski told Dr. Walewski: "I bring you joyful news. I have been delegated by the leadership of the Jewish Fighting Organization to report to the Command of the Jewish Military Union that at one o'clock in the morning representatives of the ŻOB will come to the ŻZW headquarters in order to sign the official act of union between the two organizations."[4]

Gutkowski also informed Walewski that at the meeting held by the ŻOB Command earlier in the day it had been decided, in view of the German moves, that in case of a sudden attack each organization would defend one of the two sectors into which the main ghetto had been divided by the commanders of the ŻOB and the ŻZW. Thus, on the eve of the German attack on the Warsaw ghetto, the two fighting organizations had coordinated their actions and, on learning of the impending attack, taken up their battle positions.

According to the report compiled by the survivors of the ŻOB Command in March 1944 and sent to London by the Government Delegate's Office, the ŻOB had twenty-three combat groups at the outbreak of the ghetto revolt. Five belonged to the Polish Workers' Party, four to the Bund, five were made up of Dror members, four of Hashomer Hatzair members, one of members of the Left-Wing Poale Zion, one of members of the Right-Wing Poale Zion, one of members of Gordonia, one of members of Akiba and one of members of Hanoar Hatzioni.[5] Thus the Zionists formed the majority, which was reflected in the command: Mordecai Anielewicz belonged to Hashomer Hatzair, Hirsh Berlinski to the Left-Wing Poale Zion, Isaac Zuckerman to Hekhalutz, Marek Edelman to the Bund and Michał Rojzenfeld to the Polish Workers' Party. Eight combat groups were in the Central Ghetto under the overall command of Israel Kanał of Akiba, five in the Brush Workshops Area under the command of Marek Edelman and nine in the Factories Area under the command of Eleazar Geller of Gordonia.

Altogether the ŻOB counted between 600 and 800 men and women. Each fighter had a revolver or a pistol with ten to fifteen rounds, four to five grenades and four to five Molotov cocktails. Moreover, two or three fighters in each of the three ghetto areas had rifles, which means that the ŻOB had only some ten rifles.[6]

The ŻOB also had one submachine gun and one light machine gun, but not enough ammunition to make full use of them.

The ŻZW had had only 150 members at the beginning of January 1943, almost all of them members of the Revisionist Party or its youth organization Betar, but grew to 400 by the time of the revolt.[7] Its commanders were David Apfelbaum, a reserve lieutenant in the Polish Army whose father had been a well-to-do merchant, and Paweł Frenkel, a journalist. In the last three months before the revolt the ŻZW was joined by proletarian elements, namely by groups of porters and smugglers led by Janek Pika, whose real name remains unknown, Krzywonos, whose real name is also unknown, and Rudy Paweł (Ginger Paul), whose real name was Pinkhas Besztimt. The ŻZW, as we already know, were fortunate in having the help of Iwański's and Ketling's organizations. While from Ketling it received weapons through a tunnel that linked the "Aryan" side of Karmelicka Street with a bunker underneath the house at Karmelicka No. 5, which was inside the ghetto, it was through another fifty-yard-long tunnel linking the ŻZW command headquarters at Muranowska No. 7 with the "Aryan" side of the street that arms came from Iwański's Security Corps. Altogether the ŻZW had at least 21 submachine guns, 8 machine guns, at least 30 rifles and an unknown number of pistols and grenades.

The main force of the ŻZW was concentrated in the Central Ghetto where Apfelbaum and Frenkel had overall command over the combat groups led by Leon Rodal, Lipszyc, Roman Wajnsztok and Złotogóra in Muranowska Street and Muranów Square. There the fighters of the Jewish Military Union had 8 submachine guns, 1 light and 2 heavy machine guns and about 300 grenades.[8] Four other ŻZW combat groups commanded by Khaim Federbusz, Janek Pika, Lazar Staniewicz and Binsztok also fought in the Central Ghetto. Khaim Łopata, Abraham Rodal and Pinkhas Besztimt commanded three combat groups in the Brush Workshops Area and there was also a combat group in the Factory Area, where the leaders were the lawyer David Szulman, Nathan Szulc and Pinkhas Taub.

Apart from the Jewish Fighting Organization and the Jewish Military Union, there was an unknown number of armed groups organized by people who worked together or shared underground bunkers. Altogether they may have numbered some 2,000 people and it was these groups that carried on most of the fighting in the second stage of the revolt, when hardly any members of the ŻOB and the ŻZW remained alive or inside the ghetto. One of these "wild groups," as they were known, was composed of orthodox Jews led by Drejzin, a chemical engineer, and Eleazar Frydenzon, a religious educationalist.[9]

The wild groups provided themselves with their own arms, which included revolvers, pistols, grenades and Molotov cocktails, by buying them from Poles or, in the case of those who were employed on the railways, by stealing them from German troop trains. The determination of thousands of Jews outside the two military organizations to die fighting can be gauged from the following account in Witold Dobrzański's diary. A Warsaw worker and member of the PPS (Polish Socialist Party), who made a living smuggling food into the ghetto, he set out with four other Polish smugglers during the first night of the revolt through the sewers with food which he sold as usual to a waiting Jewish smuggler. On the way back from the ghetto the Polish smugglers led a party of forty Jewish women, children and old people through the sewers into the Polish part of the city. The following night Dobrzański and his companions again made their way into the ghetto carrying 150 rounds of ammunition for VIS pistols, bread and vodka.[10] His ammunition must have been bought by the wild groups.

Next to the spirit of the people, the chief factor that determined the nature of the revolt was the system of underground bunkers and tunnels built by the two military organizations and thousands of ordinary ghetto dwellers. Following the growing number of Soviet air raids in the second half of 1942, the Jews under the guise of building air-raid shelters began to construct secret hideouts, bunkers and underground passages that led outside the ghetto walls or opened into the sewers. When the revolt broke out, the underground ghetto was so extensive and labyrinthine that it determined the nature of the fighting.[11]

Six years later, while waiting for his trial in the Mokotów Prison in Warsaw, Stroop returned several times to the subject of the underground ghetto in his conversations with his two cell-mates, the SS officer Gustav Schielke and the Pole Kazimierz Moczarski. One day in November 1949 he reminisced:[12] "The fighting in the ghetto was really tough. Whatever others may say, I shall always hold that the Jews had prepared themselves well for the battle and that they had demonstrated great fighting qualities. How strong and organized was the resistance of the Warsaw Jews is shown by the fact that we destroyed a total of 631 bunkers. It makes no difference whether they were combat bunkers or residential bunkers, for each residential bunker could at any time become a source of aggression and a base of armed resistance. Can you imagine, Herr Moczarski, how much time, money and effort must have been expended by the Jewish engineers and technicians to have built so many bunkers unbeknown to us? This was a truly impressive achievement!"

The fact that an entire underground system of bunkers had been built by the Jews without becoming known to Dr. Hahn's Sicherheitsdienst, Stroop told Moczarski on another occasion, also proved that there had been few traitors among the Jews, ". . . even though Dr. Hahn* claimed that he had the entire Jewish community honeycombed by his agents and informers, I do not believe that such was the case, for it is my opinion that the percentage of traitors or people inclined to commit treachery was not higher among the Jews than among other peoples—among the population of the General-Government in particular. The percentage among the Jews was rather lower. Why do I think so? Because had it been otherwise, we would not have run into so many surprises in the ghetto and at least some of the hundreds of bunkers, whose construction had required months of labor and large amounts of building materials, would have been revealed to us by our agents. But, as a matter of fact, we had to search for them as though we were blindfolded, acting like drunken children in a fog, and, apart from generalities, we knew nothing about the underground organization in the ghetto. It was I who found traitors and occasional informers in the course of the fighting."[13]

* SS Standartenführer (Colonel) Dr. Ludwig Hahn, chief of the Security Police (Sipo) and Security Service (SD) in Warsaw throughout almost the entire German occupation. An Austrian, he was a member of Einsatzgruppe I commanded by SS Brigadeführer (Major-General) Bruno Streckenbach at the time of the German conquest of Poland in September 1939, commanding one of its Einsatzkommandos. The Einsatzgruppe I was made up of Austrian Nazis who later played a major role in the extermination of Polish Jewry because of their high positions in the SS and police machine in the General-Government. Sentenced to life in Hamburg on July 4, 1975.

The battle plans and hopes of the Jewish fighters were also summarized by Anielewicz at the last meeting on April 18 between the ŻOB command and the leaders of the combat groups in the Central Ghetto. In the first phase of the fighting, Anielewicz told them, the Jews would exploit the element of surprise to deliver as many blows as possible against the enemy's forces. Then would come the second stage, which would be one of partisan warfare in view of the enemy's overwhelming superiority in fire power. "We shall wear down the enemy by ceaseless attacks from gates, windows, ruins, in daytime and at night," the twenty-four-year-old leader told his comrades-in-arms. "The basis of our plan is the ghetto labyrinth. The Germans will be forced to fight for months in the ghetto. *If we receive as many weapons, ammunition and explosives as we need, then the enemy will pay with a sea of blood.*"[14] As we shall see, the battle plan of the Jewish Fighting Organization was almost completely realized as far as it depended on the Jews. Where it failed, the failure was due to the fact that the Home Army, which was the only underground organization with large amounts of arms and ammunition, made no serious effort to supply them to the fighting ghetto.

II

At six o'clock in the afternoon of April 18 the Polish police began to surround the ghetto walls and at two in the morning on April 19 the Poles were joined by Ukrainians, Lithuanians, Latvians and German gendarmes, who set up machine gun positions and sentries every twenty-five meters. This was followed by the dispatch of patrols composed of Poles and Latvians into the ghetto. The Jewish fighting organizations, which had warned the people to go into their hideouts and bunkers, did not attack the patrols but went on with their preparations for battle. They also covered the walls with posters calling on the Jews to die with honor and hoisted Polish white-red and Jewish white-blue flags, as well as at least one red flag, over the highest buildings in the ghetto. There was also a streamer near the ghetto wall calling on the Poles to rise against the Germans.

At five o'clock in the morning of April 19 Sammern-Frankenegg led his force into the Central Ghetto. We do not know how large it was, for in his report Stroop spoke only of sixteen officers and 250 SS men and did not bother to mention the Ukrainians, Latvians and Polish police.[15] The column was headed by the remnant of the Jewish ghetto police, of whom more than a dozen had been shot when they refused to take part in the operation. After the Jews came Latvians, Lithuanians and Ukrainians, who were followed by fifteen Renault tanks and armored cars, lorried infantry with heavy machine guns, ambulances, field-kitchens and a signals unit. The column was accompanied by a car with a powerful loudspeaker, through which the Jews were called upon to report willingly for "resettlement." After entering the Central Ghetto through the Nalewki gate the column moved up Nalewki Street towards the Nalewki-Gęsia intersection, where part of it turned into Gęsia Street and then into Zamenhof Street, which ran parallel to Nalewki Street. Having established themselves in the two main thoroughfares of the Central Ghetto, the cutthroats under Sammern-Frankenegg's personal command were then to proceed with the rounding up of the inhabitants.

But the Jews were waiting for the Nazis at the Nalewki-Gęsia intersection. There three combat groups led by Zachariah Artsztejn, Lutek Rotblat and Henryk Zylberberg armed with the only light machine gun and submachine gun in the possession of the ŻOB had taken up positions in the corner houses and in the Brauer Factory. As soon as the head of the column of singing Nazis crossed the intersection, the Jewish fighters opened up with their machine gun, their two or three rifles and used their grenades and Molotov cocktails. The Nazis fled in panic, leaving a number of dead and wounded. The fighters then ran into the street, firing their pistols at the Nazis who tried to recover the wounded and the dead, and proceeded to collect the weapons, uniforms and helmets from their fallen enemies.

To help his men who had been defeated at the Nalewki-Gęsia intersection, Sammern-Frankenegg sent a lorried unit of Germans. The German SS men stopped at the intersection and tried to crush the Jewish resistance by using flamethrowers. They failed to kill a single member of the three combat groups and by eight o'clock, after some two hours of fighting, withdrew and left the Jews in possession of the battlefield.

The detachment which had turned into Gęsia Street and then advanced along Zamenhof Street did not fare any better. When it reached the intersection of Zamenhof and Miła Streets, it found itself facing the central stronghold of the ŻOB, whose command bunker was at Miła 39. This was linked with the bunkers under the houses 67, 62, 52, 47, 44 and 38 and the bunker at number 35 in the parallel Niska Street. Here the ŻOB Command prepared for the enemy a classical ambush in the best traditions of the German Kessel. The column headed by the Jewish ghetto police and three light tanks reached the turning into Miła Street when the four combat groups led by Ber Braudo, Aaron Bryskin, Mordecai Growas and Leyb Gruzalc went into action.

They allowed the ghetto police to pass and then attacked the Nazis with grenades, Molotov cocktails and with their two or three rifles. One of the tanks was set on fire by Molotov cocktails and blew up with the crew inside. The Nazis scattered and tried to find shelter in the gateways and house entrances. Where there was not enough room to shelter everybody, the Germans took it from the Ukrainians by force. After a quarter of an hour SS officers with riding-crops in their hands appeared in the street and whipped the Ukrainians out of their hiding places. The column reformed and tried to advance behind a second tank, but the Jews hit the tank with a home-made bomb and set it on fire. At the sight of this the civilians left their hiding places and rushed into the street to feast their eyes on the sight of the dead and wounded murderers.

The ŻZW units involved in the fighting were Khaim Federbusz's group in Gęsia, Pawia and Zamenhof Streets, Lazar Staniewicz's and Binsztok's groups in Nalewki and Franciszkańska Streets, and Pika's group in Miła Street. A remarkable eyewitness account of the exploits of Pika's men was written down in November 1945 by Jacob Smakowski, one of them. Smakowski was born in Warsaw in 1924, the son of a poor house painter. He was sixteen when the Germans occupied Warsaw and a few days later he was seized in a street by the invaders and with thirteen other Jews taken to the site of the Polish parliament. There they were ordered to dig deep pits and bury in them Polish students, whom the Germans brought in lorries and shot. On the third day Jacob escaped and returned to his parents and sister at No. 19, Pańska Street.

To save his family and himself from starving to death, Jacob became a smuggler of food from the "Aryan" side into the ghetto. He had several hairbreadth escapes, including one when he saw six other smugglers shot dead by the Germans as they climbed the ghetto wall. In the Great Liquidation he did everything in his power to save his parents and sister, but was unable to rescue his mother and sister from the train that took them to the gas chambers of Treblinka. Eighteen-year-old Smakowski swore to himself that he would revenge them and the first opportunity occurred towards the end of January 1943. When his father was beaten up and robbed of his pitiful possessions by two German Werkschütze at his place of work, Jacob invited them to his lodgings on the pretext of selling them vodka. There he got them drunk, killed them and buried their cadavers in the cellar of his house. He took their pistols and in March joined the ŻZW. At midnight of April 18 he was with a group of seventy-five ŻZW fighters awaiting orders. His account follows:*

> We were sent to Miła Street where half of our group went into the courtyard of No. 29 and the other half into the courtyard of No. 28. I went into No. 29 because I knew well the house. Other groups went to Muranowska, Wałowa and Franciszkańska Streets. Our commander was Pika Finkel. He was dressed like an SS man and we were dressed like the Latvians. We waited. As day broke about 1,000 Latvians, Lithuanians, Ukrainians and German gendarmes** marched into the ghetto. When the gendarmes marched into Zamenhof Street and were halfway up the narrow Miła Street, our commander fired his pistol to signal us to open fire. We fired at the Germans and killed many. When the Germans inside and outside the ghetto heard the firing, they fled panic-stricken.

In his report for April 19 Stroop told Krueger that one tank and three armored cars had been used in the attack and admitted the loss of only one tank, which he claimed had been set on fire twice. He also mentioned the loss of six SS men and six Trawniki men "in the first attack." How many the Nazis really lost in the fighting which lasted half an hour we do not know, but it was considerably

---

* Jakub Smakowski ("Czarny Julek"), "Fragment pamiętnika," *Biuletyn Żydowskiego Instytutu Historycznego*, No. 2/94, 1975.

** Poles and Jews called all the SS police formations "gendarmes." The Germans in question were an SS Ordnungspolizei battalion. The Latvian, Lithuanian and Ukrainian cutthroats formed part of the SS Schutzpolizei.

more than the casualties admitted by Stroop. As for the Jews, they lost only one dead, a ŻOB fighter. The victory of the Jews was so decisive that, to quote Stroop again, "This attack caused the withdrawal of the units used in the fighting."

Completely shattered by the failure of his plan, Sammern-Frankenegg hurried to the Bristol Hotel where Stroop was staying and at half past seven in the morning told him: "Everything is lost in the ghetto, we are no longer in the ghetto, we cannot get inside the ghetto, we have a number of wounded and killed." "Sammern wanted to wire Cracow and ask [Krueger] that they should send Stukas, so that the ghetto would be destroyed by bombs and aircraft."[16] But Stroop refused to go along with Sammern-Frankenegg's proposal, since it would have meant leaving to the Luftwaffe the honor of wiping out some 70,000 defenseless Jews. He therefore drove to the ghetto to see for himself what was happening and took over the command of the operation. Thus, although Sammern-Frankenegg was officially removed from his post on April 24 and posted to Croatia where he was killed by partisans in September of the same year, Stroop became the virtual SS and Police Leader of the Warsaw Distrikt on the morning of April 19.

On his arrival in Warsaw Stroop has seen Ludwig Fischer, the Governor of the Warsaw Distrikt, and Lieutenant-General Rossum, the commander of the Warsaw garrison. Fischer had told him that should a revolt break out in the ghetto, it must be crushed at once before it could lead to a general uprising in the city, while Rossum warned him that if the revolt spread to the entire city, the garrison and police forces would not be enough to suppress it.[17] Stroop was therefore determined to use all necessary force and every means of mass terror to break the ghetto revolt within the shortest possible time. According to his report the average daily strength of the force which he used to crush the revolt and destroy the Warsaw ghetto was as follows:

Staff Headquarters	6 officers
	5 NCOs
Waffen SS:	
Third Battalion of Panzergrenadiers	4 officers
	440 other ranks
First Cavalry Battalion	5 officers
	381 other ranks

Ordnungspolizei:
First Battalion, 22nd SS Police Regiment	3 officers
	94 other ranks
Third Battalion, 22nd SS Police Regiment	3 officers
	134 other ranks
Technical Section	1 officer
	6 other ranks
Polish police	4 officers
	363 other ranks
Polish firemen[18]	166 other ranks

Sicherheitsdienst:[19]
	3 officers
	32 other ranks

Wehrmacht:
Third Battery, 8th Light Anti-Aircraft Regiment	2 officers
	22 other ranks
Detachment of the Training Armored-Train Battalion at Rembertów	2 officers
	42 other ranks
Detachment of the 14th Reserve Sapper Battalion	1 officer
	34 other ranks

Alien Guard Units:
Battalion of Trawniki men[20]	2 officers
	335 other ranks

Thus, according to Stroop, the daily average total of his force numbered 36 officers and 2,054 other ranks. But his general report does not enumerate the 100mm. howitzer, which he mentioned in his daily reports, the flamethrowers and the part played by the Luftwaffe. Moreover, it omits to mention the Third Battalion of the 23rd SS Police Regiment, which he enumerates in his daily report for May 15. Nor does his report agree with the statement made by his adjutant, Captain Karl Kaleske, to Polish interrogators while he was being held by the British. According to Kaleske, the Third Battalion of the Panzergrenadiers and the First Cavalry Battalion had each around 1,000 men, which was the usual strength of such formations.[21] Kaleske's figures are thus closer to the number quoted in Report No. 149 of the Department of Internal affairs of the Government Delegate's Office dated April 20, 1943. According to the well informed Polish intelligence service, "the ghetto was entered by strong units with a total strength of 5,000 men."[22]

Nor does Stroop's report convey even an approximate picture of the disparity in fire power between his force and the Jewish fighters. Even if one accepts the number of men in his report, their armament consisted of no less than 135 submachine guns, 69 light machine guns, 13 heavy machine guns and 1,358 rifles, as well as a number of anti-tank guns and 120mm. and 81mm. mortars.[23] And, of course, they had all the ammunition they needed.

It was with such a force that Stroop resumed the assault on the ghetto at midday. Supported by a battery of field guns sited in Krasiński Square, which bombarded the Jewish positions in Nalewki Street, his men again attacked with the support of tanks and armored cars the ŻOB positions at the intersection of Nalewki and Gęsia Streets. To help them, Stroop called on the Luftwaffe and several Heinkel-217s bombed targets that were pointed out to them by Luftwaffe observers.[24] After holding out for six hours and using up all their home-made bombs, grenades and Molotov cocktails, the Jewish fighters withdrew to the adjoining Majzels Street. But before withdrawing they set on fire the Werterfassung warehouse in Nalewki Street, where the SS stored property looted from their Jewish victims. To mark their victory, the SS men and their henchmen broke into the hospital at 6, Gęsia Street and threw the sick and the nurses into the flames, killed the new-born babies by smashing their heads against walls and disembowelled the mothers in the gynecological ward.

At four in the afternoon the SS reached Muranów Square and became engaged in even fiercer fighting with the ŻZW combat groups commanded by Apfelbaum, Frenkel and Leon Rodal. The ŻZW fighters occupied a block of houses in Muranowska Street from 7 to 21. They were entrenched in number 7, which they defended successfully with the aid of a machine gun until eight in the evening, when Stroop ordered his men to leave the ghetto. In the other houses the Jews used guerrilla tactics: they moved their positions by climbing over the roofs or passing from one house to another through lofts, tunnels or holes in the walls. They were so successful that they destroyed another armored vehicle and captured two machine guns from the Germans. At the same time other combat groups of the ŻOB and the ŻZW fought smaller actions in Sapieżyńska, Bonifraterska, Lubeckiego and Stawki Streets.

The fighting during the first day of the revolt was not confined to the two fighting organizations. Wild groups attacked the Germans or defended houses against them in Smocza, Gęsia, Lubeckiego, Niska, Zamenhof and Stawki. In Szczęśliwa Street two self-defense bodies fought in number 13 and in the Oksako Factory.[25]

Before night fell, the entire Nazi force withdrew from the ghetto. According to Stroop's report for April 19, his men had managed to capture only 380 Jews, none of them fighters, so that the Jewish military organizations could claim to have won an undisputed victory during the first day of the revolt. They had won it without any help from outside, for the promise given by Colonel Chruściel to come to the aid of the fighting ghetto resulted in a single heroic gesture without military importance.

On Chruściel's orders a plan to help the fighting ghetto had been worked out by the leaders of the Warsaw Diversion Command (Kedyw) of the Home Army in January 1943. Captain Józef Pszenny, whose *nom de guerre* was Chwacki, was put in charge of the operation because he led one of the oldest and best armed Kedyw sabotage units. It was decided that Captain Pszenny and his men would blow a breach in the ghetto wall in Bonifraterska Street, which would allow a large number of Jews to escape in the direction of the Gdańsk Railway Station and the Żoliborz suburb, and from there to the Kampinos forests. It was also decided that the action would be carried out by Pszenny on the first day of the revolt without waiting for further orders from his superiors.[26]

At four p.m. on April 19 Pszenny briefed the three sections that were to carry out the diversion and two hours later the twenty-five men armed with Sten guns were in Bonifraterska Street, which was crowded with Poles watching the fighting in the ghetto. The Germans allowed the crowds to gather freely around the walls of the ghetto because many of the Poles expressed their sympathy with what the Germans were doing. The Jewish-Polish writer Adolf Rudnicki, who watched the destruction of the ghetto from the "Aryan" side, recalls in his *Easter* that the destruction of the Warsaw ghetto took place during the Jewish Passover and the Christian Easter, which coincided in 1943. "As soon as the words were heard: 'You may go, the mass is finished, halleluiah, halleluiah!' the congregations hurried from the overcrowded churches, their souls still aglow, all vernal, with freshly cut flowers in their hands, towards the walls to watch the spectacle. To watch Warsaw's Paschal spectacle.... As long as there was daylight they hung out under the walls. They gazed, they talked, they regretted. They regretted the goods, the properties, the legendary Jewish gold, but, above all, the flats and houses, 'the finest houses in the city.' They said: 'Could not King Hitler have solved this question in some other way?' ... Behind the walls the people were dying convinced that human bestiality had reached its limits. And, indeed, what more could there be? But we, who were on the spot, saw how tiny, how insignificant is human conscience. The explosions shook the earth and the streets but not the people." It was in the almost ideal conditions offered by such a crowd that Pszenny's men spent an hour preparing their two mines in a house entrance. But before they were ready a carload of Polish policemen unexpectedly appeared in the street. One of Pszenny's men fired at the first policeman to jump out of the car and this was the beginning of a battle with the policemen and Germans, in which two of Pszenny's men were killed and four wounded without being able to explode the mines against the wall. In fact, the mines were abandoned in the middle of the street where they exploded blowing to pieces the bodies of the two dead Poles.[27]

According to the Polish historian Władysław Bartoszewski, "the balance of the armed action carried out by Chwacki's unit under the walls in Bonifraterska Street on April 19, 1943 must be appraised to have been negative from a military point of view. For although over a dozen German and Polish policemen participating in the criminal extermination of the ghetto were killed, the order of the commander of the Warsaw Region Home Army Command to breach the wall was not carried out. ... The fiasco had been undoubtedly caused, apart from the objective difficulties due to the choice of time and place as agreed with the ŻOB, *by the lack of necessary fighting experience*."[28] That Pszenny and his men displayed much more gallantry than efficiency and cool-headedness there is no doubt, but that was not the real cause of their failure. For even if they had managed to breach the wall, very few Jews could have escaped in view of the attitude of the Polish crowd and the absence of any organized help by the Home Army to make their flight possible. If the Home Army leaders had really wanted to help the ghetto, they would not have contented themselves with the symbolic action of one platoon, but would have staged, as promised by Chruściel, half a dozen or more similar attacks at the same time and backed them up with units positioned in such a way as to help the Jews who had managed to escape through the breaches in the walls.

But, of course, such an operation could easily have led to a general uprising in Warsaw and this the Home Army Command was determined to avoid at all costs.

III

During the night of April 19 to 20 groups of Jewish fighters left the ghetto and attacked the enemy in the neighboring streets, while others lobbed grenades and Molotov cocktails from the walls. The total effects of their attacks are not known, except that grenades thrown from the ghetto wall in Bonifraterska Street killed one German gendarme and one Polish policeman in Sapieżyńska Street.[29]

April 20 was the Führer's birthday and to celebrate it Stroop began the day by presenting the Jews with an ultimatum that unless they surrendered, the Judenrat members would be shot and the ghetto levelled to the ground. When the Jews ignored the ultimatum, Stroop sent his force into the ghetto and in the fighting that developed all the three areas of the ghetto became involved.

The German attack was opened by the guns sited in the Krasiński Square and Bonifraterska Street, which shelled the Jewish positions inside the Central Ghetto. One force resumed the assault on the ŻZW positions in Muranowska Street, and especially the combat groups entrenched in the house No. 7/9,* over which a Polish and a Jewish flag were still flying. The SS jumped out of their lorries in Muranów Square and as they advanced towards the houses in Muranowska Street they were received with bursts from two machine guns positioned in a house at the corner of Muranowska and Nalewki Streets. Having suffered a number of casualties, the Germans retreated in search of cover. Half an hour later they received reinforcements in the shape of five self-propelled anti-aircraft guns,[30] which first directed their fire against the machine-gun positions and then systematically shelled the houses. When the guns stopped their bombardment, some 300 SS men stormed the ruins and after hand-to-hand fighting captured eighty fighters who had completely run out of ammunition and Molotov cocktails. Many of

---

* It was one building with a double number.

the captives were wounded, but all eyewitness accounts left by civilians who watched the scene from their hideouts agree that the captured Jews displayed no signs of fear as they were marched off to be shot by the killers from the Security Service. In the end the SS captured the flags, but the fighting was far from over.

The ŻZW had been able to offer such efficient resistance because their supply of ammunition and arms had been replenished by Iwański's organization. A section of his unit under the command of Sergeant Józef Lejewski-Grabarz had brought a consignment of arms and ammunition through the tunnel leading from 6, Muranowska to 7/9, Muranowska on the first day of the fighting. The same Lejewski was to bring two more supplies of arms and ammunition in the following six days and to take a number of wounded fighters, women and children with him to the "Aryan" side.[31]

By nightfall most of the group that had defended number 7/9 were wounded and without ammunition. About twenty of them made their way through the tunnel and were transported in coffins by Iwański's men to a villa in the woods between Michalin and Józefów, fifteen miles southeast of Warsaw. From there Iwański hoped to move them to partisan units, but their presence was discovered by a Polish policeman, who on April 22 brought a force of German gendarmes and Polish policemen to their hiding place. In the fight that followed the Germans and their Polish henchmen killed eight men and six women; those who managed to escape attacked a Polish police post at nearby Otwock and freed a group of Jewish girls. Only two or three in the end succeeded in joining a small partisan detachment organized by the Polish Socialists in the Grójec District.[32]

Equally tragic was the fate of a group of seven left in the tunnel. On April 21 they made their way to the "Aryan" side and hid in the loft of 6, Muranowska until Iwański could organize their escape to the partisans. One of the Polish inhabitants of the house was a member of the *Sword and Plough* Organization, which was closely linked both with the National Armed Forces and the Gestapo, and he betrayed the Jews to the Germans. The Jews defended themselves, but several were taken alive and only one or two managed to escape.[33]

While the fighting was going on in Muranowska Street, other

Nazi units were busy in Miła Street. A detachment passing through Majzels Street fell into an ambush laid by a ŻOB combat group and lost several dead, while the Jews escaped without losses and joined their comrades in Miła Street. In Miła Street the Jews had hoisted a red flag and to capture it Stroop called on the Wehrmacht specialists with their flamethrowers, who set house after house on fire. An eyewitness account speaks of a young boy, mortally wounded, firing a machine gun from a roof in Miła Street until he died from his wounds.[34]

At three o'clock in the afternoon another Nazi force commanded by Stroop himself attacked the Brush Workshops Area, which was defended by five ŻOB combat groups led by Hirsh Berlinski, Jurek Blones, Jurek Grynszpan, Henokh Gutman and Jacob Praszke; three ŻZW combat groups led by Abraham Rodal (a brother of Leon Rodal), Khaim Łopata and Pinkhas Besztimt; and several wild groups. The overall command was exercised by Marek Edelman. Each of the ŻOB combat groups consisted of fifteen to seventeen fighters, including two or three women; the youngest fighter, Lusiek Blones, was fourteen years old, while the oldest, the carpenter Abraham Diament, was forty. The fighters each had a pistol, a Polish VIS or a German Lueger, one or two grenades or a home-made bomb of great explosive force with a fuse that had to be lit before it was thrown, several home-made iron bombs and a quantity of Molotov cocktails. Diament, a former sergeant in the Polish Army and a crack shot, had a Mauser rifle and so did two or three other fighters. But they were all so short of ammunition that when in the evening of April 19 Edelman managed to purchase twenty rounds of pistol ammunition, he divided them among his men, who on the average had only ten to fifteen cartridges each.[35] The ŻZW groups were better armed and had more ammunition.

A detachment of some 300 Nazis marched up Wałowa Street to the main gate leading from the "Aryan" side into the Brush Workshops Area. There, in the middle of the "Aryan" street and three meters from the gate, the Jews had buried a mine containing several hundred kilograms of iron. As the factory guard opened the gate for them and the first ranks of the Nazis entered the ghetto, the Jews exploded the mine electrically. Marek Edelman put the number of the Germans killed by the explosion at 100—no doubt an exaggerated figure; the ŻOB report on the day's fighting gave the number of German dead as twenty-two.[36] The survivors fled, leaving behind them the dead and the wounded.

Two hours later the Germans returned, advancing along Wałowa Street in single file and clinging to the walls. Thirty Nazis who entered through the gate were received with grenades, Molotov cocktails and two bombs and only a few escaped unscathed.[37] But once again Stroop ordered his men to capture the Brush Workshops and this time the Nazis penetrated into the area from several directions. But this time too they met with determined resistance and suffered losses due to Jewish grenades and Molotov cocktails. The Jewish fighters found that their pistols were of little use because of their short range, but their few rifles claimed many victims. Diament, hidden behind a barricade of mattresses, killed six Nazis despite the intense fire of a German machine gun aimed at his position in a fourth-floor window. The victory of the Jews was so complete that the Germans, for the first time in the history of the Final Solution, sent three officers with white cockades in their lapels to propose to the Jews a fifteen-minute truce in order to be able to remove their dead and wounded. In return for the truce they offered the Jews a peaceful transfer to the Trawniki and Poniatowa labor camps with all their belongings. Bullets, grenades and Molotov cocktails were the Jewish reply.

Like Sammern-Frankenegg before him, Stroop had failed to break the Jews in battle despite his overwhelming fire power. He therefore ordered his men to stop their assault against the Brush Workshops Area and called on the Wehrmacht gunners and the Luftwaffe for help. The gunners brought up a 100mm. howitzer and three anti-aircraft guns and at about six in the afternoon began systematically to shell the houses. Nevertheless, when night fell and Stroop withdrew his men from the ghetto, the Brush Workshops Area was still in the hands of the Jewish fighters.

While in the Central Ghetto and the Brush Workshops Area it was the Germans who had taken the offensive, such was not the case in the Factories Area. There Toebbens and Schultz had continued their efforts to persuade the Jews to report for "resettlement" but without success. The mass of workers had gone into their bunkers and hideouts and several wild groups had joined the ŻOB and ŻZW. Having been left alone on April 19 the Jewish fighters were determined to come to the help of their comrades in the Central Ghetto and the Brush Workshop Area as early as possible and the opportunity presented itself at six o'clock in the morning of April 20.

At that time a Nazi column led by a band and a tank made its way through the "Aryan" part of Leszno Street towards the ghetto gates. As the column passed houses 74 and 76, which overlooked the "Aryan" street, the fighters in the houses opened up with pistols and rifles and flung grenades and Molotov cocktails at the SS men, killing eight. The tail of the column scattered; some of the Nazis broke into the houses on the opposite side of the street, placed their machine guns in the windows and opened up against the Jewish positions, while others used mortars. The head of the column hurried on and made its way through Nowolipie Street into Smocza Street in the direction of the Central Ghetto. In Smocza Street the Jews had buried a mine, but it failed to explode. However, undeterred by the failure they attacked the tank with Molotov cocktails and set it on fire.[38] Instead of continuing on its way, the column was therefore forced to fight in the no-man's-land between the Factories Area and the Central Ghetto.

According to Stroop's reports for April 20, his casualties for the day amounted to only nine men: two dead Wehrmacht gunners who formed the crew of a 28mm. anti-aircraft gun used as an assault gun, and six SS men and one Trawniki man wounded. Thus, unless one rejects all the Jewish and Polish reports on the course of the fighting as figments of imagination, Stroop's figures cannot be accepted. However, in the same reports Stroop admitted the fiasco of his force when he informed Krueger that his nine assault detachments had captured only 505 Jews and that in the Brush Workshops Area only twenty-eight Jews had turned up for transportation. Thus, once again, the Jewish fighters and the unarmed mass of ghetto dwellers had triumphed—and triumphed without almost any help from outside. For apart from the assistance brought by Iwański and his group to the ŻZW in the Muranów area, the only armed actions undertaken by the Polish underground against the Nazis were carried out by the People's Guard.

Shortly before six in the afternoon of April 20 a group of ten People's Guardsmen approached the heavy machine-gun position manned by SS men in Nowiniarska Street near the Krasiński Square. The group was commanded by Franciszek Bartoszek, a painter and one of the most daring fighters in the Warsaw People's

Józef Pszenny "Chwacki"

Franciszek Bartoszek "Jacek"
(1911–1943)

Niuta Tejtelbaum "Wanda Witwicka,"
Wanda
(1917–1943)

Leon Rodal
(?–1943)

End of April 1943: the burning ghetto viewed from the Zoliborz section

The ghetto in flames (Stroop's picture)

Guard, his friend Zygmunt Bodrowski, also a well-known painter, Jerzy Duracz and Niuta Tejtelbaum. The position was guarded by Polish policemen and Bartoszek's plan was that one of his men would mingle with the crowd, fling a grenade at the SS men firing the machine guns and flee with the crowd, whilst the others of the group held back the pursuing policemen with their pistols and grenades. The man charged with the task joined the gaping crowd, but hesitated in carrying out his orders. Finally, Bartoszek lost his patience, pushed his way through the crowd, ordered a Polish policeman in German to let him pass and walked up to the machine gun position. There he produced his Lueger, shot dead the four SS men, turned round, fired at the nearest two Polish policemen and ran. His comrades also opened fire at the Polish police and the entire group fled together with the crowd without suffering any losses.[39]

For Niuta Tejtelbaum this was not the first action against the Germans. Born in 1918 into a Hassidic family in Lodz, she had joined the illegal Communist cell at her lycée and was expelled from school when the cell was discovered by the police. However, she succeeded in obtaining admission to Warsaw University and graduated with a degree in history and psychology a few months before the outbreak of the war. In the Warsaw ghetto she was one of the first to join the Polish Workers' Party and as she was blonde and blue-eyed, she was ordered by her organization to leave the ghetto and shortly before the Great Liquidation joined the People's Guard. She helped to organize the first partisan units of the People's Guard and acted as a liaison agent between the Polish Workers' Party and the Anti-Fascist Bloc in the ghetto. She also distinguished herself as a fearless fighter. Looking no more than sixteen with her blond pigtails, which were so long that she could sit on them, she entered on one occasion a well-guarded German building, shot dead a Nazi officer in his own office and walked out looking as innocent as only a killer with Nordic features can look. On another occasion she entered the house inhabited by a Gestapo officer, penetrated his bedroom and shot him dead as he tried to hide under his eiderdown.[40] But what made her widely known as "Wanda with the pigtails" was her part in the terrorist actions carried out by the People's Guard in Warsaw in October and November 1942.

As we already know, on October 8 the sabotage units of the

Warsaw Home Army Command blew up the railways lines around Warsaw in six places. On October 16 the Germans hanged fifty prisoners, thirty-five of whom were Communists, announced that the hangings were in retaliation for the sabotage actions carried out by Communists, and to make it quite clear that Jews and Communists were the same thing, buried the fifty victims in the Jewish cemetery after they had swung for a day from their gallows. To revenge the crime, the People's Guard created three combat groups, which on October 24 carried out three terrorist actions. One group damaged the printing works of the collaborationist paper *Nowy Kurier Warszawski*; a second group led by Bartoszek attacked the Mitropa Restaurant in the Central Railway Station and killed six and wounded fourteen German officers; and the third group, which included Niuta, attacked the German Café Club at the corner of Jerozolimskie Aleje and Nowy Świat, where it killed four and wounded ten officers.

In retaliation for the terrorist actions the Germans arrested fifty hostages and imposed on the city a contribution of one million zlotys. But on November 30 four combat groups of the People's Guard numbering nineteen fighters invaded the City Savings Bank in Traugutt Street and without firing a shot got away with 1,052,443 zlotys. Niuta Tejtelbaum was in the group led by Bartoszek. To conclude her story, she fell into the hands of the Gestapo in July 1943, stood up to all the tortures that the Germans could think of and died without betraying any of her comrades.[41]

The other action undertaken by the People's Guard on April 20 was led by Jerzy Lerner, a Jew whose *nom de guerre* was Lerski. With four other men he set out to attack the SS and Polish police post at the corner of Okopowa and Gęsia Streets and thus give some Jews a chance to escape through the Jewish and Catholic cemeteries, which adjoined the western wall of the ghetto, towards Żoliborz and the Kampinos forests. But their grenades did not explode and they were lucky to get away alive when the Germans replied with their submachine guns.[42]

On April 21 the fighting continued in all the three ghetto areas. In the Brush Workshops Area, which had been bombed and shelled for hours the day before and which was partly on fire, Stroop did not expect to meet with any more resistance. However, as soon as his cutthroats tried to move into it, they met with the resistance of seven combat groups. In the courtyard of 36, Świętojerska the Nazis were received with rifle and pistol fire by the wild Hamer Group and beat a hasty retreat; they also ran into organized resistance when they entered 32, Świętojerska, while at 4, Wałowa an armed group of carters drove the Nazis out of the house. Once again the Nazis withdrew and artillery, bombers and sappers with flamethrowers and explosives took over. By nightfall the incendiary bombs turned the Brush Workshop Area into a sea of flames, and hundreds of people in hideouts and bunkers were burned or suffocated. After nightfall the five ŻOB groups led by Edelman abandoned the Brush Workshops Area and made their way to the Central Ghetto, their boots sticking in the asphalt that had become like molten lava or smoldering from the red-hot pavement stones. The only passage into the Central Ghetto was through a six-foot-wide breach in the wall, which was guarded by twelve German gendarmes, Ukrainians and Polish policemen. As the Jews approached it under a hail of bullets, a searchlight was directed at the breach, but one of the fighters by the name of Romanowicz put it out of action with a single shot and the Jews raced through the openings.[43]

In the Central Ghetto fighting had gone on throughout the day in Zamenhof, Franciszkańska, Niska, Szczęśliwa, Pokorna and Wołyńska Streets. In Zamenhof Street a combat group entrenched in the police building at number 20 had for several hours beaten back all German attempts to seize it. Finally, after losing several dead and wounded, the Nazis called on the sappers who used flamethrowers and dynamite to set the house on fire. But the main effort of Stroop's force was directed against the Factories Area, where the Jews refused to report for "resettlement" despite the efforts of Toebbens and Schultz to convince them that they could save their lives by working in the Poniatowa and Trawniki "labor camps." Schultz addressed the workers in the yard of his factory; when they refused to carry out his orders, the SS marched in and the workers scattered and took refuge in their bunkers and hideouts. The ŻZW and ŻOB combat groups received the Nazis with grenades and Molotov cocktails and killed four in the yard. The SS men then proceeded to blow up the bunkers, but met with fierce resistance and had to retreat from the factory grounds when the fighters set the warehouses on fire.[44]

The fighting spread from the factories to Karmelicka, Nowolipie, Smocza and Nowolipki Streets, where both ŻOB and ŻZW combat groups fought on until they completely ran out of ammunition, grenades and Molotov cocktails or were overcome by flames, gas or smoke. But although the losses of the combat groups were heavy, they were neither destroyed nor broken. On the contrary, their spirit was such that although the ghetto had been bombed and shelled for ten hours on April 21 and they were almost without ammunition, some groups sought out the enemy. Thus the ŻZW combat group commanded by Nathan Szulc and Pinkas Taub emerged from their bunker at 25, Nowolipie Street, made their way to a nearby church occupied by Nazis and attacked them.[45] The ŻOB Command could therefore write at the close of April 21 in its Communiqué No. 4: "Our fighters are fighting on magnificently. The morale in the fighting units is excellent. Our losses in men are relatively small. We are short of ammunition. We shall fight on as long as we are alive."[46]

The same day a Polish eyewitness of the fighting wrote in an underground Polish paper:[47]

> In the course of two wars I have been in many battles, but none had the same shattering effect on me as the one I witnessed yesterday. Through the flames of raging conflagrations, to the roar of anti-tank guns, field guns and mortars, German sappers made their way towards the Jewish positions and placed their dynamite charges. They also used flamethrowers. After this softening up the German infantry stormed the positions and was thrown back time after time by the Jews. I counted fifteen dead and 138 wounded Germans in a single sector. The Jews had machine guns and a large quantity of grenades. They defended themselves furiously and with determination. The tanks and armored cars were received with bottles filled with petrol. I saw a burning German tank from which the burned crew was being taken out.

Nevertheless, in his reports for April 21 Stroop was able to inform Krueger that his tactics had produced results: his men had managed to round up 5,200 Jews during the day.

IV

In his first report for April 22 Stroop told Krueger: "Setting houses on fire produced during the night the result that the Jews, who despite all our searches had remained hidden so far in the lofts, cellars and other hideouts, have begun to appear in the open to escape the flames in one way or another. Encircled by flames, the Jews in large numbers, entire families of them, have been jumping from the windows or lowering themselves with the aid of knotted sheets. Measures have been taken to liquidate both the first and second. All through the night there was firing again from the houses which we assumed to have been cleared." Thanks to the spreading fires he could claim the capture of 6,400 Jews at the close of April 22.

On April 22 the fires joined up and engulfed Świętojerska, Franciszkańska, Wałowa, Nalewki and Zamenhof Streets. Thousands of Jews were burnt alive; hundreds who had jumped from burning houses and had not been killed at once lay in the streets, their bones broken, parts of their bodies charred, suffering unimaginable agony, often begging in vain for a bullet from the Germans and their Lithuanian, Latvian or Ukrainian henchmen.[48] The Pole Józef Małecki,[48a] a member of the General Staff of the People's Guard who was in overall charge of the assistance given to the Jews by his organization, found himself watching the ghetto from Powązki. "The contempt for death and the Germans displayed by the inhabitants of the ghetto was without parallel," he recalled fourteen years later. ". . . Standing in the midst of a mass of people near Dzika Street I could observe the behavior of the ghetto inhabitants in the houses in Miła Street. The houses were set on fire by special Nazi detachments. The people hiding in the houses fled from the flames from one storey to another. When the flames reached the fourth floor, which was the top one, the murderers 'magnanimously' put up a long ladder and proposed to the Jews to use it. Not a single person took advantage of their offer. . . ."[49]

Many of the Jews sought refuge in the sewers, but Stroop had taken measures against them too. Already on the first day of the uprising he had ordered the Warsaw water and sanitation board to block the sewers underneath the ghetto and then to flood them. His scheme failed because the Jews, helped by some Polish workers employed by the board, removed the blockages. Stroop then ordered that creosote be poured into the ghetto sewers and when this also failed to stop the Jews from using them, his Wehrmacht experts proceeded to throw gas grenades into them and to boobytrap the manholes.

Throughout the day there was sporadic fighting in Świętojerska, Franciszkańska and Muranowska Streets, while in the Factories Area the Jewish combat groups beat back most attempts of the Nazis to storm the houses which they used as strongholds. The SS men mostly confined themselves to bombarding the Jewish positions with mortars while waiting for the Wehrmacht sappers to use dynamite and flamethrowers. Although no longer able to coordinate their actions, the ŻOB and ŻZW combat groups fought everywhere and so did groups of anonymous Jews in defense of their bunkers. Jewish resistance was so fierce that in his reports for April 22 Stroop had to record the first death of an officer, SS Untersturmführer (Second Lieutenant) Otto Dehmke, who was blown up by one of his own grenades when it was hit by a grenade thrown by a Jew. At his trial in Warsaw Stroop recalled that his men had been unable to capture a house at the corner of Muranowska and Nalewki Streets and that after two or three days of fighting Dehmke and his assault unit broke into it. It was then, Stroop recalled, that Dehmke and another German were killed and the assault unit was forced to retreat. According to Kaleske, Stroop revenged Dehmke's death by having the SD execute several hundred Jews on the spot.[50]

On April 22 the small Polish left-wing combat organizations made several attempts to help the fighting Jews. At half past four in the morning a People's Guard unit commanded by Franciszek Bartoszek blew up the rails near the Western Railway Station and later in the day another group led by him set on fire a troop train in the hope that their actions would slow down the transportation of the captured Jews to Treblinka and the camps in the Lublin region.[51] Shortly after midday a larger group of the People's Guard led by Józef Podkański, a tramway worker, made their way towards the wall in Bonifraterska Street, but were all captured by the Germans and shot on the spot.[52] According to Stroop's report, twenty-five died shouting, "Long live Poland! Long live Moscow!" At about the same time a PLAN combat group led by Więckowski carried out two attacks: one unit attacked a Lithuanian detachment in the Muranów Square area, as a result of which a number of Jews managed to escape into the "Aryan" streets, while a second unit attacked some SS men in Pańska Street, near the Factories Area. A year later, in the course of the Warsaw Uprising, Więckowski was killed with a group of survivors of the ŻZW in the Wola suburb.[53]

On April 20 Governor-General Frank had informed Hitler through Lammers, the chief of the Führer's chancellery for state matters, that "Since yesterday we have in Warsaw a well organized rising in the ghetto, which we have already been forced to deal with by the use of artillery."[54] The nature of the ghetto uprising must, however, have been kept from other Nazi leaders both by Hitler and Himmler, for Goebbels recorded in his diary on April 25: "From a report reaching me from the occupied areas I gather that a truly grotesque situation obtains in Warsaw. The Jews tried to leave the ghetto by subterranean passages. Thereupon these underground passages were flooded. The ghetto is now under artillery fire. When such conditions prevail in an occupied city, it certainly cannot be said to be pacified. It is high time that we evacuated the Jews as quickly as possible from the General-Government."[55] Himmler, however, who knew very well what was happening in Warsaw and was aware that the original plan to liquidate the ghetto in three days had failed, ordered Krueger on April 23 to liquidate the uprising without regard to the losses which total annihilation would cause to the armaments industry. "On April 23," Stroop recalled in the introduction to his report, "the Reichsführer SS ordered through the Higher SS and Police Leader [Krueger] in Cracow that the clearing of the Warsaw ghetto be carried out with the utmost toughness and ruthlessness. I therefore decided to destroy totally the Jewish quarter through burning down all the housing blocks, including the housing blocks around the armament factories. One factory after another was systematically emptied and then destroyed by fire."[56]

The systematic burning of street after street did not break the spirit of the Jewish fighters. On April 23 the strongest resistance was put up by the combat groups in Leszno and Nowolipie Streets, where Stroop's battalions concentrated most of their efforts on rounding up the workers of the Factories Area. At the same time the Jews also began the systematic burning of factories and warehouses to prevent the removal of the machinery and raw materials by the Germans. Also on April 23 Nathan Szulc and his comrades set out with explosives from their bunker at 5, Karmelicka Street for SS Obersturmführer Brandt's Gestapo headquarters at 103, Żelazna Street, determined to blow them up. However, they encountered a German patrol and in the battle that followed most of them died, but not without killing and wounding several Nazis.[57]

On April 23 the Polish underground organizations made their maximum effort to help the fighting ghetto. The commander of the Warsaw People's Guard was Dr. Henryk Sternhel, a Jewish physician who had fought in the International Brigades in Spain. As medical officer of the Adam Mickiewicz Battalion of the Polish Jarosław Dąbrowski Brigade, Sternhel had distinguished himself both as a doctor and commander. After the fall of the Spanish Republic he was interned with other Poles in France and when France collapsed he managed to join the French underground. In 1942 he and several dozen Polish veterans of the International Brigades made their way to Poland, where they were to play a most important role in organizing the People's Guard and its first partisan detachments. On April 23, Gustaw, as Dr. Sternhel was known, took command of one of the three four-man teams that set out to help the Jewish fighters. The second team was led by Michał Tetmajer and the third by Jerzy Lerner. The task of the three groups was the same: to approach the walls of the ghetto and to attack with grenades any group of SS men or Polish policemen they met, or should they fail to meet such groups, to attack SS and police posts.

Sternhel's team arrived in Freta Street at half past five in the afternoon and saw a Gestapo car stop outside a house, which probably served as a transit point for Jews escaping from the ghetto. While four gendarmes remained in the car, the others invaded the house. Sternhel's team lobbed two grenades at the car, killed the Germans and got away safely.[58] Teams Two and Three joined up against their orders with the intention of capturing a car and then attacking the Germans from it, but at the corner of Gęsia and Okopowa Streets somebody in the Polish crowd recognized Lerner as a Jew and demanded to see his identity papers. Lerner produced his pistol and opened fire, but his companions lost their heads and proved of no help to their commander. Pursued by a Polish policeman, Lerner ran into Leszno Street, where he was cornered by German gendarmes in the gate of a house. After shooting dead three Germans, he blew himself up with his only grenade.[59] The report of the People's Guard General Staff on the three actions concluded that Lerner's companions had displayed "insufficient military training," but praised the three fighters who had accompanied Dr. Sternhel, two of whom were the Jews Solomon Szlakman, whose *nom de guerre* was Stefan Koluszko, and eighteen-year-old Rysiek Moselman. Both Szlakman and Moselman had acted as liaison men between the ghetto and the People's Guard.[60]

The same day the Home Army also carried out its second major action to help the Jews. After the failure of Captain Pszenny's attempt to blow up the wall in Bonifraterska Street, Lieutenant Jerzy Skupieński, whose *nom de guerre* was Jotes, was ordered on April 22 by the Diversion Command to take his special unit from the Wola suburb and to blow on the following day a breach in the ghetto wall in Okopowa Street between Dzielna and Pawia Streets. However, at the last moment Skupieński informed his superiors that he was incapable of carrying out the mission and Captain Jerzy Lewiński, known as Chuchro, who was the commander of all the Diversion Units of the Home Army Warsaw Region Command, had to undertake it himself. With two other officers and four soldiers he arrived in Okopowa Street at midday on April 23, his plan being to approach with a sapper carrying a mine the locked gate at the corner of Pawia and Okopowa Streets and to blow it up, while the others of his group covered his retreat. But the group ran into several German, Ukrainian and Latvian sentries and patrols, so that Lewiński and his companions never even managed to get near the gate. The group had to beat a hasty retreat, in the course of which it killed and wounded several Germans without suffering any losses.[61] Thus Colonel Chruściel's promises of attacks "all along the ghetto walls" combined with actions to cause "several breaches in the wall from the side of the Powązki Cemetery and Stawki Street" produced two inefficient and unsuccessful operations without the slightest military effect on the fighting in the ghetto.

The same day Ensign Zbigniew Stalkowski and five of his comrades of Detachment DB 19 of the Diversion Command set out to help the fighting Jews by attacking Nazi units marching towards the ghetto. They arrived in Bankowy Square, south of the Factories Area, but met no German columns or lorries. They therefore killed a German policeman in Rymarska Street and another policeman in Orla Street, and, warned by one of their comrades that a car with German gendarmes was approaching from Zimna Street, scattered and mingled with the crowds in a nearby street market.[62]

A much more impressive action was carried out on the same day by Tadeusz Kern-Jędrychowski and fifteen former Boy Scouts. The older Boy Scouts formed their own units in the Home Army, which were known as the Grey Ranks (Szare Szeregi). Kern-Jędrychowski was an instructor at the officers' training school for the Grey Ranks in the Żoliborz district; at the outbreak of the ghetto revolt his cadets wanted to know why the Home Army was not coming to the aid of the Jews and those of them who had schoolfriends behind the ghetto walls refused to accept his explanations. They demanded to be allowed to carry out some action to help the fighting ghetto and Kern-Jędrychowski agreed to lead them. They decided to attack the SS guardroom in Konwiktorska Street, which overlooked the wall along Bonifraterska Street, and they carried out the operation much more effectively than their elders in the Diversion Units. They fired at the guardroom, then at the SS men as they ran out, and withdrew without suffering any losses after killing three Germans and wounding one.[63]

Another Home Army unit that refused to remain passive was the Sad (Orchard) Platoon, whose commander was Lieutenant Jerzy Morro. On learning of the outbreak of the ghetto revolt, the platoon met in the afternoon of April 19 to hear from their commander what were the orders from above. When Morro told his men that he had had no orders, twenty-one-year-old Tadeusz Zuchowicz proposed that they should pass their twenty kilograms of pistol ammunition to the Jewish fighters. Morro accepted Zuchowicz's proposal and succeeded in contacting the Jewish fighters, with whom it was agreed that at eleven p.m. on April 23 Morro's men would find a brick marked with chalk in the ghetto wall along Bonifraterska Street. They would then remove the brick and pass the ammunition through the hole to a waiting Jew.

Zuchowicz with three other men transported the ammunition to the Polish hospital in Bonifraterska Street on April 23 and shortly before eleven o'clock crept up to the wall, undetected by the Germans who were operating a searchlight in the vicinity.[64] However, in the darkness they could not see the chalked sign and it was already ten past eleven when they finally heard the noise of bricks being removed from the ghetto side of the wall. Zuchowicz removed the bricks on his side and an emaciated hand stretched out through the opening to get hold of the ammunition, which it passed on to another invisible fighter. After handing over the ammunition the Poles also gave the Jew the three grenades, which apart from pistols they had carried for their own defense, several packets of cigarettes and a note scribbled in the darkness which said: "Glory to the heroes. Our hearts are with you," and was signed by Zuchowicz and his companions. The Poles then shook the emaciated hand of the invisible Jew, replaced the bricks, fixed them with putty passed to them by the same hand, and successfully withdrew to the hospital where they spent the night.[65] One wonders whether theirs was not the most effective help brought to the Jews by a Home Army unit during the entire ghetto uprising.

Such was the sum total of the main armed efforts of the Home Army to help the ghetto. But according to Chruściel, "The action continued for a whole week before Easter, the most energetic in its execution being groups consisting of a crack platoon each that operated near the cemeteries and in Franciszkańska and Stawki Streets.... I cannot answer how far our assistance made it possible for Rakower's group (300 men) to break through."[66] The Rakower group was a wild group made up of porters who fought in the area of Miła, Wołyńska and Ostrowska Streets. On April 20 Rakower and nine of his comrades managed to fight their way to the Jewish cemetery and after reaching Żoliborz were helped by members of the Home Army to get to the Kampinos forest where all trace of them disappeared.[67] Chruściel's transformation of Rakower's ten-man group into a 300-strong detachment inevitably makes one skeptical about his other claims. Especially as in reply to Mark's requests for further details he answered that he could no longer remember which of his men had taken part in the operations and that the reason why their deeds had not been mentioned in the underground Home Army press was that "Both the Polish people and the Germans knew who in Warsaw was capable of such actions and it was therefore superfluous to make them public. There were, besides, certain sections of the Polish public, fortunately not numerous, whose attitude towards the Jews was unsympathetic or outright hostile."

V

Forsaken completely not only by the Allies but, apart from a few hundred noble individuals, by their own compatriots, the fighters of the Warsaw ghetto went over to the second stage of their revolt on April 23. Writing to Zuckerman on that day Anielewicz informed him:[68]

> ... What we have experienced cannot be described in words. We are aware of one thing only: what has happened has exceeded all our dreams. The Germans twice ran from the ghetto. ... I have the feeling that great things are happening, that what we have dared is of great importance. ... Beginning with this evening we are passing to partisan tactics. Three combat groups will set out into the ghetto tonight. They have two aims: armed reconnaissance and the capture of arms. Remember that pistols are of no use to us. We use them rarely. We badly need grenades, rifles, machine guns, explosives. ... Keep well, my dear. Perhaps we shall meet again. But what really matters is that the dream of my life has come true. Jewish self-defense in the Warsaw ghetto has become a fact. Jewish armed resistance and retaliation have become a reality. I have been the witness of the magnificent heroic struggle of our Jewish fighters.

No more weapons or ammunition from the Home Army reached the Jewish fighters despite Zuckerman's desperate pleas for them. Nevertheless, the ŻOB and ŻZW fighters did not give up their struggle. Nor did thousands of completely defenseless Jews, whom only fire and gas could force to leave their bunkers and hiding places. In the Muranów Square area, Stroop reported on April 24, his men surrounded a factory and tried to enter it. "As some of the Jews resisted, I ordered it to be set on fire. Only when the front of the houses and the adjoining building had become an inferno of flames did the Jews appear. A number of them were on fire; they tried to save themselves by jumping from the windows or balconies into the streets below where they had previously flung beds, blankets and other soft articles. All the time one could observe that again and again the Jews and bandits [i.e., the fighters], notwithstanding the gigantic conflagration, preferred to go back into the flames rather than fall into our hands. Until the end of the action the Jews continued to shoot, so that by the end of the day a unit of sappers had to make their way into the concrete building under the cover of a machine gun."

Also on April 24 combat groups continued to defend their positions in the Factories Area. There ŻOB and ŻZW fighters fought in houses 74, 76 and 78, Leszno Street, 67 and 68, Nowolipie Street and 21 and 41, Nowolipki Street. The Germans set on fire eight houses in Nowolipki Street, but the Jewish fighters retreated over the roofs, throwing grenades and Molotov cocktails on the SS men in the streets, and burned down the Wehrmacht warehouses in Smocza Street. Stroop then ordered the entire area to be burned down.

On April 25 Stroop reported: "If last night one could observe over the former ghetto only the reflections of fires, this evening one can see a gigantic sea of flames." Nevertheless, his men managed to capture alive only 1,690 Jews and killed in fighting 362 Jews. On April 26 he informed Krueger that all his detachments had encountered resistance and that while 362 Jews had been killed in battle, 1,330 had been forced out of their hiding places and "immediately annihilated."

On April 26 the Jewish fighters suffered a heavy blow: one of their arms caches exploded when the house in which it was situated went up in flames. Probably expecting that the explosion would break the morale of the fighters, Stroop once again presented the Jews with an ultimatum, which they rejected. At the close of the day the ŻOB Command sent to Zuckerman a report on the situation, which is the last known to have reached the "Aryan" side. The short letter written by Anielewicz concluded:[69]

> The number of our losses, that is, the victims killed by shooting and by the fires, in which men, women and children have been consumed, is immense. Our last days are approaching. But so long as we have arms in our hands we will continue to fight and resist.
>
> We have rejected the German ultimatum demanding our capitulation.
>
> Aware that our last day is at hand, we demand from you to remember how we were betrayed. The day of payment for our spilled innocent blood will come. Send help to those who in the last battle may escape the enemy's hands, so that they can carry on with the fight.

Whom did Anielewicz and his comrades have in mind when they wrote of betrayal? There can be little doubt that they referred to the leaders of the Home Army and the Government Delegate's Office, whom in his letter of March Anielewicz had accused of indifference to the fate of Warsaw's Jews and of "a cynical game with our fate." On the seventh day of the uprising, faced with the failure of the Home Army to keep its promises to help the fighting ghetto with supplies of arms and such attacks on the Germans as had been agreed with Colonel Chruściel, the ŻOB Command had every reason to believe that "the venom of anti-Semitism is continuing to poison Poland's ruling circles, despite the so tragic experiences of the last three years."

On April 27 there was some of the fiercest fighting in the history of the ghetto uprising. In the Factories Area Stroop's assault detachments concentrated on eliminating the nests of Jewish resistance that still prevented them from rounding up the thousands of workers for transportation to Treblinka, Trawniki and Poniatowa. In the yards of the Toebbens and Schultz factories Toebbens and two deputy directors, a German and a Jew, warned the workers at eleven in the morning that unless they reported for transportation by one o'clock in the afternoon, the factories and the people inside them would be turned into a pyre. The unarmed Jews, many of whom had not eaten since the uprising began, were on the point of giving up their resistance when ŻOB fighters appeared. Toebbens and his German deputy director at once fled and the fighters attacked the SS surrounding the factories. But by the end of the day the remaining bunkers used by the ŻOB combat groups in Nowolipki and Nowolipie Streets were blown up, while those in Leszno Street were flooded. Those of the fighters who could not escape fought to the last bullet or Molotov cocktail and then took cyanide; only a few fell alive into the hands of the Nazis.[70]

In the Central Ghetto Stroop was forced in the afternoon to send an assault force of 320 men into Niska Street, which in previous reports to Krueger he had described as destroyed and cleared of Jews. Unable to enter a block of houses where they had discovered Jews, the SS set it on fire. The Jews, according to Stroop "kept shooting until the very end when they jumped, frequently from the fourth floor, after having previously thrown beds, mattresses, etc., into the street, but always they did so only when there was no longer any other escape from the fire." It was probably on that day that the Pole Paweł Gołąbek, who had found himself trapped in the ghetto by the outbreak of the revolt, saw Stroop in Niska Street. "Stroop was sitting on a stone in Niska Street surrounded by high-ranking officers," he recalled at Stroop's trial in Warsaw in July 1951. ". . . I saw two old people, two young people and a child on a balcony. The house was on fire. When the flames enveloped the house and reached the balcony, the young woman addressed Stroop. She told him that he ought to be ashamed that the German people, who had produced Goethe, had also produced him who dared to do what he was doing. 'I do not beg you for mercy,' she said, 'because I know that I will not receive mercy from your hand, but remember that for what you are doing to us today you will not escape punishment.' At that moment the flames engulfed the balcony and the Jews began to burn. They had no other way out but to jump. The first to jump were the two old people, then the mother who took the child in her arms and jumped from the balcony shouting defiantly, and after her the man. Then Stroop got up and told the SS men to finish off those who had jumped from the balcony."[71]

The fighting in Niska Street remained engraved on Stroop's memory, for he recalled it in great detail when reminiscing to his two cell-mates in the Mokotów Prison. On April 26, he told them, he sent against the Jews seven assault detachments of seventy men each plus one officer in command. But although each detachment was by now familiar with the area where it was operating, Stroop explained, "The operation proceeded slowly. All the detachments met with resistance, which they were unable to liquidate without bringing in the sappers, flamethrowers and even artillery. Each operation took from one to four hours. It was a question of capturing strong points and hideouts, for not a single Jew emerged willingly from a bunker that day. We were compelled to blow up every entrance leading to a cellar or a corridor, as well as a number of courtyard gates and ground floors. The fighting was no joking matter! We were becoming increasingly and painfully aware that we were now fighting the most determined of the insurgents, the élite of the Jewish Fighting Organization. . . . On Tuesday, April 27, I used a new tactic. From 0900 to 1500 hours smaller detachments—there were twenty-four altogether—searched the Restghetto, captured about 800 Jews and shot about 100 who resisted, many offering armed resistance. And after 1600 hours we attacked the fortified houses in Niska Street. I used some 400 picked SS men and all the Wehrmacht men under my command for that purpose. We fought until nightfall, till 22.30 hours. The method used in the battle for Niska Street was the same as the one we had used before: our men approach their objective; the first exchange of fire; artillery is brought up; a brief assault follows. If we suffer casualties, I order the flamethrowers to the fore. All this time our machine guns never cease firing. The conflagration spreads—we set the buildings on fire in accordance with the direction of the wind—and we move behind it. We advance ever so slowly. We are on the lookout for moving targets. The Jews are jumping from windows, balconies, attics, roofs. My crack shots are firing at the Jewish 'paratroopers.' Some of the Jews are in despair and resigned to their fate. Others are combative and aggressive to the very end. They curse us. They swear at us. Some sing the Polish national anthem, others the Psalms. . . ."[72]

The main battle was fought again in Muranowska Street. The badly wounded Apfelbaum and Frenkel, with the survivors of the ŻZW combat groups in the Central Ghetto and of the groups which had withdrawn from the burnt-out Brush Workshops Area, had once again reoccupied the ruins of 7, Muranowska and dug their way to the tunnel linking their previous headquarters with 6, Muranowska on the "Aryan" side of the wall. On April 26 Jan Pika had made his way through the tunnel and reached Iwański with a request from Apfelbaum for arms and ammunition and help in evacuating the wounded. The Pole, fully supported by his wife Wiktoria, took his sixteen-year-old son Roman, and accompanied by his brother Wacław, his second-in-command Władysław Zajdler-Żarski and fifteen other men, all of them armed with submachine guns and grenades, made his way through the tunnel and joined Apfelbaum on the morning of April 27. Their expedition was, however, reported by a traitor in an anonymous letter to the Nazis, and to deal with the Jews and Poles Stroop sent a battalion of Latvians commanded by Lieutenant Diehl, who with his Schutzpolizei unit had had extensive experience not only in murdering defenseless Jews but also in fighting Soviet partisans.[73]

But the Jews were ready for the Latvian cutthroats. One group was positioned with a machine gun in the corner house of Nalewki and Miła Streets, a second group lay in the ruins of what had been

38, Nalewki and a third group defended the ruins of 7/9, Muranowska. Furthermore, a ŻOB combat group joined the battle in Muranów Square. At midday Diehl and his Latvians accompanied by two tanks approached through Nalewki Street and were allowed by the Jews to reach Muranów Square before being attacked. Iwański and his men let the tanks pass and then he flung a grenade at the SS men, who were armed with submachine guns and grenades. At this agreed signal Iwański's and Apfelbaum's men opened up at the Nazis from all the sides of the square. A twelve-year-old boy, about whom Iwański remembered that he was called Yankel, the Yiddish diminutive for Jacob, destroyed one tank with Molotov cocktails and was killed in performing his deed. The second tank tried to withdraw, but it was set on fire by the ŻOB unit. The Nazis retreated and called on the Luftwaffe for assistance. A German plane then dive-bombed the Jewish positions and only then did the Latvians resume their attack.[74]

Of Iwański's group ten died in the battle or from the wounds they had suffered in it. Among the dead were Iwański's son and his brother Wacław, while Iwański himself was badly wounded. The losses of the Jews were equally heavy. The leaders of the ŻZW, Apfelbaum and Leon Rodal, the men who had defended the Jewish and Polish flags on the first and second day of the revolt, were mortally wounded in the fighting. Both Iwański's group and the Jews had used up their ammunition and therefore, when darkness came, it was decided that Iwański's men would evacuate the wounded fighters and a number of sick and children, altogether 34 persons. Apfelbaum refused to be evacuated and died inside the ghetto on April 28 or 29, while Leon Rodal died while being carried through the tunnel.[75] Iwański recalled that "The rescued were placed in layers inside two hearses—we had previously prepared a wooden structure to prevent the ones at the bottom from being suffocated by those on the top—and then we put the lids on and placed the metal wreaths on top. Hearses with wreaths did not attract attention, they looked natural. The badly wounded were taken to hiding places in the city, most of them to my flat, while the lightly wounded and the sick were placed outside Warsaw."[76]

Although the battle had lasted from morning until nightfall, Stroop in his report for 27 April put his losses at two SS men and one Trawniki man!

But the fighting in the Muranów area was far from over. Smakowski's diary provides us with an eyewitness account of the actions of a single fighting group, the one led by Pika:

> It must have been the 28th of April. In Muranów Square the Germans ordered captured Jews to take off all their clothes, then searched their clothes, took their money and gold, ordered them to dress and marched them off. When night came we attempted to reach the "Aryan" side, but when about one hundred of us tried to get over the Muranowska-Pokorna wall, the Germans opened fire at us from the houses on the "Aryan" side, from where the Poles had been removed. About fifty of our group were killed and the survivors retreated.
>
> Later the Germans made a breach in the wall where we had tried to escape and placed there ten gendarmes armed with rifles, who fired at every Jew attempting to get out. The following morning Pika noticed fifteen gendarmes come through the breach in the wall and make for our house, because during the previous night they had observed that we had been firing at them from it. Pika, in his SS uniform, advanced towards them and said in a loud voice: "*Ja, ja, hier sind Juden da.*". ("Yes, yes, there are Jews here"). They saluted and Pika led them into the courtyard to show them where the Jews were. We were on the ground floor and when the gendarmes reached the middle of the courtyard, we opened fire and killed the fifteen of them.
>
> Later we raised over our corner house, No. 42 Nalewki Street and No. 17 Muranowska Street, two flags, a white-red one and a white-blue one, to show that we were not giving up, that we were insurgents. Poles watched through binoculars how we fired at the Germans and the Germans fired at us. Next to the flags on the fourth floor we placed a bomb, which we concealed under rubble and stones, so that those who attempted to take down the flags would be blown to pieces. We made the flags out of table-cloths; I sewed them together in our bunker. The Germans drove up in tanks. When they approached our house, we opened fire and withdrew to No. 40, Nalewki Street and from there to No. 38, where the Braun workshops were, and there we hid on the staircase of the fourth floor. That was our last chance. We reckoned that as soon as the Germans approached we would open fire and withdraw. Should it prove impossible, we would shoot ourselves, for each of us kept his last bullet for himself. Some had cyanide for this purpose.
>
> A number of our lads withdrew to No. 15, Muranowska Street. We saw the tanks stop outside no. 42, from where nobody fired at them. Behind the tanks came Germans and Ukrainians. The Ukrainians

went up to the fourth floor and approached our flags. Suddenly there was a terrific explosion, the wall collapsed and buried the invaders. The same night we learnt that a dozen or more of them had been killed. The flags were fixed to a wall and next to it we had dug a hole, so that in order to reach the flags the Germans would be forced to step where the bomb was buried. And this is what happened.

After our success we moved to No. 6, Wałowa Street. There we were reached by a boy who had fled from the bunker under No. 42, Nalewki Street. He told us that the Germans had dragged out of the bunker more than forty Jews and shot them in the courtyard. Several managed to escape through a back exit. They did it in retaliation for our flags. In our group was a lad whom we called "The Yellow Mellon." He proposed that we mine our gateway and kill the Germans who tried to come near us. We placed mines on both sides of the gateway, then we barricaded it and then placed dynamite above it. As soon as the Germans approached, we lit the fuse. The mine exploded and the group of Germans was killed. The explosion was so great that the gateway became impassable.

The Aktion was then in its second week. Two weeks passed since the outbreak of the uprising and the Germans had still not managed to get through. For us it was a convenient defensive position, for opposite us there were also ruins. Unable to get at us through No. 6, Wałowa Street, they tried through No. 32, Świętojerska Street. We let them come through there because we had placed a mine and when their tank rolled over it, the tank and its crew were blown up. The Ukrainians then opened up. We retreated to No. 6, Wałowa Street, but they succeeded in taking alive a number of our lads.

VI

The heavy losses suffered by the ŻOB and ŻZW in the Factories Area brought the dreaded moment when the surviving fighters had to accept the fact that their only chance of continuing the struggle against the Germans was to leave the ghetto and become partisans. This stage had been anticipated by the Jewish fighters and their friends and, as we already know, Iwański's group had risked their own and their families' lives to help their Jewish comrades leave the ghetto. Also Ketling and his PLAN organization were as good as the Security Corps. On April 27 thirty-six members of the ŻZW, five of them women, were in the bunker at 5, Karmelicka, which was linked by a tunnel with the "Aryan" side of the street, when a messenger arrived from their PLAN friends. He led them through the tunnel and sewers to 13, Grzybowska Street, which until the Great Liquidation had formed part of the ghetto, and there he left them after telling them to wait until his organization found a way of conveying them to Międzylesie near Otwock, where they would become the nucleus of a partisan detachment.[77] In fact, only a few of the group succeeded in joining the Polish People's Army, the joint military and partisan organization formed by the Revolutionary Party of Polish Socialists and the PLAN in May 1943. The majority died in the "Aryan" part of Warsaw.

As we know, the ŻOB had been promised by Colonel Chruściel that when the time came, the Home Army would help them and other Jews to leave the ghetto through the sewers. After April 23 Isaac Zuckerman made desperate attempts to contact Chruściel and make arrangements for such an evacuation, but despite Woliński's help did not succeed: he was either unable to meet the people who could give the orders for such an operation or told that the Home Army was unable to help. However, the People's Guard with its few hundred members found it possible to do what the mighty Home Army regarded as impossible.

The task of evacuating the Jewish fighters was entrusted by the People's Guard to Małecki, but the actual operation was carried out by Władysław Gaik, a Polish worker born in Siberia where his father had been banished by the tsarist authorities for his revolutionary activities. Gaik's assistants were the Jews Stefan Koluszko, a former Yiddish actor whose real name was Solomon Szlakman, Moselman, Zołotow and Szejngut. Contact between the People's Guard and the ŻOB during the ghetto uprising was chiefly maintained by three Jews: Tevye Szejngut of Hashomer Hatzair; eighteen-year-old Rysiek Moselman of the Polish Workers' Party; and eighteen-year-old Jurek Zołotow, also a member of the PPR. All three were to die in battle on the "Aryan" side while performing their duties. It was one of them that on the night of April 27, when of the twenty-six streets in the ghetto twenty were ablaze, reached the remnants of the ŻOB combat groups in the Factories Area with the news that the People's Guard had made plans to rescue them.

The ŻOB leaders gathered in a cellar in Leszno Street and decided that their only alternative was to leave the ghetto. Twenty-

Regina Fuden "Lilit"
(1922–1943)

Simkha Ratajzer

Mira Fuchrer
(1920–1943)

Leyb Rotblat "Lutek"
(1918–1943)

Nazis forcing women prisoners to strip

Captured Jews led toward Umschlagplatz

one-year-old Regina Fuden of Hashomer Hatzair set out on the perilous mission of informing the combat groups of the decision and succeeded in finding all except two. Only forty fighters were able to undertake the passage through the sewers: their seven badly wounded comrades had to be left in a bunker in the care of Leah Korn. The forty swore that they would send a party to save the wounded, but two or three days later the Germans discovered the bunker and murdered them before they could be rescued.

After setting on fire the warehouses at 72, Leszno Street the forty ŻOB fighters led by Regina Fuden went down the manhole opposite house number 56 in the same street. It was eleven o'clock at night on April 28. Guided by Regina Fuden, they crawled through the sewers all through the night and the following day and emerged through the manhole at the intersection of Ogrodowa and Żelazna Streets during the night of April 29. Regina Fuden insisted on going back and guiding those groups which had remained in the ghetto. Accompanied by Solomon Barczyński, also a member of Hashomer Hatzair, she made her way back through the sewers. Neither she nor Barczyński was to meet their comrades who had escaped from the ghetto; she was last seen badly wounded in the knee after a clash with the Germans.[78]

The other thirty-eight fighters made their way to 27, Ogrodowa where Ryszard Tryfon, a Polish worker, hid them in the loft. On April 30 Gaik and Szejngut arrived in a furniture van driven by Stanisław Tarczyński and carried some twenty fighters to the Łomianki woods on the outskirts of the Kampinos forests, four miles north of Warsaw. Those of the fighters for whom there was no room in the van were hidden by Tryfon in a cellar until they too could be moved out of Warsaw, but their hiding place was denounced by a Pole to the Gestapo and on May 6 the Nazis invaded the building. The Jews refused to surrender and fought until most were killed; the few who fell alive into the hands of the Germans were shot on the spot.[79]

Another group of ŻOB fighters commanded by Benjamin Wald had followed the same route as the forty guided by Regina Fuden and reached the same manhole a few hours later. However, having learnt of the escape of the Jews, the Nazis now guarded all the manholes in the area. As soon as Wald's group emerged from the sewers, they were attacked by an overwhelming force and died to a man after having used up their last few bullets and grenades.[80]

Also on April 29 a group of the surviving ŻZW fighters in the Central Ghetto led by Abraham Rodal made their way through the tunnel in Muranowska Street and by nightfall reached the Michalin woods near Otwock. The historians of the ŻZW do not tell us how many they were and how they reached their destination, but it seems highly improbable that they could have crossed the Old Town, a bridge over the Vistula and the suburb of Praga without the help of their Polish friends from Iwański's or Ketling's organizations. Their arrival in the woods was at once reported to the Germans, who surrounded them with a strong force of gendarmes and Polish police. However, the Jews managed to break through the ring and took a decision that must appear very odd. Namely, they decided to return to the immediate neighborhood of the ghetto and seek shelter in a bunker at 13, Grzybowska Street, from where they hoped to establish contact with their PLAN friends and with their help join a partisan unit. But odd as their decision may appear, it was dictated by hard facts: they were all alone in the suburban countryside of Warsaw and reckoned their chances of meeting a Pole willing to hide them until the German pursuit had ceased to be minimal. And so they made their way back to Warsaw and miraculously reached 13, Grzybowska where they joined the group who had arrived there on April 27. On May 2 a further handful of survivors from the ŻZW combat groups in the Factories Area made their escape through the sewers and went into hiding at 8, Grzybowska.[81]

The fighters who remained in the Factories Area carried on the fight. On April 30 the remnant of the ŻZW combat groups set on fire the Wehrmacht supply stores in Przejazd Street on the "Aryan" side of the ghetto wall and ŻOB fighters during the night attacked Nazi patrols in Leszno and Nowolipie Streets. As for the Central Ghetto, on May 1 the ŻOB survivors held meetings at which they sang the Internationale in a gesture of supreme defiance of the Nazi New Order. Moreover, to mark the day, the ŻOB groups decided to send out several parties in daytime "with the task of bagging the largest possible number of Germans."[82]

Shortly before midday a group of fighters dressed in German uniforms and helmets under the command of Mordecai Growas set out from the ŻOB Command bunker at 18, Miła Street and attacked a Nazi unit outside 47, Nalewki Street. The Germans fled, leaving behind three corpses, and returned in large numbers, but were unable to come to grips with the Jews, who disappeared in the ruins. The remnant of the combat groups, which under Edelman's command had withdrawn from the Brush Workshops Area and established a new base in a bunker underneath Franciszkańska, also sent out three parties. The success of the Jewish hunters was such that in the afternoon Stroop ordered his gunners to bombard the ruins, since he was unable to set them on fire. And in his daily report for May 1 he informed Krueger that his men had captured 781 Jews and killed 245 either in battle or because they resisted. He also reported that among the captured one Jew, on the point of being loaded into a train in the Stawki railway yard, suddenly produced a revolver and fired three shots at a police lieutenant without hitting him. "The Jews captured today," Stroop informed his superior, "had all to be dragged out by force from the bunkers. No voluntary surrender from uncovered bunkers was recorded today."

To his cell-mates Stroop recalled the incident with the captured Jew in the following words: "On the same first of May I witnessed an extraordinary event. The prisoners were rounded up in an open space. Some were in an utter state of depression, but others remained defiant. Humble but defiant. I was standing not far away, surrounded by my bodyguards and observing those men. Suddenly there was a cracking noise and I saw a young Jew, aged between twenty-five and twenty-eight, firing a pistol at one of our police officers. He fired three shots with the speed of lightning. One bullet hit the officer in the hand. We all opened up at the Jew from wherever we happened to be. I managed to snatch my pistol out of the holster and shoot the Jew in the body as he fell. He was dying, but he stared at me with eyes full of hatred and do you know what he did? He spat in my direction. When my bodyguards saw it, they cut his body to ribbons with bursts from their submachine guns until he looked like a long, flattened sack of meat."[83]

Before the end of the day the Germans discovered the bunker in Franciszkańska Street occupied by Marek Edelman's combat groups. When the SS men found one of the entrances into the bunker and lobbed grenades into it, the Jews replied with their pistols from inside. With all their attention riveted on the entrance, the Nazis did not notice the group of Jewish fighters who had left the bunker through another exit and attacked them from the rear with their few grenades. At the sounds of the battle the main force of the Jewish fighters emerged on the surface and, after inflicting several casualties on the Nazis, forced them to retreat. Abraham Diament, who was in the group which had outflanked the Germans, again shot several with his rifle before being killed himself.

On May 2 Stroop sent a larger force against the Jews and this was again defeated in a battle which Edelman described as "technically one of the finest," fought by his men.[84] On May 3 the Germans again returned and were again held at bay by the Jewish fighters who, according to Stroop, "fired simultaneously with revolvers held in both hands." In the end the Nazis managed to throw gas grenades into the bunker and this forced the surviving half of the fighters to withdraw. Some fifty men and women under Edelman's command found shelter in the bunker beneath 22, Franciszkańska Street, which had been built by the ghetto garbage collectors, while a few others made their way to the bunker at 18, Miła Street, to which the ŻOB Command had withdrawn after losing its own bunker. The Germans failed to capture a single live Jew.[85]

On May 1 Goebbels recorded in his diary:[86] "Reports from the occupied areas contain no sensational news. The only noteworthy item is the exceedingly serious fighting in Warsaw between, on the one hand, the police and part of our Wehrmacht, and the rebellious Jews on the other. The Jews have actually succeeded in making a defensive position of the ghetto. Heavy engagements are being fought there which even led to the Jewish Supreme Command's issuing daily communiqués. Of course this fun won't last very long. But it shows what is to be expected of the Jews when they are in possession of arms. Unfortunately some of their weapons are good German ones, especially machine guns. Heaven only knows how they got them." The state of anxiety in the highest Nazi quarters recorded by Goebbels explains why on May 2 Krueger himself arrived from Cracow and accompanied Stroop on a tour of the ghetto to find out why it was taking him so long to liquidate the Jews.

Stroop took Krueger to the northern boundary of the ghetto where in Stawki Street his men proceeded to capture the Transavia and Wiśniewski-Serejski works. The Transavia Works, where Jews

had been employed repairing aircraft parts, was defended by a
ŻOB combat group led by Edward Fondamiński, the secretary of
the Polish Workers' Party organization in the ghetto. In 1936 Fondamiński had graduated at the Warsaw Polytechnical School with a
degree in electrical engineering and in 1941 one of his professors
had offered him and his wife shelter, but both had chosen to share
the fate of the Jews in the ghetto. On May 2 Fondamiński and his
comrades defended one of the last buildings in the Central Ghetto
until Stroop gave his men the order to set it on fire. One of the
officers who had daily accompanied Stroop since April 19 was SS
Obersturmführer (Lieutenant) Franz Konrad, who as chief of the
Werterfassungstelle was responsible for seizing everything of value
that could be taken from live or dead Jews. In 1946 he was arrested
by the Americans in Austria and ultimately handed over to the
Poles, who tried him together with Stroop in July 1951 and hanged
him for his crimes. During his interrogations by the Americans he
recalled about May 2, 1943:[87]

> The entire row of houses in the area had been set on fire. There
> remained a house standing all on its own. As SS Obergruppenführer
> Krueger with his suite and Stroop with his staff were walking along
> the burning street, a man approached them and reported that at the
> back of the house Jews were trying to escape from the flames by
> climbing to the roof through the dormer-windows in the garrets. . . .
> The entire company went into a house entrance and in the evening
> light observed the people illuminated by the flames in their actions of
> desperation. A number of people had already reached the roof while
> others appearing through the dormer-windows were trying to reach it
> by climbing a narrow ledge. . . . The men were ordered to open fire at
> the people who were on the ledge. . . . The most terrible thing was to
> watch the children over three or four years old, who had the courage
> to try to save themselves by climbing the ledges three or four floors
> above the street. They too were shot down. A number of the wounded
> got caught during their fall on the open windows or balconies. . . . In
> order to prolong their agonies, no bullet was wasted on the people
> suspended in mid-air . . .

Six years later, in his prison cell, Stroop told his cell-mates that
"Krueger was worried because the Grossaktion was taking so long.
But when he realized on the spot how difficult the situation was,
how stubborn and determined the Jews were, how even the softest-

looking Jew could transform himself into a fanatical fighter, when he saw the *Haluzzenmaedeln*, when he heard the reports of the SS officers and the views of Dr. Hahn and Dr. Kah, he changed his attitude. As we parted he said to me: 'I now understand that in a situation so novel to us it has been difficult to achieve lightning successes. . . .' Krueger's inspection was favorable to me personally and raised greatly the morale of my staff and all my soldiers. . . . Krueger also told us to photograph everything. At the final conference he held in my residence in Szuch Avenue, he said: 'This will be precious material for history, for the Führer, for Heinrich Himmler, as well as for future historians of the Third Reich, for National Socialist poets and writers, for the education of the SS, and will document our efforts and the hard and bloody sacrifices that the Nordic race and the Germans have had to make in order to dejudaize Europe and our entire planet.'"[88]

Yet Jewish resistance did not cease. During the nights of May 3 and 4 parties of Jewish fighters dressed in German uniforms went out hunting for the German patrols that Stroop now sent into the ghetto after dark. Others set on fire the Wehrmacht fuel dumps in Stawki Street. In Leszno Street, which had been completely burnt out, the SS Nazis expected to round up only a few survivors when they entered it on May 6, but they met with armed resistance from wild groups and ŻOB fighters, which was so intense that in his daily report Stroop admitted higher losses than usual: one dead, one badly wounded and one SS Unterscharführer (sergeant) lightly wounded. On the following day the last ŻOB bunker in Leszno Street was captured by the SS men with the use of gas, but the resistance of wild groups did not cease. In fact, it appears to have become even more determined, for while in Stroop's earlier reports the number of Wehrmacht sappers engaged in blowing up houses and bunkers had ranged from 18 on April 20 to 43 on May 4, on May 6 it was 75 and on May 8 it was 74. As the sappers were employed in reducing Jewish resistance points by the use of dynamite and flamethrowers, many of the Jewish hideouts must have successfully beaten off the SS men before their occupants were blasted, burned alive or gassed. In fact, on May 7 Stroop again informed Krueger in his daily report that "The only and best method of annihilating the Jews remains therefore to cause fires."

No doubt his conclusion was influenced not only by the resistance which his men encountered in Leszno Street, but also by what happened in Smocza Street. About the continuing Jewish resistance in that street we know from Władysław Świętochowski, a Polish fireman who with his mates was ordered to keep the fires from spreading to the "Aryan" side. He recalled:[89]

> At the corner of Smocza Street I saw a young man, a Jew who had probably been flushed out of his hideout, run across an open space towards the nearest ruins. Two Germans with submachine guns were running after him. The young men fled up the skeleton of a staircase, climbing higher and higher with great dexterity. He was still being pursued; he climbed on to a balcony; he looked round and saw the Germans aiming their submachine guns at him. With the speed of lightning he threw a grenade, which exploded. The Germans were badly wounded, perhaps killed. We fled. The insurgent got away.

Świętochowski also recalled about the fighting in Smocza Street:

> One day I saw in my sector ten dead Germans and fascists of the auxiliary formations, as well as many wounded being taken away by German Red Cross ambulances. As I heard at the time, the number of casualties among the Germans and their auxiliaries was much higher.

More light on the nature of Jewish resistance during the same period is shed by the reports of the Polish police.[90] The report for May 5 and 6 said: ". . . Patrols armed with submachine and machine guns are watching in a number of streets the smoldering ruins of houses. Scared SS men are anxiously peering into the shadows of the ruins, expecting at any time a bullet in the side or the back. Jews emerge from bunkers underneath the smoldering houses and frequently wipe out weaker German patrols to a man. . . ." On May 7 the Polish police report recorded: "The ghetto seemed to have come to life again. The Jewish dead came out of their bunkers and cellars and again opened a fusillade. There are big losses on both sides. Explosions continued all through the day and the night, as well as small-arms fire." The report for May 8 and 9 said: "Heavy firing and explosions both on the territory of the ghetto and along the walls. Light anti-tank guns used [by the Germans] in cellars, various underground hideouts and bunkers. Victims on both sides, both inside the ghetto and along its boundaries. Thus in Długa Street a Jewess shot dead two Germans and went berserk, firing wildly until she was disarmed. At the corner of

Długa and Miodowa Street a completely exhausted Jew was forced to emerge from a sewer—he surrendered. Apparently the blocking of the manholes and the flooding are working."

In 1949, in his conversations with his German and Polish cellmates, Stroop frequently returned to the difficulties that he and his men had encountered as a result of Jewish partisan tactics, in particular after May 1. Questioned on this subject by Gustav Schielke, Stroop recalled: "After the first week's fighting in the ghetto I began to pay increasing attention to those reports, which suggested that the Jews were moving about like cats at night, that under cover of darkness they were regrouping, delivering their mail, transporting food, water and ammunition from their stores and answering our fire with fire. During my briefings I drew the attention of my officers to the fact that I had no idea how to deal with the problem. Then came the night of April 30 to May 1, which was bloody for us. The Jews shot three of our men, including two Polish policemen of the cordon surrounding the ghetto, and killed two SS men. There were over a dozen fire fights. My adjutant had to wake me up during the night. I was mad at the new complication. On May 1 I consulted experts on how to deal with the matter. This gave rise to gossip in the little intriguing world of my countrymen in Warsaw that in daytime I was capturing and killing Jews, but at night I was exposing my men to a certain death."

However, SS Hauptsturmführer (Captain) Alfred Spilker, a prewar policeman from Hannover who belonged to Dr. Hahn's Sicherheitsdienst, came to Stroop's rescue. He found an expert on partisan warfare in urban conditions in the person of an SS paratroop officer of Skorzeny's organization, who happened to be passing through Warsaw. "He advised me," Stroop recalled, "to select the cleverest SS men who had been trained in diversionary activities and organize them in night patrols, which were to follow the tactics of partisans and not of regular troops. I telephoned General Krueger, who himself had been an expert on day and night street fighting, and he accepted my plan. He told me to organize at once five such patrols of nine SS men each, and to prepare another five similar groups to be ready for any eventuality. It took me a couple of hours to pick my men.... On May 1 at 2200 hours, I briefed my new partisan formation. I told them to move through the ghetto using backstreets and alleys, and at irregular intervals of time. Their task was to observe the movements of the enemy's units and patrols, to discover bunkers, to track down and liquidate the enemy. I gave them first-rate equipment: submachine guns with large amounts of ammunition, grenades, knives, Very pistols, rubber-soled boots. They carried nothing that shone at night. Even their faces were blackened. I told them to put on under their uniforms waistcoats made of steel mail, which were impervious to daggers or pistol bullets. And this is how the 'nocturnal partisan war' started in the ghetto."

However, Stroop admitted, the Jews proved more than a match for his picked SS killers, even though they had no Tommy guns and their weapons generally consisted of a few home-made grenades and a few pistols with a few rounds of ammunition. Asked by Schielke how successful his partisan patrols had been against the Jews, Stroop replied: "My men did not prove themselves the most skilled and cunning in those operations. They made too much noise and found it difficult to take the Jews by surprise. . . . Despite constant improvements in our methods of partisan warfare, we were unable to liquidate the nightly actions of the Jews. We killed a number of Jews. I don't remember how many, but I would guess about thirty daily. We too had several badly wounded and several lightly wounded. One SS man was shot in the belly. We flew him at once to the Sudetenland, but the poor fellow died there. This happened night after night, because the Jews, who were better than we at such warfare, stubbornly continued to make use of the nights for their communication and supply activities, and also for fighting."[91]

VII

By May 8 hardly any members of the two fighting organizations remained in the Factories Area. The ŻZW group in the bunker at 13, Grzybowska Street had sent Abraham Rodal and another man into the ghetto during the night of May 5 with the mission of bringing back as many comrades as they could find. They did so successfully and set out again on the following night, but on the way back the party ran into a force of Germans and Polish policemen and in the fight Abraham Rodal and most of his group were killed.[92] It was probably also during the same period that Paweł

Frenkel, who commanded the ŻZW in the Central Ghetto after Apfelbaum's death, made his way with nine others to 11, Grzybowska Street where his organization had another hideout.[93]

Among the forty ŻOB fighters whom Regina Fuden had led safely through the sewers of the Factories Area on April 29 was the Bundist Zalman Frydrych, to whom the ŻOB Command had given the task of reaching Isaac Zuckerman and informing him that the time had come to evacuate the survivors of the organization in the Central Ghetto.[94] On receiving Anielewicz's message from Frydrych, Zuckerman again tried to obtain the help of the Home Army but ran into a stone wall. He therefore turned to the People's Guard and together with Małecki and Gaik worked out a plan for rescuing the Jews by bringing them out through the sewers. But before Gaik could find men who knew the sewers and were willing to act as guides almost a week passed, so that it was only on May 8 that two Polish workers, Wacław Śledziewski and Czesław Wojciechowski, and Simkha Ratajzer, one of the forty who had escaped from the ghetto on April 29, set out on their rescue expedition.

After many hours of wandering through the sewers they reached the manhole at the corner of Zamenhof and Stawki Street and at two o'clock in the morning of May 9 Ratajzer emerged on the surface, leaving the two Poles in the sewer. He made his way through what had been Franciszkańska, Nalewki, Miła and Zamenhof Streets and found no sign of life in what had been the ŻOB positions. Convinced that none of the ŻOB fighters had survived, Ratajzer returned to the sewer and with the two Poles set out on their return passage.

The three men had, indeed, arrived too late to lead Anielewicz and his comrades out of the ghetto. Stroop had reported to Krueger on May 7: "The location of the bunker of the so-called 'Party Leadership' is already known. Tomorrow it will be opened by force." To discover the Jewish hideouts Stroop's force used listening devices operated by Wehrmacht experts, dogs and a small number of Jewish captives, including children, whom they terrorized into committing acts of treachery by promising to spare them or their nearest and dearest. During Stroop's trial Edelman told the court how the SS men had captured a group of children and had tried to make them reveal the whereabouts of the ŻOB Command bunker, but the children refused to do so and were murdered on the spot.[95] Nevertheless, as the Nazis blocked all the five known exits when they attacked the bunker on May 8, one may assume that they had obtained the information from a Jew.

Anielewicz and his staff had occupied a bunker under 29, Miła Street when the revolt broke out. From there they had to move to 7 and 9, Miła and, finally, to 18, Miła, where there was a large bunker built by the gangster and criminal confraternity, who made the ŻOB fighters welcome. Altogether the bunker housed some 500 people, of whom 100 to 120 were members of the ŻOB. Among them were Anielewicz and his wife Mira Fuchrer; Fondamiński and his wife; Arye Wilner; Michał Rojzenfeld, the Communist member of the ŻOB Command; and three combat group leaders: Ber Braudo, Leyb Gruzalc and Leyb Rotblat. When the Germans attacked the bunker in the afternoon of May 8, the ŻOB members had only a few rounds of ammunition left and had not eaten for days. However, it never occurred to them to surrender. They intended to use the tactics they had successfully used before: one group was to defend the entrance discovered by the Nazis, while other groups left through the other exits and attacked the enemy from the rear and flanks.

But the enemy blocked all the five exits and when the ŻOB fighters refused to surrender, the Germans threw gas-grenades into the bunker. The non-combatants then left the bunker, but the ŻOB fighters received with bullets the Nazis who tried to penetrate inside. The Germans then again offered to spare those who surrendered and when the ŻOB fighters did not reply, they threw in more gas-grenades. Determined not to be taken alive, the fighters then decided to kill themselves. Leyb Rotblat, the leader of the Akiba combat group, shot dead his mother, Maria, who had been the protector of the ghetto orphans, and, according to one source, his Polish wife Halina, who had shared his fate in the ghetto. According to other sources, he shot dead his mother and sister.[96] The others followed his example and only four, who had not died by their own hand or from the effects of the gas, discovered a sixth exit and managed to reach the surface without being seen by the Germans. The survivors, Tosia Altman, Michał Rojzenfeld, Yehuda Węgrower and Menakhem Bejgelman, collapsed in the rubble and were found there during the night by a patrol belonging to Edelman's group. They were all killed later on the "Aryan" side.

Edelman's group based in the garbage collectors' bunker at 22, Franciszkańska Street had sent Aaron Bryskin with a number of fighters on the night of May 8 to find a way out of the ghetto. Bryskin's party emerged through the manhole in Tłomackie Street, which until the Great Liquidation had formed part of the ghetto, and ran into Polish firemen and Nazis. Unable to return to the manhole, Bryskin's group fought their way through the Germans and ultimately found a hiding place in number 14 in the nearby Miodowa Street. There they held out until May 27, when they were betrayed to the Germans by the house porter. After killing and wounding a number of Polish policemen and German gendarmes, the Jews all fell in battle except for one, who was captured alive by the Germans. A few days later Gaik, carrying out the sentence of the People's Guard, shot dead the Polish traitor.[97]

On the following night Edelman again sent two parties in search of an escape route. One party followed the passage through the sewers taken by Bryskin, but when they tried to open the manhole in Tłomackie Street they heard German voices and were received with bullets. But the other party led by Israel Kanał and Tsivya Lubetkin by an extraordinary stroke of luck met Ratajzer and the two Poles on their way back through the sewers.

Guided by three men, Edelman and Berlinski led some fifty fighters, including the four survivors of the Command bunker, through the sewers. Their goal was the manhole at the corner of Prosta and Twarda Streets, not far from Grzybowska Street, so that they had to make their way underneath almost the entire length of the ghetto. They crawled in impenetrable darkness through sewers 70 to 80 centimeters in diameter, now and then forced to dismantle the obstructions erected by the Germans, at any time likely to trigger off one of the numerous boobytraps, or to be gassed, or torn to pieces by grenades lobbed through the manholes, or simply drowned in excreta that frequently reached up to their mouths. What made their progress even more difficult was that Tosia Altman, apart from having been gassed, was also wounded in the head, while Rojzenfeld and Węgrower felt so weak that they kept begging to be shot. Their comrades refused to abandon them and Berlinski gave them the six cubes of sugar he found in his pocket, which, according to him, saved their lives.[98]

Finally they reached their destination and their guides left them to report to Małecki, Gaik and Zuckerman. The guides returned during the night with a pot full of soup and the news that between five and six in the morning of May 10 a lorry would arrive and they would be taken in it to Łomianki to join their comrades. At half past five they heard firing; when eight o'clock came and there was no sign of their rescuers, some shouted: "Let's get into the street! We've been sitting in shit for thirty hours! We'll perish in the sewers if we don't get out at once. Let's get out and fight!"[99] The leaders, realizing that to emerge in daylight in their physical condition would mean death for everybody, refused to give way. However, they agreed that a group of fifteen men should make their way to another manhole, while all the others would wait until nightfall and then try to cross Warsaw.[100] The fifteen went off to their deaths, while the thirty-four led by Edelman and Berlinski stayed and were rescued.

At nine in the morning on May 10 Gaik and Szlakman arrived in a lorry driven by Tarczyński and stopped outside the manhole, watched by hundreds of people from the surrounding houses. The two were covered by Major Małecki, Moselman, Zołotow and two others. Not far away was a Polish police station and in full view of the manhole was a bar frequented by policemen. Gaik and Szlakman entered the bar, found two policemen there, produced their pistols and threatened to kill them if they did not behave themselves.[101] It took almost half an hour to get the fighters out of the manhole. When this was done, the lorry drove them through Żoliborz to Łomianki, where they met the fighters who had arrived in the woods on April 30.

The daring escape of the Jews was at once reported to Stroop, who ordered all the manholes in the district to be guarded by SS men and Latvians. The result was that when the fifteen fighters, including one girl, emerged from a manhole, the Nazis were waiting for them and in the fight that followed not one of the Jews was taken alive.[102]

Only a few hours after helping to save the thirty-four ŻOB fighters, Moselman and Zołotow died in battle. They had agreed to meet in Bankowy Square, only a few streets from the scene of their triumph, probably to arrange the transportation of arms and ammunition to the men and women who were still fighting in the ghetto. But they were recognized by a Polish informer, who at once brought a detachment of Polish police. In the ensuing fight Zołotow was mown down by a hail of bullets, while Moselman managed to throw a grenade which badly wounded a policeman, and, although hit by several bullets, he escaped as far as the Saxon Gardens, where he was finished off by German soldiers.[103]

On the following day it was the turn of Paweł Frenkel and nine of his ŻZW comrades to be betrayed to the Germans by a Polish informer. The ten had been waiting in their hideout at 11, Grzybowska Street for their PLAN friends, who were due to transport them on May 12 to the Lublin region to join a partisan detachment, which was probably the one commanded by the Jew Szelubski. But on May 11 the Gestapo surrounded the house and demanded their surrender. For a whole day Frenkel and his comrades defended themselves with their pistols and grenades and killed four Germans before being overcome by superior firepower. Frenkel and six others died in the battle, but three of the ŻZW fighters fell alive into the hands of the Germans and were murdered by them.[104]

Let us now see what happened to the ŻOB fighters whom Gaik and Szlakman had transported to Łomianki. This is how Isaac Zuckerman recalls the events in a letter to the author of this book:[105]

> On May 9 I informed the Home Army that the fighters were in the sewers and on May 10 I was given an oral reply that the Home Army was unable to organize their rescue. But after the Home Army had learnt that the fighters had been rescued, I received from them instructions to convey them to Volhynia by our own efforts and with the use of our own arms.
>
> I rejected their proposal at once for the following two reasons:
>
> (1) The first reason I gave them was that it was quite impossible for Jewish fighters to march hundreds of kilometers from central Poland to Volhynia because of their appearance and the hostile attitude of the population. That would be a death march.
>
> (2) The second consideration which I had to take into account was that in Volhynia there were three principal forces engaged in fighting and murdering one another: Ukrainian nationalists, Soviet partisans and the Polish Home Army, which were all far from friendly to Jews. Is it necessary to spell out what would have been the fate of the Jews?
>
> Although I already knew enough about the attitude of the Home Army to Jewish armed resistance and to Jewish fighters, I still did not

imagine at the time that one of their groups would a few months later murder our fighters near the Bug River.

The position of the Jews in the Łomianki woods soon became critical because in the meantime the Germans had selected it as a place for carrying out executions of Poles. The Germans were therefore likely to discover their presence at any time. But once again the People's Guard came to the rescue of the Jewish fighters. On May 20 or thereabout Gaik again achieved what the mighty Home Army dared not undertake. He hired a lorry, dressed himself and two other men in the uniforms of German gendarmes, crammed some forty Jews into the lorry and, with the two "gendarmes" pretending to be escorting prisoners, drove from Łomianki south into Warsaw, then through the city and across the Vistula into Praga, and from there north-east to the woods in the Wyszków area.[106] What happened to the Mordecai Anielewicz partisan detachment organized by the ŻOB fighters in the Wyszków woods we already know.*

Let us now see how General Bór-Komorowski justified General Rowecki's and his own failure to carry out their promises to the ŻOB. The late general's recollections of the events were as follows:[107]

> When it became clear that further defense was impossible, we decided to save the survivors of the fights. During the night Home Army units gained control of the manholes in the vicinity of the Jewish district. They were opened and surrounded by armed guards. A reception base had been prepared for the survivors in the forests near Otwock (about twenty miles south-east of Warsaw), where they were to rest, receive clothing and food and then proceed in small groups by night and under escort to further bases in the provinces. Our intention was to form partisan detachments in eastern Poland from these gallant survivors, which was indeed their only chance of safety. However, when our men got through the sewers to act as guides, they found that the remaining resistance groups were composed almost entirely of defenders in such an advanced state of nervous and physical exhaustion that they were quite unable to attempt the underground journey. Only about 100 people took advantage of this means of escape.

---

* See Reuben Ainsztein, op. cit., p. 413. Almost all its members fell in battle against Germans, to whom they were betrayed by Poles, and the NSZ (National Armed Forces).

Bór-Komorowski's version of the events is not only pure invention, but a disgraceful attempt to rob the Security Corps and the PLAN of their achievements. Had the Home Army made any attempts to help the Jews who were seeking escape through the sewers, Colonel Chruściel in his letter to Bernard Mark would certainly have mentioned them. Moreover, according to Colonel Chruściel the concentration area of the Home Army for Jews who had managed to escape from the ghetto was in the Kampinos forests, west of the Vistula, and not in the Otwock woods, east of the river. However, it was in the Michalin woods near Otwock that Iwański and Ketling tried to establish a partisan base for the survivors of the ŻZW. Thanks to them a total of 140 ŻZW fighters, including a number of those who hid in Grzybowska Street, reached the Michalin woods and created a partisan detachment, which formally constituted part of the PAL, the Polish People's Army, which had come into existence in May 1943.[108] But Michalin was too near Warsaw and neither the Jews nor their Polish friends had any experience in partisan warfare. The presence of the Jews was reported almost at once to Stroop, who immediately concentrated a large force of SS and gendarmes in the Otwock woods. In their attempts to break through the German ring, one-third of the ŻZW fighters died; the remainder escaped but were unable to reorganize themselves in a partisan detachment.[109] Some made their way to the Lublin region, where they joined People's Guard or Soviet partisan detachments. Others survived in hiding in the Warsaw area until the Polish uprising of 1944, when they joined the PAL and Security Corps units and were almost all killed in the fighting or after the surrender.

A year later, at the outbreak of the Warsaw Uprising, the paper strength of the Warsaw Region Home Army Command was 50,000 men and women, while in the uprising the actual strength of the Home Army units was between 25,000 and 28,000 soldiers.[110] On the other hand, the fighting strength of the Security Corps units during the uprising was 620 men, that of the Polish People's Army was 120 and that of the People's Army, i.e. the former People's Guard, was around 600.[111] Thus it follows that the three organizations, which together were able to mobilize only some 1,400 men, were responsible for rescuing most of the Jews who escaped from the ghetto. One is therefore justified in believing that if the Home Army had done as much as Iwański's and Ketling's organizations or the People's Guard, not hundreds but thousands of Jews could have been saved.

Of course, it would not be true to say that no Jews were helped to escape from the ghetto by members of the Home Army. The Home Army in Warsaw comprised representatives of every social, political and religious section in Polish society, except the Communists. There were therefore bound to be people in it who found it beyond their moral endurance to accept the line of their leadership that nothing must be risked to help the Jews. The actions of the former Boy Scouts led by Kern-Jędrychowski and Zuchowicz of the Sad Platoon are the only examples of Home Army units acting against the line, if not orders, of the Home Army Command, but there were an unknown number of individual members of the Home Army who acted similarly. It was the moral plight of such individuals that made Jerzy Andrzejewski write *The Passion Week*, whose intellectual hero, Julian Małecki, sets out on his own to help the fighting and dying Jews because he is no longer able to justify his inactivity either by telling himself that the right moment has not come yet for the Home Army to fight the Germans or that however horrible the crime, Hitler is the instrument that history has chosen to rid Poland of her Jewish problem. And with the intellectual honesty that in 1938 led Andrzejewski from the anti-Semitic and fascist camp to open expressions of solidarity with Hitler's Jewish victims, he had his hero killed by Polish Nazis for helping the Jews.

But the number of Małeckis in the Home Army was so small that we again meet the name of Tadeusz Zuchowicz when we look for them—the same Zuchowicz who had persuaded his comrades in the Sad Platoon to give their pistol ammunition to the ghetto fighters. Zuchowicz set out through the sewers in search of Jews whom he could rescue. He met twelve ŻOB fighters who, contrary to Bór-Komorowski's version of the events, still had enough moral and physical stamina to follow the Pole to a hideout in Czerniakowska Street, from where he later conveyed them to the partisans in the Wyszków forests.[112]

VIII

With the death of the ŻOB and ŻZW leaders and the escape of over 160 ŻZW fighters and the two groups of ŻOB fighters, resistance in the ghetto entered a new phase. In his report for May 8 Stroop told Krueger that only 3,000 to 4,000 Jews remained alive in the ghetto, but as late as May 22 Goebbels was to enter in his diary: "The battle of the Warsaw ghetto continues. The Jews are still resisting. On the whole, however, resistance is no longer dangerous and has virtually been broken."[113] The Jews who carried on the fight belonged to the ŻOB, the ŻZW and to wild groups. They were unable to coordinate their actions and they had practically no contacts with the underground Polish organizations outside. Yet they carried on a partisan war against the Germans and their henchmen until July 1943.

Of the ŻOB fighters there remained the combat groups led by Zachariah Artsztejn and Henryk Zylberberg,[114] and a group led by Simon Mellon, a member of Hashomer Hatzair. Mellon's group, which numbered twenty-five men and women armed with eight pistols and eight grenades, had its base in the rubble of Świętojerska and Wałowa Streets. Other groups were led by Joseph Farber, Anielewicz's former adjutant and also a member of Hashomer Hatzair, and by Isaac Blausztejn, a member of Dror. Of the ŻZW fighters there remained two groups led by Khaim Łopata and Janek Pika. Other groups about whose actions fragmentary accounts have remained were led by Lazar Szerszen, who had escaped from Treblinka, Moses the Bolshevik, the Szermans, Kreński, Prywes, Kaplan and Simon Kaufman.[115]

The conditions in which the Jews had to fight after May 10 were infinitely more difficult than they had been during the first ten days of the uprising. Not only did they depend almost completely on what they could find underneath the ruins of the small hoards of food that had been hidden by the murdered Jews, but they also had the greatest difficulty in finding water. Furthermore, mountains of rubble did not provide the same cover as the ruins of houses.

On the night of May 10 partisans attacked Nazi patrols and on May 11 Kaufman's and Kaplan's group lobbed grenades and fired at Nazi units in Gęsia Street, so that the Polish police report dated May 11 said: "During the day there was intermittent firing in the ghetto, but during the night it was heavier and there were explosions." On May 13 Stroop reported to Krueger: "When liquidating a bunker there was a regular exchange of fire, the Jews firing not only 0.8mm. and Polish VIS pistols, but also throwing egg-shaped

Polish grenades at the SS men. After part of the occupants had been dragged out of the bunker and were on the point of being searched, one of the women, as had happened often before, produced with lightning speed an egg-shaped grenade from her knickers, pulled out the pin, threw it at the soldiers and jumped back into the hideout." The same day Sarah Rozenblum, who with a group of comrades was defending a bunker at 3–5, Bonifraterska Street, flung a grenade at the Nazis who were on the point of throwing gas-grenades into the hideout and killed several Germans.[116] Jewish resistance on May 13 must have been very effective indeed to make Stroop admit in his report that his losses for the day amounted to two SS men dead and three SS men and one policeman wounded.

On the night of May 13 and 14 the Red Air Force carried out the heaviest air raid on Warsaw since the outbreak of the German-Soviet war.[116a] Several Jewish groups took advantage of the bombing and attempted to break out of the ghetto, but only a small number succeeded in making their way through holes in the ghetto wall in Bonifraterska and Mylna Streets. During the bombing other groups of Jews attacked Germans who were patrolling the ghetto walls on the "Aryan" side.[117] Also on the following two nights groups of Jews, who according to General Bór-Komorowski were too exhausted to be saved by his soldiers, again tried to break out of the ghetto, but without success. In his report for May 14 Stroop complained that it was impossible to obtain any information from captured Jews on the still undiscovered bunkers and that Jewish fighters operated in German uniforms and helmets. One of his assault units had had a fire fight on May 14 with a "gang" of ten to fourteen Jews on the "Aryan" side of the roofs of a block of houses situated on the ghetto boundary. In the afternoon of May 14, Stroop went on in his report, the activities of his men had been watched by SS Gruppenführer (Lieutenant-General) Maximilian von Herff, Chief of Personnel in the Reich Chief Security Office. Also the reports of the Polish police registered the fact that "On the 15th and the 16th of May there was heavy firing in the ghetto. In daytime there were powerful explosions and at night intense firing on the borders of the ghetto. One could hear small-arms, submachine and heavy machine gun fire."

On May 16 Stroop reported to Krueger that he had completed the Grossaktion in the Warsaw ghetto by accounting for 56,065

Jews and that to mark the occasion he had had the principal Jewish synagogue in Tłomackie Street blown up. On May 24, in reply to a demand for further details, Stroop informed Krueger that apart from the 56,065 Jews accounted for by his men, 5,000 to 6,000 Jews had perished in the explosions and fires. Thus only a few hundred Jews remained alive in the ghetto. They included several bands of children who roamed through the ruins until they died of hunger or were caught by the Germans or the Polish police and murdered. Many of the children could have escaped through the holes in the walls to the "Aryan" side, but they knew that even there they would not be safe unless they had the very good fortune to meet one of those Poles whom Ringelblum called "the good spirits." "The longer the fighting went on," Małecki recalled on the fifteenth anniversary of the outbreak of the ghetto revolt,[118] "the more often individual Jews got out of the ghetto in search of shelter and the more frequently there appeared emaciated children in rags who begged for bread. There were always warm hearts who despite the risks they ran gave them shelter for the night or showed them the way out of the city. Unfortunately, my memory also recalls other facts. I recall three children from the ghetto with sacks full of rusks and bread in Sienna Street. They were stopped by two representatives of Poland's golden youth, who handed them over to a German patrol that arrived from Sosnowa Street. The gendarmes did not waste any time. One of them seized the youngest child by his legs and smashed his head against a wall and another gendarme shot the other two dead."

But the fighting in the ghetto did not stop on May 16. By then the fires had died out and this created more favorable conditions for the Jewish survivors, because they could move at night without being seen. Dressed in German uniforms and their boots wrapped in rags so as to be able to move without making a noise, the Jewish fighters set out nightly in search of German patrols. On May 18 the Polish police recorded that "Jewish detachments crawl out of the ground and make surprise attacks on the Germans. When night comes, the SS men withdraw from the ghetto."

On May 19 Mellon's group clashed with a German unit armed with a machine gun at the corner of Gęsia and Nalewki Streets. A well-aimed grenade killed two SS men and the Jews withdrew with captured weapons and ammunition. On the same day and May 20 the Germans captured the last bunkers in Miła Street, which were defended by Simon Kaufman and a few other survivors.[119]

The groups led by Artsztejn, Blausztejn and Farber continued to operate in Nalewki Street until the end of May, when the street simply ceased to exist. Artsztejn and other survivors then moved to Bonifraterska Street, where on June 3 they ran into a Nazi unit. They fought back but were too exhausted by hunger to lob their grenades far enough to hit the Germans. They lost four men and one girl as against three German dead and a few days later, when trying to reach the "Aryan" side, Artsztejn was killed and his group ceased to exist. On June 5 it was the turn of Jan Pika, the last commander of the ŻZW group, to die in a clash with the Germans.[120]

After May 20 the Germans again met with resistance in what had been Nowolipki and Nowolipie Streets and did not liquidate the last nests of resistance until the end of May, so that the Polish police reports for the period recorded: "On 27, 28, 29 and 30 of May there was heavy firing by day and by night, especially in the night from May 29 to 30 and during the day, when there was heavy fighting on both sides in the Przejazd and Leszno area. The Jews tried to break out into the Aryan side."

On May 30 Zylberberg and a few survivors of his group went down the manhole at the corner of Smocza and Nowolipie Streets and sought a way out of the ghetto through the sewers. "I shall not try to describe what it was like, I could not do it," he recalled twenty-seven years later.[121] "Thousands of corpses were rolling in the swirling current of the flooded sewers. In every branch of the sewers there were Jews waiting for a miracle that could never happen. The people would join up in groups, then would separate again and attempt singly to reach the surface. Many times we ran from the gas-grenades which the Germans kept dropping through the manholes. Those who could no longer escape died. We had no food, not even a crumb of bread. Driven on by hunger we crept out at night and like rats we scratched under the rubble in search of a crust of bread or a potato peel. I was gradually losing my strength, my body was covered with ulcers, my legs, encrusted in excreta and other filth, looked as though they were leprous."

On their twelfth day in the sewers, when Zylberberg and his companions were lying in the sludge waiting for their end, there appeared a Jew with a torchlight who told them that he had come to guide them to safety. They followed him and altogether thirty Jews emerged through the manhole at the corner of Pańska and Wronia Streets to find themselves surrounded by fifteen SS men armed with submachine guns. Convinced that they had been trapped, the Jews climbed into three lorries which drove them across the Vistula into Praga, where they turned north. When the lorries were stopped by the gendarmes at a roadblock on the outskirts of Praga, Zylberberg heard the SS men tell them in German that they were taking the Jews to their place of execution. The three lorries by-passed Legionowo and drove on to the Chotomowski forest, where they stopped and the Jews were told to get out. They did so expecting to be shot, but heard one of the SS men say in Polish: "You are free. We have saved you."

The SS men turned out to be members of the Home Army. Zylberberg and his companions were divided into groups of four, placed with peasant families and ultimately incorporated in Home Army partisan detachments. Zylberberg found himself in Jan Gustek's detachment, which operated near Kraśnik in the Lublin region. In July 1944 Zylberberg and several of his companions were ordered to make their way to Warsaw, where they were given the task of transporting arms to the various points where the Home Army units were to pick them up on the outbreak of the planned rising. Zylberberg fought through the uprising and thanks to his "Aryan" looks and false papers escaped summary execution when the Polish insurgents surrendered to the Germans.

The rescue of Zylberberg and twenty-nine other Jews by an unidentified Home Army detachment is the only known case confirming Bór-Komorowski's claim that the Home Army saved some of the ghetto fighters. However, both the fact that the rescuers took the Jews to the forests north of Legionowo, which is in the opposite direction to the Otwock woods where according to Bór-Komorowski the rescued Jews were taken, and the fact that this daring rescue in bright daylight has never been mentioned by Home Army historians, prove that the operation was carried out by a detachment acting on its own initiative and possibly against the orders of the Home Army Command.

While Zylberberg and the last of his group were wandering through the sewers, on the surface other groups of Jews were still fighting. In its reports the Polish police recorded that "in the night of June 1 to 2 the situation in the ghetto appears to have become somewhat worse. [Polish] citizens kept in the Pawiak prison are shot on the territory of the ghetto and their corpses are burnt on the site of their execution. There are various rumors alleging that the Jews have interfered with the executions and even attacked those who were carrying out the shootings. Today the ghetto borders were surrounded by strong SS formations and armored cars were introduced into the ghetto.... According to information received from the Gestapo, the German losses suffered during the liquidation of the Jews have proved too high in relation to the number of the Germans engaged in the liquidation." And on June 8, *Głos Warszawy*, the newspaper of the Warsaw organization of the Polish Workers' Party, reported that "In the last few days the last surviving ghetto defenders carried out several sorties outside the walls, killed several gendarmes and compelled the Germans to increase their garrison." The Home Army's intelligence service reported on June 15 that the Germans were continuing to send every night patrols of Ukrainians and Latvians armed with sub-machine guns and grenades into the ghetto and therefore "It may be concluded that there are still considerable numbers of armed Jews who are determined to defend themselves."[122]

In Bonifraterska Street several groups of bakery workers carried on guerrilla warfare throughout June until they fell in battle or died from their wounds, hunger and thirst or, in a few rare cases, succeeded in reaching the "Aryan" side. On June 5, Moses the Bolshevik's group attacked a German force in Bonifraterska Street and suffered heavy losses, but a few managed to break through the ghetto wall. Another group of young people operated in Majzels Street, where in one attack on the Nazis it lost two girls.[123]

During the same period the only help the Jews received from outside was from Iwański's group and a few individual Poles, who penetrated through the sewers with food, ammunition, a few grenades and pistols. Of those Poles a number were denounced to the Germans by the National Armed Forces and killed.[124] As for Iwański, he has described his own and his group's activities as follows:[125]

> Later, up to the middle of June, the ghetto was entered by our patrols,

which maintained contact with the Jewish fighters battling in the ruins, the so-called Rubblemen. We supplied them with ammunition, grenades, food, bandages and on our way back we took the wounded. We could evacuate only as many as there were in our patrols, for each of us could bring out only one Jew. One moved through the sewers dragging one wounded in a specially made sack, with openings for the legs and a grip at the head. The sewers were of different sizes, sometimes one had to bend in two and in such a posture cover a good distance—and one moved in filth. One therefore had to hold up the head of the wounded as high as possible or one would arrive with a corpse.

There were no big battles, but there occurred clashes between our patrols and German scouts searching the ghetto area. The evacuated Rubblemen were mostly taken to my flat. There they were washed, given first aid and their rags burnt at night. Once, while she was washing the wounded, my wife Wiktoria passed out. It turned out that our second son, [eighteen-year-old] Zbigniew, was in one of the sacks. Wounded during a clash, he had died while being transported. Thus we lost both our sons, and I lost also both my brothers, for apart from Wacław there also died, at the same time as Zbigniew, my brother Zbigniew. I lost my dearest and nearest, I lost my health, I was wounded eleven times, and in 1943 my wife caught TB from a Jewess we were hiding. But how else could one have acted in those days? . . .

The fighting continued in the first half of July. In the rubble of Zamenhof and Pawia Streets a group led by Herszberg fought on until their last round of ammunition and their last Molotov cocktail. In Wałowa Street Mellon's group waylaid a marching Nazi unit that was singing the *Horst Wessel Lied* and saw it run. The Nazis returned with large reinforcements, but failed to capture the Jews who again received them with bullets and grenades and then disappeared in the rubble of Franciszkańska Street. Later Mellon's group met in their bunker at 34, Świętojerska Street and decided to send a delegation to the "Aryan" side to ask the Polish underground for arms and ammunition, so as to enable them to carry on the fight on the territory of the ghetto.[126]

To put an end to the last survivors of Warsaw Jewry, the Germans proceeded in the second half of July to blow up the mountains of rubble and ruins. It was a long and costly operation, but it worked: bunkers, cellars, underground passages and accesses to the sewers, which were the last source of water, were systematically destroyed, thus reducing even further the terrain where the Jews could still operate. Moreover, the Jews had a new enemy to contend with. For while a few Poles risked their lives bringing food and arms to the Jews in the ghetto, others organized in gangs visited the ghetto at night in search of loot. The Jews attacked the two-legged hyenas and thus acquired a few weapons.[127]

The fighting effectiveness of the last Mohicans of the Warsaw ghetto can be deduced from the citations accompanying the awards of Iron Crosses to Major Bundtke and Captain Ederer of the 22nd Schutzpolizei Battalion. The Bundtke citation said: "After the withdrawal of the Waffen SS units, the battalion was left on its own to carry out its task. Because the enemy knew of the reduction in our forces, individual bands again resumed their attacks. In the intensified fighting against well-armed and well-led bands it was necessary to deal with the remaining nests of resistance in the ruins, cellars, underground sewers.... In a number of attacks Bundtke personally took command, setting his soldiers an example of courage...."[128] As for Ederer, "During the operations in the former Jewish district in Warsaw in July 1943, he took a personal part in an armed engagement with nine armed bandits and was instrumental in rendering them harmless. In June 1943, while dealing with a bandit nest in the former Jewish district in Warsaw, he distinguished himself in fighting the Jewish-Bolshevik bandits."[129]

In September the Germans again sent large forces of gendarmes and police into the ghetto to wipe out the surviving groups of Jews, whom neither thirst nor hunger had yet destroyed. One group is known to have fought its way out of the ghetto on September 23, 1943.[130] An unknown number of Jews armed with grenades, pistols and a few submachine guns remained even after September; after they had killed several gendarmes, the Germans once again proceeded to blow up the ruins in October 1943. The long months of winter, when the tracks left in the snow betrayed the Jews, typhus and hunger accounted for most of those who had survived after October. Nonetheless, in June 1944 a group of Jews attacked a detachment of German gendarmes passing through the ghetto and killed three with grenades.[131] At least one Jew, David Białogród, is known to have survived in the wilderness of the ghetto until August 1, 1944, the day of the outbreak of the Polish uprising.[132]

IX

Jacob Smakowski's unpublished diary provides a unique account of the partisan war waged by the Rubblemen and the last Mohicans of the Warsaw ghetto. Unable to capture No. 6, Wałowa Street, the Ukrainians set it on fire and Smakowski and his three comrades had to jump down to the roof of a neighboring two-storey house to escape being burned alive. Two of them fell to their deaths, a third, Leyb Binenfeld, was badly injured, but Smakowski got away with a badly gashed leg, the wound being caused by the corrugated iron roof on which he landed. Both spent three days in a bunker at No. 8, Wałowa Street, whose occupants shared with them their water and food. On the third day Smakowski and Binenfeld left the bunker because they felt that the Germans were getting too close to it and spent about a week on the staircase of a burnt-out annex in the courtyard of No. 24, Franciszkańska Street.

After a week Smakowski suggested to Binenfeld that they should go back to the bunker to find out what had happened to its occupants. "When we got there," Smakowski recalled, "we saw that the house and the bunker had been destroyed by fire and the people gassed. We learnt that before dying the people in the bunker had fought back desperately. The Germans had seized an Orthodox Jew and tortured him until he showed them the entrance to the bunker. The Germans wanted to blow up the entrance, but could not get near it, for the Jews defended themselves stubbornly and killed seven Germans. In the end the Germans used gas and the Jewish fighters were suffocated."

Convinced that sooner or later the Germans were bound to discover all the bunkers, Smakowski gathered twenty Jews and on the night of May 12 led them through sewers into Powązkowska Street. Unfortunately, a Ukrainian unit was guarding a coal depot near the manhole and as the Jews emerged into the street, they killed almost all of them. Smakowski and Binenfeld, who were still in the sewer helping the women to climb up the manhole, heard the shooting and escaped back into the ghetto. This time Smakowski found shelter in a bunker at No. 18, Muranowska Street, where one of the twenty-eight occupants was a sick woman. Her husband, ignoring Smakowski's warnings, cooked food for her in the daytime. "One day, when I dozed off, he made a fire again in daytime,"

Smakowski recalled. "Without saying a word I got up and left through the tunnel. I was followed by my mates, Gutek and Cegiełka, and by Mrs. Cymes. We camouflaged the entrance to the bunker behind us. Half an hour later the fire attracted the murderers. The gendarmes arrived, dragged the Jews out of the bunker and shot them in the courtyard. Then they covered them with wood and burned them. After a time they left. We observed the massacre from the stairs. Mrs. Cymes went out of her mind. She kept crying: 'Oh, my two sons! They shot my two sons!' When it got dark she said she wanted to look out of the window to see what was going on. She opened the window and threw herself from the fourth floor."

Smakowski and his two mates found shelter in a bunker at No. 45, Nalewki Street. Its occupants quarrelled every night over their portions of soup and, despite Smakowski's warnings, raised their voices. They were heard by one of the patrols the Germans sent out every night. When night fell on June 21 the Germans surrounded the house and burst in.

> The young people made a quick escape and hid. The gendarmes caught Dr. Korman, who because of his old age did not manage to escape. They took him to their post and tortured him to make him lead them to the "bandits." In the morning of June 22 they brought him to the house and he showed them the entrance to the bunker. A German armed with a rifle and carrying a candle was the first to enter it. I had the presence of mind to push my pistol into a pot and to bury my few pieces of gold. I was calmer than the others because at night, when the others used to go outside to cook and inhale fresh air, I had dug a tunnel to No. 43, Nalewki Street, covered the entrance with a board and camouflaged it. But when the German appeared, he took me completely by surprise: it was half past five in the morning, I was still asleep and we were quite unprepared. When the trap was opened, we expected to see one of our own people. The German threatened us with his weapon, called out: "Hände hoch!" and made us leave the bunker. Outside I saw Dr. Korman and sixty Germans. They ordered us to line up and to take off our clothes and then searched us thoroughly, especially the women . . . They took our money.
>
> I stood calmly and smiled. I no longer cared what happened to me. What could I do? Was I to weep and beg for mercy? Of course not, I was going to die with dignity. An SS man walked up to me and asked: "Why are you smiling?" I replied: "I don't care, I'm seventy today."

The German reached for his Parabellum and struck me three times on the nose. (It is still crooked.) Then he told me that he was going to kill me with a special type of dum-dum bullet. He turned to Dr. Korman and said: "Well, Korman, do you have anything else to tell us?" Dr. Korman answered that he had nothing else to add. The SS man ordered him to step forward and shot him in the back. Then they marched us, naked and with our hands raised, to the Judenrat at No. 11, Zamenhof Street.

I knew that when we reached the Judenrat they would finish us off. I therefore said to the baker Kagan: "Moniek, tell them that you have money and we may still escape." I approached one of the SS men and whispered: "Sir, we have hidden our gold." He left us outside a gateway under the guard of two SS men, one of whom was the notorious executioner Paul Haendtke. They took us back to 45, Nalewki Street, and before reaching it we heard shooting. We realized that the others had been shot outside the Judenrat. When I asked an SS man what was happening, he replied that they were only shooting for practice. When Kagan's wife realized what had happened, she seized her child and tried to run away. She was shot down at once.

When we entered the courtyard of No. 45, Nalewki Street, two SS men stayed with Kagan and I and Haendtke made for the bunker. I was the first to enter the tunnel, for he felt certain that I could not escape because I was naked. As soon as I was inside the bunker I reached for my pistol hidden in a pot, cocked it and turned round. Haendtke was just making his way into the bunker. I saw only his head and outstretched hands—in one he held a candle. I fired three bullets into his head and when I saw that he was dead, I dragged him inside. I pulled out the planks which shored up the tunnel and it immediately collapsed burying the entrance to the bunker. I then pulled the topboots off the dead SS man's feet, took his pistol and documents, as well as his cigarettes and matches. I buried his boots in the sand. (I am still wearing them today.) Then I made my way through the tunnel I had dug to No. 43, Nalewki Street. Before escaping I heard the Germans shouting from the courtyard: "Herr Haendtke, Herr Haendtke! Der Hund ist schon tot?" (Mr. Haendtke, Mr. Haendtke! Is the cur dead?") I called back: "Ja, ja, ich komm' heraus." ("Yes, yes, I'm coming out.")

From No. 43 I jumped on to the staircase of No. 3, Kupiecka Street, I sat there till nightfall. At one in the morning I decided to return to No. 45, Nalewki Street to find some clothes and matches, for without matches it was impossible to survive. There I found Kagan lying dead next to his wife. The SS men had removed Haendtke's corpse, for I did not find it inside the bunker. I found there the boots and a pair of trousers, as well as Kagan's gold and money, and made my way to No. 4, Wałowa Street.

I found my maternal uncle there. His bunker was still safe. Complete silence reigned in the brushworkers' area, so that it was generally believed that no live Jews remained there. In fact, my uncle Dek, his children and eighty other Jews were hiding in the bunker. In the third courtyard of No. 34, Świętojerska Street, seventeen persons were hiding underneath an oven. There were also twenty Jews in Morawes' bunker under the ruins of No. 10, Wałowa Street, and smaller groups of four or five Jews hiding on the staircases. I stayed there from June 22 to August 30. Because there was total silence in the area, the Jews began to think that they were safe. They spoke in loud voices and walked in the open without taking necessary precautions. I told them about my experiences, about what had happened to the bunkers at Nos. 45, Nalewki Street and No. 18, Muranowska Street. They retorted: "You and your experiences! The Aktion is over." But the Germans were vigilant and every night sent out patrols which we could not hear, because they wrapped their boots with rags.

It was August 30, one o'clock in the afternoon. Our man at the entrance to the tunnel leading to the bunker heard the trap being raised. He rushed into the bunker and said: "Folks, we've been betrayed!" I never expected our bunker would be discovered. The trap was in No. 4, Wałowa Street. A 100-meters-long tunnel had been dug underneath the rubble to No. 20, Nalewki Street, but there was no exit. So all was lost. I managed to bury my pistol and money before the Germans entered the bunker. There were more than eighty of us when we left the bunker. By then the Germans used to kill the Jews wherever they captured them. Until May 15 they had taken them to the *Umschlagplatz*, but after that date, to prevent them scattering on the way, they shot them on the spot. When the Germans penetrated into our bunker, they assured us that if we left without resisting, we would be taken away to work. Once they had got us into the courtyard, they ordered us to undress and took all our possessions.

When they noticed me they said: "Ach, du schwarzer Hund! Du bist da? Heute haben wir dich gefangen!" ("Oh, you black cur! So you're here? We've got you today!") They taunted me, pushing their pistols into my face. I thought to myself: It's all over. If all the Jews are doomed, why should I be an exception? And yet I said to myself that I must escape. I learnt that they had found my photograph after Haendtke's death among the clothes we had taken off in the courtyard. They found it in my clothes and had been searching for me ever since. They put me aside in the courtyard and placed the other Jews against a wall. The Jews did not weep, they did not scream, they faced death with dignity. Then they intoned in singing voices: "*Shma Israel!* We are dying to sanctify Thy Name!" The mothers kissed their children and comforted them, telling them: "Don't be afraid, my child, it must be so . . ." But the children sobbed bitterly. Then the Germans ordered them to place their hands on their heads. I heard the shots and nobody escaped. Then I was ordered to fetch boards, any kind of wood, books and anything flammable from the cellars. I had to place it all over the bodies of the murdered Jews. Then they poured petrol over the pyre and set it alight. With my own eyes I saw the Jews burning, including my uncle Dek, three male cousins, one female cousin and a woman aged eighty.

Then they said to me: "You will not burn after your death, but alive." They tied my hands and feet and flung me into the back of a car. Two gendarmes watched me. I heard them say that I was being taken to the Azazel Theater in Nowolipki Street, which was occupied by German women recently evacuated from bombed cities in Germany. They were entertained with the spectacle of Jews being burned alive. Young, handsome Jews were brought to the Azazel site, petrol was poured over them and they were turned into live torches. On the way there they whipped me mercilessly with their riding-crops. When we reached the Gęsiówka between Gęsia and Zamenhof Streets, I flung myself out of the car and realized that the effort had freed my hands. At the same time I became aware of an excruciating pain in my leg caused by a bullet. Bullets were ricochetting from the stones all around me. The car had turned round and stopped beside me. The Germans got out and one of them seized my hair and raised my head. I was almost unconscious and my heart had ceased to beat. He peered into my face, smashed my head into the ground and said: "Schade eine Kugel. Der Hund ist tot." ("A pity to waste another bullet. The cur is dead.") They kicked my face and drove off.

That was my miracle. I continued to lie there, naked, my head, arms and legs turned into a pulp. Blood was pouring from me. I went on lying and pretending that I was dead. But out of one eye I saw two Polish policemen coming towards me. One of them said: "I told you, he's dead." And he added: "Can't you see, the Germans have finished him off. What a handsome lad." And they went away. I lay there for a few more minutes until I saw them enter Więzienna Street where their Gęsiówka station was. As soon as they disappeared I gathered my last strength, rose to my feet and ran to the house at No. 18, Gęsia Street, which had belonged to the Jewish Council. I managed to climb to the fourth floor where some of the staircase remained. I found there food, rusks, sugar, a few rags and even a few zlotys. I covered my nakedness; I gradually became my old self. I stayed there almost seven days. I found there a calendar on which the people who had preceded me had marked their last days. They had been there from April 19 to June 28. I also found a pot with cooked *kasha* which had gone moldy, rusks covered with butter, and the bones of the people who had not managed to eat them in the courtyard. I said to myself that they were all that remained of the people who had been burned there. Human tibias and other bones strewed every courtyard.

As soon as I felt better I made my way to the brushworkers' area where I felt at home. On the staircase of No. 8, Wałowa Street, I met four lads: Felek Bogusławski the butcher and Abraham Jelień, both from Lodz, Moniek—I cannot remember his surname—from Warsaw and a certain Płocki. We spent the days on the stairs, talking, telling each other stories, reading and playing cards. I managed to read there a novel about Rasputin and several other books I had found. There was silence in the area. It was already the beginning of October. We did our cooking at night on the staircase and searched the cellars for food. At that time young Poles from the Polish underground began to enter the ghetto and photograph the dead. One of them belonged to the Home Army and had sold us arms at the beginning of 1943. When he saw me he was delighted and exclaimed: "Blackie, you're still alive!" We established a regular contact with him. I gave him clothes and he brought us food. And this is how we carried on.

At the beginning of November, it must have been on the 6th, he and two other Poles came to us and said: "Lads, follow us —there are more Jews around." They led us to Szczęśliwa Street, where the Transavia buildings had been. I had no idea that any Jews could have survived there. How could one have hoped that any might have escaped? But there must have been some ninety of them—and what lads they were! Strong lads with firearms, all wearing topboots, and they had good bunkers supplied with food. When the time had come to go into the bunkers they did so and were still there. They remained on their guard and nobody had discovered them. They, too, were in contact with the same Poles.

The young Poles wanted us to help them rescue twenty-five Home Army officers when they were being taken to the ghetto to be shot. The plan was to attack the lorry taking them to their place of execution. A group of fifteen Poles arrived to help us. Being well acquainted with the ghetto, I was chosen to be in overall command. And this is what followed. On November 7 we heard the noise of approaching vehicles and a few minutes later we saw the prisoners, their hands tied with barbed wire and their eyes blindfolded with black rags, and all of them naked. First came SS men on a motorcycle with a sidecar, the lorry with the prisoners followed and another motorcycle with a sidecar brought up the rear. I had placed the lads in the ruins of a house in a Karmelicka Street, behind paneless windows, and as soon as the convoy drove from Leszno into Karmelicka Street we opened fire. The first one to act was a lad of the group from Szczęśliwa Street. He lobbed a grenade which exploded beside the leading motorcycle. All the SS men were killed. My own group wiped out the SS men on the second motorcycle. We wasted no time getting on to the lorry and untied the hands of the officers and removed the rags from their eyes. When they saw our German uniforms they said: "What the hell?" and did not want to get down. We told them: "We, Jews, have freed you. Quick into the sewer, they'll be firing at us from the Pawiak!"

And this is what happened. As soon as the Ukrainians saw the burning vehicles and heard the shooting, they opened fire and killed four Jews and three Poles. At the manhole there was panic. Those who managed to get inside the sewer stayed alive. The Ukrainians were firing at us from a two-storey-high watchtower. I led almost the entire group of one hundred men through the sewers to the "Aryan" side. I brought them to Freta Street and at night we made for a monastery in Piwna Street which served as a hideout. Shortly afterwards the Jews and the Poles made their way to the forests. Motor vehicles had been laid on to transport them to the forests in the Lublin region. As for me, I decided to spend a little time on the "Aryan" side. Captain Zygmunt Kazimierczuk of the Home Army, whom I had freed in the ghetto on November 7, gave me his address—his parents lived at No. 13, Świętojańska Street—and asked me to come to him whenever I was on the "Aryan" side, because he wanted to show me his gratitude. After two days with him I returned to the ghetto.

On January 11, 1944 Smakowski and Leyb Binenfeld left the wilderness of the ghetto ruins and found shelter in Kazimierczuk's flat. But Smakowski did not hide there. Several times he made his way back to the ghetto with food for a group of Jews hiding in a bunker at No. 34, Świętojerska Street. When the Poles rose on August 1, 1944 he joined immediately a Home Army unit and took part in the fighting that led to the capture of the Pawiak prison. His military record was such that he was promoted to a staff sergeant, a rank not easily given to a Jew. He was wounded defending the barricades in Świętojerska Street, but after spending two days in a hospital he returned to active service and used his unique experience to help the Home Army units in the Old Town escape through the sewers into central Warsaw. There he fought on with his unit in Królewska Street and the Saxon Gardens until Bór-Komorowski's capitulation. Before this happened Smakowski and thirty other Jews had built an underground hideout at No. 36, Wspólna Street, provided it with water and food and there they held out until January 17, 1945, when the Red Army finally forced the Germans to abandon Warsaw.

X

The Warsaw Ghetto Uprising was not only the culmination of armed Jewish resistance to Nazism. It was much more, because in the course of it thousands of completely defenseless Jewish children, women and men demonstrated a refusal to acknowledge the power of brute force that had no parallel in the history of European resistance. Judged in purely military terms, it was the biggest anti-German battle fought on Polish territory since September 1939, for the Germans had deployed only 1,910 men against the partisans in the Zamość area in February 1943 and 1,630 men in the anti-partisan *Osterwegen* operation in the Parczew forests of the Lublin region in April of the same year. The first operation had lasted ten days and the second, three days. *Gwardzista*, the mouthpiece of the People's Guard, was therefore only stating a fact when it said on May 20, 1943: "The heroic resistance of the Warsaw ghetto has now lasted a month. It is the biggest and longest act of armed resistance in occupied Europe. (That is, outside Yugoslavia, where the fighting has assumed the nature of a national uprising.)"

This view of the military importance of the Warsaw Ghetto Uprising is not shared either by Reitlinger or Hilberg in their histories of the Final Solution. Reitlinger describes the Warsaw Ghetto Uprising as "the first national military struggle of the Jews since the rebellion of Bar Kochba in the reign of Hadrian,"[133] which is historically inaccurate, and then goes on to belittle its military significance. Stroop, he argues, used only 1,100 regular troops to destroy the ghetto, whereas in the operation against "the Partisan Republic of Lake Palik" in Byelorussia, in which the Germans claimed to have liquidated 12,000 partisans and civilians, they had

had to use 16,662 men and lost 127 German dead as against only sixteen dead and ninety wounded in Warsaw, "though this may have been understated to please Himmler." But even apart from the fact that on Stroop's own admission he used twice as many men as Reitlinger tells us, the comparison is quite meaningless. In the Lake Palik operation the Germans had to use 16,662 men to surround and comb an area of forests and swamps as big as several English counties and in the end almost completely failed to bring to battle the partisans, so that almost all the 12,000 killed were defenseless peasants and Jews. In the Warsaw ghetto, however, Stroop was able to concentrate day after day his entire force and call on the help of the Wehrmacht and the Luftwaffe against static objectives. Yet, despite his overwhelming fire power, he found it impossible to break the Jews in battle and had recourse to wholesale destruction by fire.

Hilberg's appraisal of the military significance of the ghetto revolt is even more denigratory, although his book appeared eight years after Reitlinger's *Final Solution*. By then enough Jewish and Polish eyewitness accounts and works of a monographic nature had appeared to provide him with a balanced picture of the events, but preferring to rely on Stroop's report Hilberg came to the conclusion that "The losses of the Germans and their collaborators consisted of sixteen dead and eighty-five wounded." He even accepted Stroop's word for it that what his men dropped in the sewers were "smoke candles" and that "Jews who mistook the candles for poison gas came up for air"[134] to be killed by the Germans. The idea that the Jews who chose to be burnt alive or drowned in the sewers rather than surrender to Stroop's cutthroats could not tell the difference between smoke and gas is interesting indeed. But it is not worth pursuing for the simple reason that at his trial in Warsaw Stroop admitted that the "smoke-candles" were gas-grenades.

At his trial Stroop also admitted that his figures of German casualties were not complete. How big the German losses really were we shall never know, but they were much higher than those accepted by Hilberg as being essentially correct. The intelligence report of the Polish Workers' Party dated April 26, 1943 put the German losses in the first two days of the uprising at 150 dead and by the time of the compilation of the report at 700 dead and wounded. It said that the SS detachment from Grochów had had seventy casualties, including the commanding officer.[135] Having been prepared by the Communists, the report may be suspected of exaggerating the successes of the Jews. But the report of the Department of Internal Affairs of the Government Delegate's Office written on April 22 put the number of dead Germans at eighty-six and of wounded at 420.[136] The report of the Jew-hating Antyk agency prepared for the Home Army Command and the Government Delegate's office at the end of April said that the uprising was being led by a Dr. Adolf Kohn and a sergeant who had deserted from the German Army and that a numerous detachment of Polish Communists and German deserters were fighting on the side of the Jews. Having provided the kind of information that could have come straight from the Nazis' propaganda offices in Warsaw or Berlin, the Antyk agents went on to say that in the first day of the uprising the Jews had "allegedly" destroyed one tank and six armored cars. And they continued: "The first two days produced the following losses: some sixty dead and wounded in the German units. Among the Polish police, twelve wounded."[137] On the other hand, the Government Delegate's report on the Ghetto Uprising written on April 24 said: "On the German side there were [on 19 and 20 April] hundreds of dead and wounded, but the ghetto continued to defend itself."[138] Finally, the Polish historian Wacław Poterański, who as director of the Central Archives of the Polish Ministry of Internal Affairs is one of the greatest authorities on the Nazi period, has calculated that in the first ten days of the Ghetto Uprising the Germans lost around 400 dead and over 1,000 wounded.[139]

While reminiscing in the Mokotów Prison about his role in the extermination of the 70,000 Jews in the Warsaw ghetto, Stroop was challenged by Schielke on the figures of German losses in his report to Himmler. One day, when describing the fighting in the ghetto during Krueger's visit, Stroop claimed that he had lost only a few men on May 2 and 3, but had suffered no losses at all on May 4, even though it had taken his men thirteen hours to clear the buildings of the Walter Toebbens and Schultz and Company factories. According to Moczarski, Schielke interrupted Stroop and vehemently told him: "'Herr Obergruppenführer [General], I am asking you for the second time not to feed us the falsified statistics! I know that in your reports prepared by that magician, Max Jesuiter, you had to quote such figures because Krueger ordered you to do so, because Dr. Hahn advised you to do so, and also because you did not want to burden yourself with the responsibility for the human losses, for the deaths of the soldiers and policemen killed under your command. But don't try to deceive *us*, your cell-mates! I repeat: nobody will believe the figures of German losses in the ghetto, which were concocted for the purposes of history and current politics.' By his silence Stroop tacitly admitted that Schielke was right and never again quoted to us his alleged losses."[140]

We also find a very different appraisal of the importance of the Warsaw Ghetto Uprising in the official Soviet history of the war, whose authors nobody can accuse of pro-Jewish bias or of a lack of understanding of what truly mattered in the life-and-death struggle against the Nazi war machine. According to them:[141]

> An event of great importance in the struggle against the German occupiers in Poland was the uprising in the Warsaw ghetto, which broke out on April 19, 1943. It was prepared and carried out by a fighting Jewish organization created inside the ghetto.... The fighting in the ghetto went on for several weeks. Having proved unable to capture the ghetto, the occupiers proceeded to destroy it house by house and to carry out bloody executions of the inhabitants. The ghetto uprising exerted a major influence on Polish public opinion and led to the intensification of the armed struggle agadeveloper the Germans.

But perhaps the military significance of the Warsaw Ghetto Uprising has been best summed up by the Polish General Jerzy Kirchmayer, the historian of the Warsaw Uprising of 1944. Kirchmayer was a lieutenant-colonel in charge of one of the staff sections in the Home Army Command, but with his colleague, Colonel Stanisław Tatar, joined the Lublin Poles after the Warsaw Uprising, which had completely destroyed his faith in the kind of Poland that the leaders of the revolt still hoped to restore. He and Colonel Tatar were arrested together with General Spychalski in the purge of 1949, in which Gomulka nearly lost his head, and rehabilitated in 1956. In his unpublished study "The Military Importance of the April Uprising," which is in the Archives of the Institute of Party History in Warsaw, Kirchmayer wrote:

> The April Uprising in Warsaw, the largest Polish resistance center

during the Nazi occupation, was of a special nature insofar as it was staged by the Jewish population, that is, by the population which was supposed to be absolutely incapable of any active, let alone armed, resistance.

The blows delivered by the Jewish fighters hurt badly the prestige of General Stroop's "heroes," who, although armed to the teeth, were forced to bring in tanks, artillery and planes against insurgents who were almost completely devoid of arms. And although it was the struggle of people driven to desperation by fascist bestiality, it showed everybody that there was only one way out: to fight! At the same time, the defeat of the insurgents proved that no time must be wasted in starting an armed struggle, that we must carry on an active and constant war against the enemy, that we must reject passivity and waiting with arms at rest in favor of a simultaneous and gigantic uprising all over our occupied land.

The Warsaw ghetto fell after a heroic fight, but the idea of armed struggle, in the name of which the insurgents had died, reached beyond the walls, survived and endured until victory. It was carried abroad by the few Jews who reached the forests and fought there, representing an element of singular determination. It was spread by Poles who in Warsaw saw Nazis unsuccessfully attempting to break the resistance of the few and almost weaponless ŻOB groups.

Thus the military importance of the Warsaw Ghetto Uprising is above all in its repercussions among the Polish people, in the fact that being an uncompromising armed deed it undermined the idea of "enduring" and "waiting" and thus contributed in a capital manner to the rise of an active struggle against the invader. The momentary successes of the insurgents toppled the Germans from their pedestal of omnipotence and proved to Poles the effectiveness of armed resistance. Thus the blood of the ghetto defenders was not shed in vain. It gave birth to the intensified struggle against the fascist invader and from this struggle there came victory.

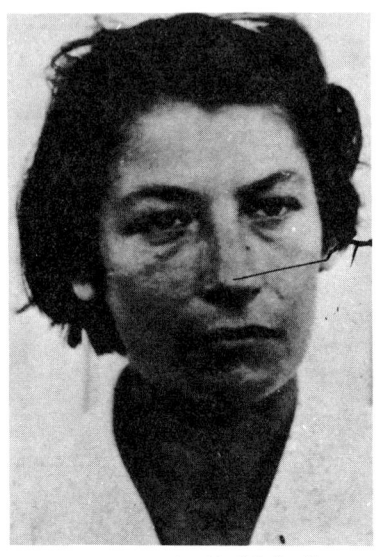

Tzivia Lubetkin "Celina"
(1914–1978)

Pola Elster
(1909–1944)

Wladyslaw Gaik
(1914–1943)

Tuvia Borzykowski
(1914–1959)

May 16, 1943: The Warsaw Synagogue blown up

Group of Jewish prisoners of Gęsia concentration camp liberated by soldiers of the AK of the "Zośka" battalion on August 5, 1944

The Epilogue

I

THE WARSAW GHETTO Uprising was not the final contribution of the Jews of Warsaw to the armed struggle against Nazi Germany.

Isaac Zuckerman, who after Anielewicz's death had become the leader of the Jewish Fighting Organization, succeeded in reestablishing his contacts with the Home Army Command on July 13, 1943 and, once again, asked it to help the surviving Jews to die fighting. He asked for two things: that the Home Army Command should allow the surviving ghetto fighters to join the Home Army units in Warsaw and in the Warsaw region, and that it should provide the Jews with arms. The arms were to be smuggled into the Poniatowa and Trawniki camps, where the deported ŻOB and ŻZW fighters had created fighting organizations and were planning revolts,[1] and supplied to the resistance organizations in the still surviving ghettoes of Częstochowa, Będzin and Sosnowiec. Neither of his requests was fulfilled.

Pressed by Woliński and the Council for Helping Jews to allow Jews to become part of the Home Army, General Rowecki had sidestepped the issue in an order addressed to his regional commanders in February 1943. The order said:[2] "I allow the creation of Jewish insurgent detachments from the patriotic Bundist and Zionist elements. Such detachments are not to be used in diversionary and partisan actions but only kept for the time when the general uprising breaks out and prepared for it. ... The arms purchased for the Jewish detachment with a view to defending enclosed communities [i.e., ghettoes] are to be stored by the Regional Home Army Commands and handed over to the detachments only in an emergency." Rowecki's order thus accepted the creation of Jewish military units inside the few surviving ghettoes, but denied them any arms and the right to take part in the armed struggle against the Germans until the time when the Home Army rose in revolt against Germany. The cynicism of the closing paragraph was so obvious that Rowecki's subordinates cannot be blamed for having completely ignored the order. According to Woliński, "In accordance with the spirit of the order, the Polish military authorities should have provided all possible assistance to the Jewish communities that were subordinated to the Jewish Fighting Organization and the Jewish Military Union. The implementation of the order, invoked many times by Jewish organizations and the people who wanted to help the Jews fight in the ghettoes, met with the unwillingness of the local military authorities. In fact, the order was carried out only in relation to the Bialystok ghetto, which according to information received from Chirurg [*nom de guerre* of Major Stanisław Weber, Colonel Chruściel's chief-of-staff] obtained, after the effective intervention of the Home Army Command, considerable material help (a car, arms, etc.)."[3] But as we already know from the story of the Bialystok Ghetto Uprising, Woliński, and possibly Major Weber himself, was misinformed on this point by the Bialystok Home Army leaders.*

Betrayed to the Gestapo by Polish fascists, Rowecki was arrested at his home in Warsaw on June 30, 1943,[4] and Bór-Komorowski, whose connections with the anti-Semitic National Party and sympathies for the National Armed Forces were well known, became the commander of the Home Army. Pressed by Zuckerman and the Jewish Coordination Committee to carry out Rowecki's order with regard to the surviving ŻOB fighters, Bór-Komorowski's Home Army Command reacted, according to Woliński, in the following manner: "The acceptance of Jews in our military units on the territory of the Skyscraper [code name for the city of Warsaw] and the Brickworks [code name for the Warsaw region] was said to be impossible, but Konar [one of Chruściel's *noms de guerre*] expressed his readiness to organize the Jews in passive insurgent units. One such unit was formed in Warsaw. One of our officers was appointed to train the unit. He arrived at the training point, fixed a meeting and did not turn up for it. Following numerous interventions, the same officer once again arrived at the training point, but in a state of

---

* See Reuben Ainsztein, *op. cit.*, pp. 534–5.

complete intoxication. Further interventions were without effect. The Jewish insurgent unit did not receive any training and ceased to exist."[5]

Such was the outcome of the Jewish efforts to join the Home Army in Warsaw after the Warsaw Ghetto Uprising had once and for all provided proof of Jewish determination and ability to fight the Germans. Had Sikorski been still alive and had Zuckerman and the Jewish Coordination Committee found a way of informing the Jewish representatives in London of what was happening, the Home Army Command might have been forced to make another gesture, as it had when it had supplied the ghetto fighters with a few pistols and grenades, which were not enough to arm a single company of troops. But with the anti-Semitic Sosnkowski in the post of commander-in-chief in London and Bór-Komorowski in charge of the Home Army, there began a new phase that was characterized by the undisguised hostility of the Home Army Command to the growing participation of Jews in the partisan movement both west and east of the Bug. Woliński described the new phase, when right-wing Home Army units combined with the fascist National Armed Forces in attacking Jewish partisans, with his usual understatement: "Very unpleasant and contrary to the spirit of the order were the actions of our detachments towards the ŻOB unit of Częstochowa, which was hiding in the Koniecpol area and attempting to come under our orders. The detachment was twice massacred by the Orzeł [Eagle] group, which was probably part of the National Armed Forces, despite the announcement by the local command that the detachment should be helped in every way."[6]

A final appeal to the Home Army Command for arms for the surviving Jews was made by Zuckerman in a letter addressed to Bór-Komorowski on November 23, 1943. In his letter he begged him "in the final hours of Polish Jewry to extend a helping hand to the Jewish centers that want to defend themselves" and went on to point out that the Jewish Fighting Organization in Będzin and Sosnowiec had fought during their liquidation with nine revolvers obtained through their own efforts.[7] His letter remained unanswered.

In view of their experiences and treatment by the Home Army, it would therefore have been only natural if the Jews still alive in

Warsaw at the outbreak of the Warsaw Uprising had avoided taking part in it and devoted all their remaining energies to seeking means of survival. But the contrary happened. They took a part in it that both in heroism and sheer numbers compared favorably with that of the Poles.

When the uprising broke out on August 1, 1944 there were in Warsaw over 900,000 Poles and at the most 7,000 people who according to Nazi criteria were Jews. Only a few hundred of the Jews had managed to escape during the Ghetto Uprising. The overwhelming majority were people who had refused to enter the ghetto in 1940 or had fled from it later and with the help of Poles had succeeded in passing as "Aryans" or had survived by concealing their Jewish identity from everybody. A third group were 380 Jews whom the Nazis had brought from Auschwitz to use as slave labor in clearing the ruins of the ghetto.

On June 11, 1943 Himmler had ordered that the former military prison in Gęsia Street be turned into a concentration camp for a Jewish labor force, whose task was to remove everything that could be salvaged from the ruins of the ghetto, fill in the cellars and sewers with rubble and earth, then cover the entire ghetto area with a layer of soil and finally turn it into a park. On June 18 SS Gruppenführer (Lieutenant-General) Oswald Pohl, chief of the SS Economic Administration, informed Himmler that 300 Jews were already in the Gęsia prison and their number would be rapidly increased. However, it was not until October 1943 that 2,000 Jews were brought from Auschwitz and on their arrival the fifty surviving Polish Jews in the Gęsia concentration camp were shot in the ruins of the ghetto. No Jews from Poland were included in the 2,000 from Auschwitz, but a number of Polish Jews who had emigrated to France, Belgium and Holland found themselves among the prisoners who came mostly from Greece, Hungary and Yugoslavia. Three days before the outbreak of the uprising, with the Red Army rapidly approaching the Vistula, one of the SS officers, twenty-three-year-old Umschuetz, entered the sick quarters in the Gęsia prison and with his submachine gun killed all the 300-odd Jews lying there. Of the surviving prisoners, 380 were left to carry out the evacuation of the large military stores on the territory of the ghetto, while the others were crammed into a train and sent off in the direction of Germany never to be heard of again. Among the

380 men left in the Gęsia prison the majority were Hungarian and Greek Jews.[8] There were also 123 Polish Jews who had been transferred from the Pawiak Prison on July 31.

On August 5 the crack Miotła and Zośka Battalions of the Home Army, supported by two captured German tanks, defeated the notorious SS brigade commanded by SS Oberführer (Brigadier-General) Oskar Dirlewanger, which was made up of German criminals released from prisons and concentration camps. In the course of the fighting they freed 348 Jews, including twenty-six women, from the Gęsia prison.* Eighty-nine of them, according to Esther Mark, were Polish citizens. The foreign Jews, among whom the largest group were Hungarians, at once asked the Poles to be allowed to join them in the fighting but were told that there was no place for them in the ranks of the Home Army. Their rejection was by no means due to the anti-Semitism of the local Home Army commanders. On August 4 Colonel Tadeusz Pełczyński, chief-of-staff of the Home Army Command, had written to Colonel Chruściel, officer commanding the Warsaw City Home Army Region, and instructed him to set up a concentration camp for the Jews of Gęsia prison. His instructions were: "Make arrangements to set up a temporary camp for all liberated Jews and other undesirable elements. Our units should receive instructions to prevent possible excesses against the Jews."** It was thus only the military situation in the Old Town that stopped the Home Army imprisoning the handful of Jewish survivors with unspecified "undesirable elements" and committing "possible excesses" against them. The Polish euphemism "anti-Jewish excesses" means pogroms, including massacre.

But the determination of the foreign Jews to take an active part in the fighting against the Nazis was such that a group of Hungarian Jews managed to send representatives to the command of the People's Army in the Wola district, which at the time was under a savage German assault. They were welcomed and led by Dr. Stern of Munkacs (Mukachevo), they formed a unit which fought together with the People's Army in the Old Town. When the Old Town fell, they were among the last of its defenders to try to escape through the sewers to Żoliborz. By then the Germans had discov-

---

* Esther Mark, "Yidn in Varshever Oifshtand," *Folks Shtime*, August 1, 1964.
** Esther Mark, *ibid.*

ered that thousands of soldiers and civilians were making their way through the sewers and systematically dropped grenades into the manholes. The Hungarian Jews led by Dr. Stern had to return to the Old Town and there most were murdered by the Germans and their Ukrainian henchmen from Kaminsky's SS Brigade.

On August 3, 1944 Zuckerman issued an appeal to all surviving Jews to join in the uprising. "After the heroic battles in the ghettoes and camps," his appeal said, "we call on all surviving Jews, both workers and intellectuals, to join the battle in the ranks of the insurgents against our common enemy for a free, democratic, just and independent Poland." As commander of the Jewish Fighting Organization, Zuckerman had offered the Home Army Command as soon as the uprising broke out the services of his Jewish detachment made up of ŻOB survivors. But after waiting for twenty-four hours for a reply, he was told by an officer that there was no room for his men in the Home Army. The twelve ŻOB survivors then joined the People's Army units fighting in the Old Town. They were all that remained of the ninety ŻOB fighters who had survived the ghetto uprising—the others had been murdered by Polish anti-Semites, betrayed to the Germans or killed fighting as partisans.

For obvious reasons, the heroism and battle record of the few hundred men and women who fought in the units of the People's Army during the Warsaw Uprising have been glorified in countless books, articles, radio and television programs since 1944. A special legend has been created around the Czwartacy Battalion—a unit forever linked with the name of Edwin Rozłubirski, a Jew. But the fact that Jews were among their finest commanders is not only passed in silence, but systematically suppressed.

The part played by Jews in the organization and leadership of the most famous unit of the People's Army deserves to be remembered. At the end of 1943 the People's Guard decided to organize in Warsaw a special duties platoon, whose tasks were to be the protection of the leaders of the Polish Workers' Party, the liquidation of spies and Gestapo agents, sabotage and diversion, and the acquisition of arms. The platoon had a strength of forty men, but in March it was expanded to a company and by May it became a battalion, which was named the Czwartacy Battalion after the Fourth (Czwarty) Regiment that had distinguished itself in battle

against the Russians during the November Insurrection of 1830.*
The first company of the battalion was made up of members of the
ZWM (Związek Walki Młodych or the Young People's Fighting
Union), the youth organization of the Polish Workers' Party created
by Hanna Szapiro-Sawicka. The Jewish girl had been one of the
organizers of the workers' volunteer battalions in the defense of
Warsaw in September 1939, one of the founders of the Polish Workers' Party and an active member of the People's Guard until she was
killed by the Gestapo. This happened on March 18, 1943 when the
Gestapo broke into her lodgings at No. 2, Mostowa Street, where
she was having a meeting with three other leaders of the Polish
Workers' Party. Hanka, as she was generally known, and the three
men defended themselves and one, Bolesław Kowalski, managed to
get away. Jan Strzeszewski and Tadeusz Olszewski were killed in
the house, while Hanka, badly wounded, managed to escape into
the street and was shot down outside No. 14, Mostowa Street.**

Members of the ZWM formed also the core of the second company, which included a platoon of former Home Army members,
while the third company consisted of militiamen of the RPPS (Revolutionary Party of Polish Socialists). The commander of the battalion was twenty-one-year-old Lech Kobyliński and the second-in-command was Edwin Rozłubirski. Both Kobyliński and Rozłubirski
had distinguished themselves as daring and successful fighters.
Thus, on April 17, 1944 Kobyliński, Rozłubirski and six other members of their unit attacked the Philips radio works in Karolkowa
Street, killed three German guards and captured a submarine gun, a
pistol and several grenades without suffering any losses. When
making their escape they killed an SS officer who was trying to
telephone for help. On June 5, 1944 Kobyliński, Rozłubirski and five
others were attacked by German gendarmes in Zielona Street, but
got away after killing five Germans, wounding several more and
shooting dead an SS officer who tried to pursue them. Only one of
the Poles was lightly wounded.***

---

* Józef Bolesław Garas, *Oddziały Gwardii Ludowej i Armii Ludowej*, 1942-1945, Warsaw 1963, pp. 38 ff.
** *Polski Ruch Robotniczy w okresie wojny i okupacji hitlerowskiej*, Warsaw 1964, pp. 321-2; letter from an eyewitness of her death, *Życie Warszawy*, 25 April 1978.
*** Garas, ibid., p. 41.

The outbreak of the uprising took the leaders of the People's Army completely by surprise. Their units were neither mobilized nor concentrated. The command of the People's Army was in the Old Town, but Kobyliński and Rozłubirski managed to reach the Old Town only on the third day of the uprising, having spent the first two days fighting with a Home Army unit commanded by Lieutenant "Sylwester" in the area of the Ministry of Communications in the center of Warsaw. At the time there was no single People's Army unit in the Old Town, which had not yet been attacked by the Germans. The fiercest fighting was in the Wola quarter, where on August 3 the People's Army had about 150 men and women, only half of them with arms, compared with the Home Army's 1,650 soldiers, about 70 per cent of them with arms, on August 5.* In the first three days of the uprising the Poles in Wola had to contend with tanks belonging to units of the Hermann Goering Panzer Division, which were trying to rejoin their division on the eastern side of the Vistula. Lack of infantry prevented the Germans from driving out the Poles. But on August 5 the SS formations of the Reinefarth Battle Group were thrown in by Obergruppenführer Erich von dem Bach, to whom Himmler had entrusted the capture and total destruction of Warsaw. Overwhelming superiority in men and firepower forced the Poles to retreat, but it was only on the 11th that the last defenders of Wola were driven out and Dirlewanger's criminals helped by formations of Vlassov Cossacks could proceed to rape, rob and murder tens of thousands of civilians. Units of the Home Army had begun to retreat from Wola to the Old Town on August 6 and among them were the survivors of the People's Army platoons.

The Old Town became the chief area of the People Army's activities. Its command headquarters at No. 16, Freta Street, where Marie Curie-Sklodowska was born, was occupied by Major Bolesław Kowalski, commanding officer of all the People's Army units in Warsaw; Captain Edward Lanota, his chief-of-staff; Captain Stanisław Kurland, chief of the Security Section, People's Army General Staff; Major Stanisław Nowicki, chief of the Propaganda Section, People's Army General Staff and editor of *Armia Ludowa*; and Lieutenant Anastazy (Menashe) Matywiecki, quartermaster of

* Garas, ibid., p. 47; Jerzy Kirchmayer, *Powstanie Warszawskie*, Warsaw 1964, p. 258.

the People's Army units in Warsaw. Both Lanota (real name: Lantner) who was known as "Edward," and Matywiecki, who was known as "Nastek," were Jews.[9]

Lanota, an engineer by profession, had been deputy chief of the Arms Laboratory, People's Army General Staff, while Matywiecki, a veteran of the prewar Polish Communist Party, was, according to Borzykowski, an active collaborator of the Jewish National Committee and used his position to help several dozen Jews who were hiding on the "Aryan" side with money, lodgings and false documents. He frequently met Dr. Berman and Isaac Zuckerman and "His deep attachment to the Jewish people emerged in his interest in the Land of Israel and everything that was being achieved there."*

The People's Army command in the Old Town tried to reorganize its forces in three battalions. Kobyliński once again resumed command of the Czwartacy Battalion, as the first battalion was called, while Rozłubirski or Gustaw, as he was known, took command of the staff headquarters platoon. The handful of ŻOB survivors joined the Second Platoon, Third Company, Czwartacy Battalion, which was commanded by Lieutenant Witek. "Witek", we learn from Borzykowski,** who himself was a member of Dror, "became very close to our group. He was not only our officer, but also an intimate comrade. He spent all his free time with us ... Brought up since his boyhood in the youth movement of the Polish Communist Party, he grew up to be a man with firm political and ideological convictions. He was completely devoid of anti-Jewish prejudices and treated everybody in accordance with one's value as a human being. ... He had none of the military stiffness of other officers and was not at ease in his official role. A true son of the people, he removed all the barriers between himself and his men, while maintaining essential discipline. Every time we saw him, a slim lad with deep, dark eyes, earnest, quiet, simple and restrained in his behavior, he made us think of a *yeshive-bokher* (a student of a Talmudical college). Some of our group called him the *halutz*. And, indeed, he had many features that justified the sobriquet. Lieuten-

---

* Tuvye Borzykowski, *Tsvishn falndike vent*, Ghetto Fighters House, Israel 1976, pp. 269–70.
** Ibid., p. 260–1.

ant Witek soon became a member of our family. He did not leave us after the collapse of the uprising and shared our tribulations regardless of the fact that by staying with Jews he was in greater danger. After losing contact with him while our group was in hiding, we met him again and maintained contact with him until liberation. A few weeks after the Red Army had marched into Warsaw, he was murdered by Polish fascists."

The positions in Mostowa Street defended by the Czwartacy Battalion were among the most crucial in the Old Town. They protruded farthest towards the Vistula between German-held streets and therefore the Germans were determined to capture them, while the Poles were equally set to hold them, for only from across the Vistula could rescue come. The Czwartacy Battalion distinguished itself by repelling German tanks that tried to break into the Old Town from the Vistula Motorway and stubbornly defended the Quebracho tannery and the Red House, which several times changed hands. The ŻOB group took part in one of the sallies that reached the Vistula. When the situation in the Old Town became critical, the ŻOB fighters, with their unique experience of the Dantesque world below Warsaw, went down into the sewers and explored them for the day when the Polish forces in the Old Town could no longer fight on.

On August 26 German Stukas scored direct hits on No. 16, Freta Street. The entire command of the People's Army in Warsaw was wiped out and there are still survivors of the Czwartacy Battalion who believe that Polish fascists informed the Germans where to drop their bombs. The three battalions of the People's Army, commanded respectively by Kobyliński, Rozłubirski and Captain Henryk Woźniak, a veteran of the International Brigades, remained without an overall commander, for Major Józef Małecki, who represented the General Staff of the People's Army in Warsaw, and Captain Ryszard Strzelecki, a member of the Central Committee of the Polish Workers' Party, had left the Old Town for Midtown (Śródmieście) through the sewers on the 17th of August. It was therefore left to Kobyliński, Rozłubirski and Woźniak to decide what to do.

Pressed into an ever smaller area of the Old Town between 19 and 28 of August, the Poles found themselves in a desperate position. The London Government's Delegate and the Home Army

Command left the Old Town during the night of 25 to 26 August, making their way to the Midtown district through the sewers. On the night of August 30 to 31 the Home Army launched a major attack on the Germans blockading the Old Town from the direction of Midtown, but the attempt to break through failed. For on learning of the attempt to break out of the Old Town, practically all the surviving civilians left their hideouts determined to follow the soldiers, and crammed the narrow streets, where they stayed despite an air and ground bombardment, mostly with rockets, that killed and maimed thousands. Units of the Home Army taking part in the attack could not get through the crowds and failed to support their comrades already engaged in battle.

Only then did Bór-Komorowski and Pełczyński accede to the demands of Colonel Karol Ziemski, who under the *nom de guerre* Wachnowski commanded the Home Army in the Old Town, to withdraw to Midtown. They ordered him to leave all his wounded and not to take any civilians. Ziemski ignored the order and on September 1 and 2 evacuated to Midtown a total of 3,000 unarmed soldiers, many of them wounded, and 1,500 armed soldiers. The evacuation had to be interrupted at seven o'clock in the morning of September 2 because the Germans poured petrol into the sewers and set it alight, and completely halted at nine o'clock in the morning when German rockets, shells and Stukas buried the manhole in Krasiński Square under a mountain of rubble. Moreover, some 800 civilians and walking wounded had made their escape through the sewers to Żoliborz. But some 2,500 badly wounded fighters and 45,000 civilians, some 5,000 of them badly wounded, were left behind. Already 35,000 civilians had been killed by German shells, rockets, bombs and bullets. Several more thousand civilians and most of the wounded in the dressing stations and hospitals were slaughtered by the German SS men and their Ukrainian, Russian, Turkoman and Azerbaijani henchmen.

The Czwartacy Battalion with the ŻOB group withdrew to Żoliborz on the night of August 27 to 28 and most of the two other battalions followed, completing their evacuation by the end of August. A well-armed platoon under the command of Rozłubirski stayed behind as part of the rearguard made up of the Home Army Parasol Battalion, WSOP (Military Service for the Defense of the Uprising) Battalion, the Wigry Battalion and a company of the

Batory Battalion. At dawn of September 1 the Germans launched a major assault on what remained of the Old Town in Polish hands and were stopped by the rearguard only a few hundred yards from the manhole in Krasiński Square. The Germans suffered such heavy losses that they entered the Old Town only in the afternoon of September 2, allowing the rearguard, which numbered many Jews, escape through the sewers to Midtown. Rozłubirski with his men also withdrew to Midtown and there fought on as part of a Home Army unit. After the war Rozłubirski stayed on in the Polish Army, reached the rank of a major-general and was forcibly retired.

The majority of the survivors of the Jewish Military Union fought in the units of the Security Corps and in the Polish People's Army (PAL) commanded by Colonel Julian Skokowski. As neither the Security Corps nor the Polish People's Army had been informed by the Home Army Command of its plans to stage an uprising, they were caught completely unprepared by its outbreak and succeeded in mobilizing only a small proportion of their members. The role of the Jews in their units was therefore considerable. And as the People's Army and the Polish People's Army fought in the Old Town and Mokotów, where the losses of the insurgents were the heaviest—33 per cent were killed and 23 per cent were badly wounded as compared with 20 and 14 per cent respectively in other parts of Warsaw[10]—very few Jews survived.

Most Jewish survivors who have written on the Jewish participation in the uprising estimate that at least 1,000 Jews fought in the Polish ranks. On the other hand the Pole Wacław Myzia, a major in the Peasant Battalions who fought with the Security Corps and the Polish People's Army units, stated after the war: "It seems to me that altogether some 2,000 Jews took part in the uprising. My opinion of the Jewish soldiers who fought in the uprising is good. They displayed a combative spirit—the feeling of fear was alien to them—and they showed great bravery and contempt for death."[11] If there were 2,000 Jewish combatants, then at least every fifteenth Polish fighter was a Jew and most of them must have fought in the Home Army. Those who fought in the Home Army units almost without exception did so under false names, which they had assumed when they became "Aryans." One of them was Nehemiah Szulkaper of Gródek Białostocki, who became Roman Rutkowski and thanks to his "Aryan" identity obtained the job of fireman on the railways—a job quite inaccessible to a Jew in pre-1939 Poland. It was as Roman Rutkowski that he fought in a Home Army unit and it was not until after the end of the war that he dared to reveal his true identity.[12] The overwhelming majority of the "Aryan" Jews who fought in the Home Army units died, however, during the uprising and their true identity died with them.

The few eyewitness accounts available testify to the legendary heroism, tenacity and enterprise of the Jews who fought in the units of the Home Army. Anna Wygonowska, a Polish woman who acted as a liason officer with the Home Army Motorized Ryszard Company in the Old Town, recalls that in her platoon alone — there were three platoons in the company — about one third were Jews. She recalls their *noms de guerre* as Biały, Filar, Gutek, Heniek, Rysiek, Szaberek, Tibor and Kalman, and describes their feats as follows:*

> Gutek and Heniek (Henryk Lederman) were the first to establish contact through the sewers with our forces in Żoliborz and maintained it as long as it was possible. The reconnaissance and preparation of an escape route to the Bank Square was the task of our platoon and took about a week. The man in command was Henryk Lederman. He led the Rudy Company as far as the manhole in the Bank Square. Then he turned back to guide other detachments from the Old Town and Midtown. He fell fighting in the Czerniaków district.
>
> The Ensign Biały (his real name was Eugeniusz Weiss), light blond and of medium height, won the admiration of his comrades. He was one of the bravest. He was wounded twice. He was killed in Czerniaków on September 16, 1944. As for Gutek, he was one of the best guides through the sewers. Always ready to sacrifice himself for others and a good comrade, totally devoted to the struggle against the Nazis, he died under the Poniatowski Bridge when after the fall of Czerniaków he and a group tried to reach Praga from the Solec.

Another eyewitness account by the Polish officer Wacław Zagórski tell us about the Jews who fought in Midtown.** His battalion was one of the two forming the task force Chrobry II, which fought in the Żelazna, Wronia and Towarowa Streets against

---

* Abraham Kwaterko, "Der Varshever Oigust-Oifshtand un der onteyl fun Yidn", *Folks Shtime*, Warsaw, July 20, 1978.
** Ibid.

Major-General Rohr's battle group made up of German SS, Kaminsky's SS Brigade of Ukrainian and Russian cutthroats and rapists, and Wehrmacht units. In an account of his role in putting down the uprising written for the Polish Institute of Contemporary History, Erich von dem Bach said: "Rohr was my finest commander. An officer of the greatest integrity on the old Prussian model, tactful, decent, incapable of any deviation . . . Short, sticky. He was a Rhinelander."* Being a Rhinelander and a professional German officer did not prevent him giving Kaminsky, who was himself of Polish origin, a free hand to commit the most unspeakable cruelties against the civilian population and the wounded Polish fighters who fell into German hands. This is how Zagórski remembers the Jews in his unit, the Lech Grzybowski Battalion made up of Home Army soldiers and PPS Militia:**

> In my battalion, which was organized in Midtown-North in the first week of the uprising, I had several dozen Jews. Two of them, seventeen-year-old Staszek, the son of the head of the Jewish community at Otwock murdered in the forests outside Warsaw, and forty-year-old Dr. Henryk Spiegler, an economist, had worked before the uprising in the secret printing shop which I ran at No. 17, Grzybowska Street. At first I did not allow them to come into the open, because I was determined to guard the secret of the printing shop. But on August 7 a German bomb smashed the building to its foundations and revealed the printing press. Both Jews escaped alive and joined my battalion. Henryk was not issued with a weapon because his sight was bad. But Staszek fought in the First Platoon of the Fourth Company in the Krochmalna, Grzybowska, Ceglana and Żelazna Streets until capitulation.
>
> In the same company we had Ensign Lolek, a fine soldier with great leadership abilities. Tall, a fine figure of a man, fair, he took over the command of his platoon when Second Lieutenant Tadeusz Micke was killed during the fighting in Chmielna Street on September 17, and beat back a heavy enemy attack.
>
> The highest reputation as a fighter was won in the company by Sergeant Michał Igra. His comrades could not help admiring his coolness and marksmanship. After the death of Błyskawica, the squad commander, he took over as leader.

* Kirchmayer, op. cit., p. 286.
** Kwaterko, ibid.

II

The Jews in the Home Army units had good reason to conceal their true identity even from their comrades, for except for the detachments composed of members of the Polish Socialist Party, Jews were not accepted and, in the case of detachments formed by members of the National Party, they continued to be treated as enemies. Moreover, the National Armed Forces had their own unit in the Old Town, the Koło (Wheel) Brigade, which numbered 600 men but of which only one armed platoon of fifty men actually took part in the fighting.[13] The Polish fascists probably killed more Jews than Germans during the uprising: in one case alone they murdered thirty Jews who had emerged from their hideout in 25, Długa Street to volunteer for service in the uprising.[14] Many of the Polish Nazis were former officers and as such were given command of Home Army units, where they did their best to intensify anti-Jewish hatreds by telling their men that the reason why the Red Army had stopped on the eastern bank of the Vistula was because it was commanded by Jews responsible for the Katyń massacre, who now wanted to take revenge on the Poles for the Warsaw ghetto. In view of the bad conscience of many of their soldiers on this subject, their propaganda was not without success.

Furthermore, the Polish gendarmerie, the so-called State Security Corps, was to a large extent composed of policemen whose record in helping the Germans to exterminate the Jews of Warsaw was second to none. The gendarmes did not just turn a blind eye to the killings of Jews by Polish fascists and common criminals in Śliska and Złota Streets, even though the murders were mostly carried out in order to rob the victims of their belongings that frequently amounted to no more than a watch or a ring, which represented the last memento of a gassed wife, husband, child or parent. The gendarmes themselves murdered an unknown number of Jews in the Żoliborz and City Center districts.[15]

We have an illuminating account of what it was like to be an "Aryan" Jew during the sixty-three days of the Warsaw Uprising in Michael Zylberberg's *A Warsaw Diary*. After making his way through the sewers out of the Old Town shortly before it was captured by the Germans, he reached with a number of Poles the center of Warsaw, where a young and elegant officer refused to accept him as a soldier because somebody in his group had denounced him as a Jew. He finally found refuge in a house in Marszałkowska Street, the principal street of prewar Warsaw, where nobody suspected him of not being an Aryan Slav. There he found that, "Again, many Jews took part in the fighting, but they did not communicate with each other as no one admitted his origin. People often talked about the responsibility borne by Jews and communists for the lack of Soviet aid during the Uprising." One night, while he was on guard duty as a member of the local civil defense organization, he and his Polish companions were approached by an officer who "had come from the front line, where the Polish soldiers were desperately battling with the Germans, not too far from where we stood. He cursed the Germans fluently, but his most vehement oaths were reserved for the Jews. He told us that he had a few Jews in his unit who pretended to be Poles. They really thought they were deceiving everyone. He, however, could recognize them with ease—by their large, fat hands!"[16]

Singularly tragic and heroic was the fate of the Jews in the Gęsia Street prison. One group of fifty men were working in the warehouses in Stawki Street loading food and military stores into trains when the uprising broke out. Most of the Jews were Hungarians[17] but among them was Chaim Isaac Goldstein, a native of Warsaw who in search of work had emigrated to Paris before the war and who was to describe his experiences in one of the most remarkable books produced by the Final Solution. A Home Army platoon liberated the fifty Jews after killing their SS guards almost as soon as the uprising began , but it took the Poles three days to capture the Gęsia Prison. In the unit that liberated the 348 Jews there was a company commanded by Captain Jerzy Morro and one of the first to break into the prison was Second Lieutenant Tadeusz Zuchowicz — the same Home Army officers who had refused to stand by doing nothing when the Ghetto Uprising broke out and on their own initiative had smuggled all the pistol ammunition of their unit into the ghetto on April 23. All the liberated Jews immediately asked to be allowed to take part in the fighting, although after the hell of Auschwitz and the slave labor in the ruins of the ghetto the right place for them was in hospitals.

Zuchowicz recalled after the war:[18] "Of the Jewish volunteers who were mechanics and electricians we organized a squad for servicing our tanks. (We had captured three tanks.) Other Jewish mechanics were posted to the rifle-repair workshop in the St. Kinga school in Okopowa Street, which was run by Warrant Officer Rafał. Most of the liberated Jews carried out auxiliary services, such as carting water, transporting the wounded and captured uniforms or any other equipment that could be indirectly used in the fighting. They also put out the fires and repaired the barricades.... About twenty who were young and stronger than the others and insisted on taking a direct part in the fighting were incorporated in our units and fought shoulder to shoulder with us. They all displayed much steadfastness, courage and a spirit of self-sacrifice. I remember how on August 9 or thereabout three German tanks attacked our positions from the direction of Powązki Cemetery. At the intersection with Okopowa Street one of the tanks was immobilized by a good shot of our Piat. The SS crew jumped out and were mown down by our bullets. The other two tanks withdrew up Powązki Cemetery, their machine guns firing long bursts. The major in command of our sector called out: 'Who will get into the immobilized tank, swing the gun round and hit the retreating tanks?' Like a cat one of our Jews leaped towards the Panther and climbed into the turret. With bated breath we watched the turret with the gun swing round slowly. The retreating tanks were already some 200 to 300 yards away when there was a roar and a flash from the barrel of the gun. One of the retreating tanks turned into a heap of iron. The second got away. The Jew, the victor, emerged from the turret with a shining face and a mouth set in an expression of determination and hatred. Our commander ran towards him, kissed him on both cheeks and pinned his own Virtuti Militari Cross on the Jew's breast."

Unfortunately, Zuchowicz's account presents only one side of the picture. For the other side we have to go to Goldstein. Soon after the Jews had been liberated from the Gęsia Street prison they found themselves, still dressed in their concentration camp pajamas, in Miodowa Street, where together with Polish men, women and children they built barricades to stop the German tanks advancing from Krakowskie Przedmieście. When the Germans approached, the civilians and those of the Jews who had no weapons sought shelter in the cellars. Goldstein and David Edelman, a Polish Jew from France who like him had been deported to Auschwitz, emerged from their cellar as soon as the German attack had been beaten off to see what had happened to their twenty-odd comrades who had fought behind the barricades. But before they got near them they heard voices shouting "Jews, Jews! Bloody Jews!" and heard two shots. Two of the Jews collapsed and their killers, with pistols in their hands, told the crowd: "We don't want Jews here! They must all be killed!" The Jews then tried to revenge their comrades, but were prevented by the crowd who pushed them into a nearby courtyard and tried to make up for the crime of their compatriots by giving them clothes to replace their concentration camp garb.[19]

The wickedness of the murders was such that as Goldstein and Edelman gazed at the burning city a few hours later, Edelman said: "Do you remember what the Bible says about the end of Sodom? It must have looked like the sight we are watching now. And who knows whether the fate of Sodom is not going to be shared by Warsaw and perhaps even the whole of Poland, for enough crimes have been committed here against Jews, apart from those committed by the Germans. . . ." Goldstein would not agree with his friend. He reminded him that Abraham had pleaded with the Lord not to punish the innocent inhabitants of Sodom for the sins of the majority and recalled all the kindnesses both he and Edelman had received from Poles. Abraham, Goldstein pointed out, had been unable to find a single innocent person in Sodom, but not all the Poles agreed with those who shouted "Kill the Jews!"[20]

A day or two after this incident Goldstein and his comrades were in Mławska Street, lying in a courtyard after a day spent building barricades. It was eleven o'clock at night when a Polish officer appeared and told the Jews that he needed twelve volunteers for a very important and dangerous assignment. Goldstein was one of the twelve Jews who followed the Polish officer to a square, where he told them that unless they could dig a trench before dawn and hide it behind a barricade, nothing could stop the Germans from reaching the nearby Vistula, from where the only help could come. Covered by two of their comrades, who were given machine guns, the ten Jews began to dig the trench "with such momentum, with such drive that the Pole looked on with amazement, wondering where people who had gone through ghettoes and concentration camps, who had been martyred by hunger and beatings, found such strength. But ours was not a physical strength but a moral force. We were driven on by our will to fight the Nazis."[21]

When the Jews had finished well before dawn, the Polish officer led them back to Mławska Street and told the lieutenant who was in charge of them: "They are heroes." Some time later, as Goldstein was talking to the lieutenant, there was a burst of submachine gun fire behind them and as they turned round they saw one of the Jews writhing in mortal agony on the ground and his killer shouldering his Tommy gun. Without a glance at his victim, the Pole walked towards them. "As he passed us, he saluted the lieutenant and said with a grin: 'That was a bloody Jew.' The lieutenant looked at me and, perceiving my emotion, excused himself for doing nothing: 'What can I do? He is not of my unit'. . . . I went up to the murdered Jew. He was a man in his forties, tall and powerfully built. He lay with his eyes open and the grimace on his face expressed the pain he had felt in the last moments of his life when he realized that he had not been killed by the enemy whom he had been fighting, but by one of those whom he regarded as his friends. . . ."[22]

In the courtyard where this murder took place there were wooden stalls where a Polish cattle-dealer kept cows and calves. One day incendiary bombs dropped by German aircraft set the stalls on fire. Many Poles were hiding in the cellars, but not one made an attempt to save the animals. "I don't know why the sight of the trapped animals should have had such a shattering effect on us, a handful of Jews who had witnessed and experienced so many horrors in the past few years and who should have been made callous by them," Goldstein recalled. "But the lowing of the cows and calves tore at our hearts. We glanced at one another and all of us, as one man, rushed towards the burning stalls. In no time at all we smashed the doors and a mountain of flesh stampeded into the courtyard. By some miracle not one of us was hurt. . . . We were surrounded by people who shook our hands, slapped our backs and offered us cigarettes. The women were particularly friendly. We were offered one of the cows, which because of her wounds had to be slaughtered. During our last few days in that courtyard we were treated like heroes and the people went out of their way to demonstrate their friendship."[23]

Some time after this incident Goldstein found himself in a Home

Army detachment defending a barricade in Okopowa Street. There were forty-two men in the detachment, including six whom Goldstein knew to be Jews. After beating off several attacks, the lieutenant in command decided that the position of his detachment was hopeless and that they had no other way out but to surrender. But before he could carry out his intention, one of his men leapt over the barricade and rushed towards the enemy, firing his Polish-made Sten gun. The six Jews and Goldstein followed him and after a moment the Poles did the same. The Nazis lost their nerve and ran, giving the Poles the time to withdraw from the barricade to a better position. The man who had rushed at the enemy was known as Stanisław Żelazo, but after his exploit Goldstein learnt from him that he was a Jewish locksmith, who in 1942 had fled from the Warsaw ghetto with his wife and children and had been sheltered by a Polish woman until they were denounced by a Polish neighbor. The Gestapo arrived while Żelazo was at work and seized his wife and children. He himself was saved from falling into the hands of the Germans by the old woman-porter of the house, who waited for him in the street and warned him of the danger.[24]

Most of the foreign Jews found themselves in the Zośka Battalion, of which Captain Morro's company formed part, and in the Parasol Battalion. The two battalions belonged to the task force commanded by Lieutenant-Colonel Jan Mazurkiewicz, whose *nom de guerre* was Radosław. Others fought in the Wigry Battalion, which formed part of the task force commanded by Major Stanisław Błaszczak, whose *nom de guerre* was Róg. After the fall of the Old Town, the remnants of the Polish forces made their way through the sewers to the center of the city, where they carried on the battle. The wounded Mazurkiewicz, who had chosen a Czech Jew by the name of Karol as his runner, was carried through the sewers by Jews.[25] In his reminiscences of the uprising Mazurkiewicz recalled: "Among the Jews liberated from the Gęsia concentration camp were several dozen reservists who had been trained in the Polish Army; they were the best element. The Jews were organized in several units. The unit in the Zośka Battalion performed auxiliary functions. Another unit of sixty men was posted to the reserve Igor Battalion. Some twenty Jews attached to my staff were engaged in delivering ammunition and recovering the wounded.

Many of them died during the fighting from German bombs. Thus an entire group of about twenty Yugoslav Jews died under the ruins of a house in Wilanowska Street, which was hit by bombs."

When the central part of Warsaw fell, the surviving Hungarian, Greek, Yugoslav, Dutch, Belgian and French Jews accompanied the Polish fighters who had refused to surrender through the sewers to the Czerniaków district and finished up on the bank of the Vistula. There most of them met their end. Among the handful who survived, Bela Harap and three other Hungarian Jews are known to have swum the Vistula through a hail of bullets and shells and reached the Red Army positions on the opposite bank.[26]

Over 200,000 civilians and soldiers died in the sixty-five days of fighting, which ended with Bór-Komorowski's surrender to SS Obergruppenführer (General) Erich von dem Bach, who until 1940 had called himself von dem Bach-Zelewski, having been no doubt as proud of his Polish origins as Nietzsche had been of his. All the survivors were then ordered by the Germans to leave the entire area of what had been the city of Warsaw and most of them were rounded up in camps, thousands ending up in the gas-chambers of Auschwitz.[27]

III

The survivors of the ŻOB found themselves with the People's Army units in Żoliborz at the moment of capitulation. Hersh Berlinski died in the Old Town. The passage of the others through the sewers equalled in horror their worst experiences during the Ghetto Uprising. Isaac Zuckerman escaped being torn to pieces by German grenades by what can only be described as a miracle, while his wife Tsivya Lubetkin and Borzykowski almost drowned.

At Żoliborz the People's Army once again organized three battalions with a total strength of 440 men and women. The ŻOB group found itself in the Third Battalion, which also included a group of ten Red Army officers and men commanded by Lieutenant Arkadiy Matosyan, an Armenian, who had all escaped from German captivity. The entire force was commanded by Captain Jan Szaniawski, whose chief-of-staff was Edward Grosglik, probably a Jew. The political commissar was Zenon Kliszko, a close friend of Gomułka who was to become Gomułka's favorite ideologist and after 1956 the chief exponent of racist anti-Semitism in the leadership of the Polish United Workers' Party that culminated in the "anti-Zionist" campaign of 1967–9.

Two groups made up of party leaders and officers, the most senior of whom was Colonel Andrzej Adrian, as well as wounded and sick soldiers, left Żoliborz for the relative safety of the Kampinos forests by the middle of September. The ŻOB group was not among them, contrary to the official version recorded by Garas.*
On the contrary, they were involved in some of the most ferocious fighting against the German 25th Panzer Division until September 23 and against Lieutenant-General Hans Kaellner's 19th Panzer Division after that date.

By then there was no escape from Żoliborz, because the Germans had completely blocked the sewers. Salvation could come only from the Red Army, which had captured Praga on the night of 13 to 14 September. The following day the First, Second and Third Infantry Divisions and the First Cavalry Brigade of the First Polish Army replaced the Red Army formations along the river and until the 19th made repeated attempts to establish bridgeheads on the western bank. A battalion of the Ninth Infantry Regiment, Third Infantry Division, commanded by the Russian Lieutenant Kononkov succeeded in crossing the Vistula during the night of 15 to 16 September and joined the Poles fighting in the Czerniaków district. The battalion was joined by a second battalion the following night. Also the following night a company of the Sixth Regiment of the Second Infantry Division managed to land at Żoliborz and the same night the two battalions in Czerniaków commanded now by the Russian Major Latyshonok were reinforced by their remaining units and received some food and ammunition. But an attempt by a company of the Seventh Infantry Regiment using amphibious vehicles to land in Czerniaków the same night ended disastrously. During the night of 18 to 19 September the company of the Sixth Regiment which had landed in the Żoliborz sector was reinforced by the other companies of its battalion and the total strength of the bridgehead rose to 400 men.

On September 18, General Zygmunt Berling, the commander of the First Polish Army, tried to establish a bridgehead north of

---

* Op. cit., p. 52.

Czerniaków, near the ruins of the Poniatowski Bridge, and from there attack in the rear Dirlewanger's cutthroats and the tanks of the 19th Panzer Division which were storming Czerniaków. But despite a smoke screen covering the entire length of the Vistula's course through Warsaw — a stretch of eleven kilometres — and massive artillery and air support, only two battalions of the Eighth Regiment succeeded in landing near the Poniatowski Bridge in the late afternoon of September 19. The force of 873 soldiers was attacked by German tanks and infantry and the remnants of the two battalions had to fight their way back to the river. Very few managed to get back to the eastern bank under the cover of darkness.

By then the Third Infantry Division had lost almost all its 223 landing-craft and seventy-eight pontoons, almost its entire strength, as well as 303 sappers.* On the following day Marshal Rokossovskiy, as commander of the First Ukrainian Army Group, therefore concluded that the insurgents could not be saved except by a major offensive, which could be ordered only by Stalin, and stopped the attempts of the Poles to come to the succor of the insurgents. The same day the Sixth Battalion of the Sixth Regiment was pushed by German tanks supported by a massive artillery bombardment into the Vistula. The last signal received from the battalion command by the Sixth Regiment was to lay a barrage over themselves in order to hit the Germans. Only a few survivors reached the Praga bank. Major Latyshonok's force fought on with the insurgents until September 23, when all resistance ceased. The fighting in Czerniaków was the fiercest in the entire Warsaw Uprising. The Germans had to storm every house in several streets and finally were held back for hours by the defenders of a single house. They took prisoner ninety-two soldiers, fifty-seven insurgents and about one hundred and twenty wounded and massacred almost all of them.** But they did not capture the Home Army commander of the Czerniaków sector, Lieutenant-Colonel Jan Mazurkiewicz, who left the district on the night of 19 to 20, using the sewers to reach Mokotów.

The First Polish Army lost over 2,000 men in its attempts to help

---

* Kirchmayer, op. cit., p. 394.
** Ibid., p. 395.

the insurgents and many of them were Jews. Some 10,000 Polish Jews had joined the Polish Army when it was organized in Russia in 1943 and the largest number of them was in the First Tadeusz Kościuszko Division. A quarter or more of its fighting strength was Jewish and its was a Jew, Captain Juliusz Hibner, who was the first man in the division to be awarded the highest Soviet military decoration, the title of Hero of the Soviet Union, after the first battle the division fought at Lenino in October 1943. A veteran of the International Brigades, he reached after the war the rank of major-general, the highest the communist rulers of Poland would give to a Jew. As the First Division was part of the Forty-Seventh Red Army which drove the Germans out of Praga, many Jews died to make it possible for the First Polish Army to reach the Vistula.

Already during the night of 10 to 11 September Captain Szaniawski had dispatched four emissaries with orders to cross the Vistula and establish a direct link with the Soviet command. They were successful and on the 14th the Russians dropped bandages and drugs and a day later a supply of submachine guns, anti-tank rifles and ammunition. But while the First Polish Army was making desperate efforts to establish a bridgehead in Czerniaków, the commander of the Żoliborz sector, Lieutenant-Colonel Mieczysław Niedzielski, refused to use his 2,000 men in a major effort to break through the thin line of German positions separating the Poles from the Vistula.* Similarly, he rejected the plans of the command of the Second Infantry Division to evacuate the insurgents to Praga during the night of 20 to 21 September.**

On September 23 Lieutenant-General Hans Kaellner's 19th Panzer Division replaced the 25th Panzer Division and began the inexorable process of wiping out the Polish insurgents. To make sure that none got away, Kaellner saw to it that all the sewers should be made impassable. On September 29 the Germans launched a general assault and drove the insurgents into an ever decreasing bag. In the evening of the same day Szaniawski proposed to the Home Army commanders that they should hold out until 2000 hours the following day, when, helped by a barrage laid down by the guns of the Russians and the First Polish Army and protected by Soviet planes, they would break through the German

---

* Kirchmayer, op. cit., p. 396.
** Ibid.

positions along the Vistula and escape to Praga. His plan was accepted. The following morning the Germans resumed their general assault and by 1700 hours pushed the insurgents into a small area bounded by Bohomolec, Mickiewicz, Krasiński, Koźmian and Promyk Streets. At that crucial moment Colonel Karol Ziemski came through the German lines and told Niedzielski that Bór-Komorowski had ordered him to capitulate.

The Home Army units accepted the order and laid down their arms, but Captain Szaniawski led a group of one hundred men and women in a desperate attempt to reach the Praga bank of the Vistula. Only twenty-eight persons, including three Home Army soldiers, broke through the German positions, reached the Vistula and either swam it or were ferried across by soldiers of the Polish Sixth Infantry Division. Among them were Szaniawski, Kliszko, Grosglik and Kobyliński, as well as two women.

The ŻOB group were waiting with their platoon in Promyk Street when the order to surrender came. A Jewish woman by the name of Jasia, who had so far survived by hiding with a Polish family at No. 41, Promyk Street, proposed that they should all use her hideout. The ŻOB group were joined by Lieutenant Witek and taking every precaution not to be seen entered the little house, which was the last in the street—beyond were the German positions and the Vistula. But outside the house they were joined by a man who told them: "I see that you want to hide. I am joining you. You want to live and so do I."* There were therefore fifteen of them, six women and nine men. Inside the house they found that the owners had gone, leaving behind them an eighty-year-old grandmother, who was both deaf and paralyzed, to be looked after by three Jewish women in their sixties and seventies, who owed their survival so far to the humanity of the Polish family and the fact that they themselves did not look Jewish and spoke perfect Polish. Their presence in the house turned out to be the salvation of the ŻOB group: every time Germans entered it the sight of the women was enought to convince them that a thorough search was unnecessary.

The women lived in the main cellar and the hideout was a tiny cellar adjoining it, the entrance of which was hidden by an old kitchen dresser. Inside it four or five persons at the most could lie

---

* Borzykowski, op. cit., p. 301.

down, but there were fifteen. After a fortnight or so Marek Edelman discovered a good hideout in another deserted house and three men, one of them Lieutenant Witek, and two women moved to it. For almost seven weeks the ŻOB group hid in the cellar, living on the few potatoes, carrots, peas and other vegetables they could find during their nightly forays into the cellars of neighboring houses. Their greatest problem was finding water, for the mains did not work. They mostly depended on the foul and dirty water they found in baths and therefore suffered the torments of thirst throughout their ordeal.

Ten days before their salvation the Germans removed the old women and Lodzia, one of the ŻOB group who pretended to be the granddaughter of Sabina, the seventy-year-old Jewish woman who by her strength of character and cool-headedness had several times saved the group from being discovered by prowling Germans. At the same time the Germans began to build a shelter next to the little house, using explosives to save themselves the trouble of digging. It was thus a matter of hours rather than days before they would discover the cellar with the Jews in it. But at midday on November 15, 1944 the Jews were saved by the arrival of several Polish and Jewish girls accompanied by Polish stretcher-bearers, who officially were looking for sick and helpless civilians that might have been left behind after the Germans had driven out the entire population of Warsaw. Their arrival at midday was an incredible stroke of good luck, for the Germans building the shelter were away having their lunch. Had they been there, they would have seen the emergence of ten human beings from a house they believed to be empty and would no doubt have seized them.

The truism that life is much more extraordinary than fiction was responsible for their salvation. The four women removed by the Germans were given their freedom outside Warsaw and happened to be seen by Inka Szwajger, who since the end of the Warsaw ghetto had lived on the "Aryan" side and liaised between the ŻOB survivors and the friendly Polish underground. She learnt from Lodzia about the plight of the ŻOB group and contacted Ala Margolis, another survivor who liaised with the Poles. Ala turned to Dr. Śwital, the head of a Warsaw hospital evacuated to a small town outside the city, and told him about the plight of a group of ten insurgents, six of them Home Army soldiers and four People's

Army soldiers, two of them Jews. Dr. Śwital was the kind of Pole who, to quote Borzykowski, "did not care whether one was a Jew or a member of the People's Army, but ready to do everything in his power to save a human being."* He obtained the necessary documents from the Germans and the Jewish and Polish girls acting as nurses were able to hoodwink all the German patrols and checkpoints and save the ŻOB group.

Several hundred Jews, including a number of Greeks and Hungarians, descended into the sewers or other hideouts and some of them held out until January 1945, when the Red Army finally liberated Warsaw. Thus Jews were among the last fighters and survivors in the city of Warsaw.

---

* Op. cit., p. 342.

Ruins of Warsaw ghetto (1945)

Notes

The Road to Resistance

1 The Catholics had their own church until the Great Liquidation of 1942. The curate of the All Saints Church, Father Godlewski, had been notorious before the war for his anti-Semitic sermons and activities. After the creation of the ghetto he did his best to help his "Semitic" parishioners and also to rescue a number of Jews. But there can be no doubt that his Christian activities under the Nazi yoke could not make good for the years he had spent poisoning the minds of thousands of Poles who might otherwise have helped their Jewish neighbors. The most unexpected people found themselves in the ghetto. "At the beginning of December 1942 the Germans brought a German soldier, who had been badly wounded on the Eastern Front, to the hospital in Gęsia Street. The duty doctor was told that the soldier was not a German but a Jew, and therefore he could not be allowed to be together with wounded Germans. The soldier came from a remote Austrian village—he was probably of Jewish ancestry, but he had no links with Jewishness. He had been brought up as a Catholic since childhood and while in hospital kept complaining that there was no Catholic church inside the ghetto where he could pray." (*Wiadomości*, No. 3, 1942, *Biuletyn Żydowskiego Instytutu Historycznego*, No. 76, 1970. *Wiadomości* was one of the underground publications in the Warsaw ghetto. The first issue appeared in November 1942 and the sixth and last in the second half of January 1943.)

2 T. Berenstein, A. Rutkowski, "Liczba Żydów i obszar przez nich zamieszkiwany w Warszawie w latach okupacji hitlerowskiej" ("The Number of Jews and the Area Inhabited by them in Warsaw during the Nazi Occupation"), *Biuletyn Żydowskiego Instytutu Historycznego*, No. 26, 1958.

3 B. Mark, *Walka i zagłada warszawskiego getta (The Struggle and Annihilation of the Warsaw Ghetto)*, pp. 50, 59.

4 Mark, *op. cit.*, p. 52. The prices were much higher after the Great Liquidation. During the Great Liquidation a loaf of bread cost 100 zlotys.

5 *Ibid.*, p. 54.

6 *Ibid.*, p. 59.

7 *Ibid.*, p. 63. Mortality per 1,000 had been 9.6 in 1938, 23.5 in 1940, 90 in 1941 and 140 in 1942. (Eisenbach, A., *Hitlerowska polityka zagłady Żydów*, p. 231.)

8 Conditions in many of the labor camps were as bad as or even worse than in the death camps. *Wiadomości*, No. 3, December 22, 1942 described them as "the practices of Oświęcim" and quoted the following examples of them: "In the middle of

November 1942 32 Jewish workers employed in the Modlin shipyard were beaten to death for being five minutes late in reporting to work. The Jews guilty of the crime were beaten to death by German soldiers (not SS men!) using clubs. It will be enough to say that after less than an hour there lay the bodies of 32 'criminals' beaten to a pulp, arms and legs severed from trunks, heads turned into tragic masks, spattered brains, disembowelled entrails. ... At Siedlce ... the German building firm Reckmann, which 'normally' liquidates every day Jews no longer capable of further efforts, allowed itself the following novelty: three Jewish workers were concreted alive inside one of the buildings being erected. The cries of the victims sent the torturers into a veritable orgy of joy. We want to emphasize that this deed was done by German civilians (not SS men or members of the Wehrmacht) ..."

9 *Black Book*, New York, 1946, p. 178.

10 *Hans Frank's Diaries*, quoted by Mark, *op. cit.*, p. 52.

11 Emanuel Ringelblum, *Ksavim fun geto (Ghetto Writings)*, Vol. 1, p. 222. The ghetto historian noted in February 1941: "Frequent cases of people foraging for food in rubbish bins. But at the same time there are flats where people daily eat oranges at 25 zlotys a kilogram, grapes and so on."

12 Mark, *op. cit.*, p. 63.

13 Ringelblum, *op. cit.*, Vol. 1, p. 370.

14 *Ibid.*, pp. 234, 314; Vol. 2, p. 68.

15 The story of Ganzweich and his organization is based on Abraham Rosenberg's study "Dos 'Draitsntl'" ("The Thirteen"), *Bleter far Geshikhte*, Warsaw, Nos. 1–2, 3–4, 1952.

16 Ringelblum noted: "The Orthodox satisfied with the ghetto. They argue—the rabbi who is the son of Samuel of Zbytków—that this is how it should be. Jews should live apart" (*op. cit.*, Vol. 1, p. 234).

17 *Ibid.*, p. 283.

18 In 1896, for the first time in Polish history, the racist principle made its appearance in Polish politics. Prince Sapieha standing as a candidate in the Galician elections to the Vienna parliament asked that only Aryans should vote for him. (*Di Yidn in Poiln*, p. 466.)

19 Leonard Stein, *The Balfour Declaration*, pp. 36–7.

20 *Ibid.*, pp. 37–41.

21 *Sefer Milkhamot Hagetaot (The Book of the Ghetto Wars)*, pp. 737–8.

22 Mark, *op. cit.*, p. 207. According to Edelman, the Jews found on him a Gestapo identity card issued in 1933. (Edelman, *Getto walczy [The Ghetto Fights]*, p. 51.) Polish sources describe the document as an Abwehr identity card, which appears more likely.

23 *Op. cit.*, Vol. 1, p. 317. Also according to Ringelblum, Szeryński refused to have his Jewish policemen carry out the hangings and this was done by a Polish policeman, Wiktor Zalek, who volunteered for the job. (*Ibid.*)

23a Chełmno-on-Ner (Kulmhof) was the first death factory and grew out of the Euthanasia Program, which Hitler is known to have planned as soon as he came to power. In fact, he told the Reich Medical Leader Wagner in 1935 "that, if war came, he would take up and carry out this question of euthanasia because it was easier to do so in wartime when the church would not be able to put up the expected resistance." (Gerald Reitlinger, *The Final Solution*, London 1953, p. 125.) About 100,000 human beings, most of them "Aryan" Germans, were murdered until the public protests of a number of Catholic and Protestant bishops and demonstrations by ordinary Germans forced Hitler to halt it. It is worth recalling, at a time when the glorification of Hitler and Nazism has reached the stage when David Irving's book claiming that Hitler did not order the Final Solution is treated seriously by British scholars, that the men whom Hitler ordered to carry out the Euthanasia Program demanded written orders and Hitler was forced to give them in a written note to Reichsleiter Philip Bouhler and Dr. Karl Brandt, the Reichskommissar for Health. As most of such Nazi documents, the crime came first and the legalization, so dear to the German mind and heart, came next: Hitler's handwritten note to Bouhler was written at the end of October 1939 and backdated as a secret decree to September 1. (Reitlinger, ibid., p. 127.)

The Euthanasia Program demanded organization and inventiveness — qualities possessed by many Germans. It also offered career prospects and these were seized by Christian Wirth, born on November 24, 1885 and a hero of the First World War. Until Hitler's rise to power he had been an obscure builder, but henceforward he was able to make a career as a policeman and by 1939 reached the rank of *Kriminalkommissar* in the Stuttgart Criminal Police Department. Before the end of 1939 he and a number of other police officers, many of them Austrians, were posted to "euthanasia duties". Wirth was posted to the Grafeneck psychiatric clinic near his native Württemberg, the first of the fourteen euthanasia killing establishments in the Reich. The victims were at the time murdered by pistol shots in the back of the neck. Wirth and his team introduced lethal injections, which proved an easier and more efficient way of murdering sick and defenseless human beings. He was therefore promoted to administrator of the euthanasia establishment at Brandenburg-an-der-Havel and there, in December 1939 or January 1940, he carried out the first gassing experiment using coal gas from a steel retort, the victims being every time 20 to 30 Germans. In recognition of his services Wirth was promoted to Inspector of Euthanasia Establishments before the end of 1940.

Before the end of 1941 gas chambers using carbon monoxide gas and disguised as shower rooms became the standard equipment of the euthanasia establishments. The new method was so efficient that on the occasion of the 10,000th gassing at Hadamar Wirth gave a party to the staff. It is worth noting that, like Hitler, Wirth had no doubts about the criminality of his actions, so that his signature has not been found on any document dealing with his work. The organization operating the Euthanasia Program was known as the Charitable Foundation for Institutional Care and it was under the same name that Wirth's teams, mostly trained at Hadamar, Grafeneck and Hartheim, operated the death factories in Poland.

In July 1941 Wirth was sent to Globocnik at Lublin and discussed the establishment of a euthanasia center, which would have been the first outside the Reich. But with the Einsatzkommandos in Russia proving that hundreds of thousands of Jews and non-Jews could be murdered by shooting, the project was not realized. However, reports from the Einsatzgruppen convinced Hitler, Himmler and Heydrich that the bullet was not the answer to the problem of genocide, especially as the massacre of naked civilians and prisoners of war turned many of the killers into useless alcoholics. Wirth's gas chambers had a special attraction for Hitler, who having been gassed in the First World War did not blame the German leaders for having introduced the diabolical weapon, but the Jews. "If, at the beginning and during the war," he wrote in *Mein Kampf*, "someone had only subjected about twelve to fifteen thousand of the Hebrew enemies of the people to poison gas . . . then the sacrifice of millions at the front would not have been in vain." Hitler's obsession with murder by gassing, vented first on "Aryan" Germans, was no secret to leading Nazis in the SS machine of genocide and led to the perfectioning of Wirth's gas chamber, which could take only 20 to 30 victims at a time. The product of German inventiveness was a gas van built by Sauer which was capable of dealing with 80 to 90 victims at a time.

The first van was tested on Jews and Slavs at Mogilev. The victims were still alive when the van was opened and they were finished off with grenades. The second test, with a modified van, was also a failure because the victims crammed into the back of the vehicle and tipped it up. However, in October 1941 a number of such vans were already in use in Byelorussia and the Ukraine for the gassing of women and children. At the beginning of November 1941 Wirth left Franz Stangl in charge of Schloss Hartheim near Linz, where with the assistance of a team of scientists and technicians he had perfected the gassing operation, and set off for an abandoned manor house in a small park near Chełmno-on-Ner. With three gas vans supplied from Berlin he set up the first death factory in Poland. At the same time other vans were sent to the Semlin camp in Yugoslavia, which was filled by Jews from Belgrade, and more than 6,000 were gassed in them. (Michael Tregenza, "Bełżec Death Camp", *The Wiener Library Bulletin*, London, Nos 41/42 1977.)

It is probable that the first victims were "Aryans": Poles and Germans from asylums in the Warthegau, for on Himmler's orders 1,200 mental patients from four hospitals in the Polish Corridor had been executed in a wood near the village of Piasnica Wielka in October-December 1939. But as far as it has been possible to establish, Kulmhof began to operate as a death factory on December 8, 1941, and from that date until January 1945 some 300,000 Polish Jews from the Warthegau and 25,000 foreign Jews, over 5,000 Gypsies, over 5,000 Soviet prisoners of war and several thousand Poles were gassed there. (H. Dąbrowska, "Zagłada skupisk żydowskich w 'Kraju Warty' w okresie okupacji hitlerowskiej" ("The annihilation of the Jewish communities in the 'Warta Land' during the Nazi occupation"), *Biuletyn Żydowskiego Instytutu Historycznego*, Nos 13–14, 1955; Edward Serwański, *Obóz zagłady w Chełmnie nad Nerem (The Annihilation Camp at Chełmno-on-Ner)*, Poznań 1964.)

24 Edelman, *op. cit.*, p. 14.

25 David Wdowiński, *And We Are Not Saved*, pp. 54–5.

26 Bartoszewski, Lewinówna, *Ten jest z ojczyzny mojej*, pp. 141–6. On the Jewish origins of General Petrykowski, as he became in the Polish Army after the war, see Mark's *Der oifshtand in Varshever Geto*, 1963 edition, p. 22. It is significant that in the Polish edition of the book, *Powstanie w getcie warszawskim*, which also appeared in 1963, there is no mention of Petrykowski's Jewish origins.

27 *Haim Lazar Litai: Matzada shel Varsha (The Masada of Warsaw)*, pp. 90–91.

28 Kazimierz Koźniewski, *Zamknięte koła (Closed Circles)*, pp. 211–67.

29 *Ibid.*, pp. 153–61; Kazimierz Drewnowski, K. Koźniewski, *Pierwsza bitwa z Ges-*

tapo (The First Battle with the Gestapo), pp. 45–59.
  30 The story of PLAN is based on Koźniewski's *Pierwsza bitwa z Gestapo*.
  31 Kott is usually described as a Catholic, but in a private communication from Koźniewski I have it that he was a Protestant.
  32 *Pierwsza bitwa z Gestapo*, pp. 77–8.
  33 *Ibid*.
  34 Kott is a central figure in Koźniewski's two books. A critical examination of Kott's activities is to be found in A. Rutkowski's "Sprawa Kotta w środowisku żydowskim w Warszawie" ("The Kott Affair and the Jews of Warsaw"), *Biuletyn Żydowskiego Instytutu Historycznego*, No. 63, 1967.
  35 Edelman, *op. cit.*, p. 8.
  36 *Polski Ruch Robotniczy*, etc., pp. 78–80.
  37 *Ibid.*, pp. 350–53.
  38 *Ibid.*, p. 132; Edelman, *op. cit.*, p. 17.
  39 *Polski Ruch Robotniczy*, etc., pp. 154–5. In the first group of six there were two Jews, Paweł Finder and Pinkhas Kartin. Among the people who were parachuted in the spring of 1942 were two more Jews, Leon Bielski and Mieczysław Heyman, the latter acting as a wireless operator. Both Szmidt-Kartin and Heyman took part in the creation of the resistance organization inside the ghetto.
  40 Mark, *Walka i zagłada warszawskiego getta*, p. 73.
  40a Ignacy Robb-Narbutt, whose real surname was Rozenfarb, was no doubt among the top partisan leaders in wartime Poland. He was also one of the organizers of the People's Guard and the People's Army. His father had been a member of the Polish Socialist Party and banished to Siberia for his revolutionary activities in 1905. Ignacy was brought up to regard himself as a Pole and it was only after the German occupation of Poland that he realized that he was a Jew. A journalist by profession, the tall, handsome and powerfully built Ignacy proved himself a fine soldier during the September Campaign of 1939. After the fall of Poland he worked as a journalist in Lvov, but when the Germans captured the city in 1941 he made his way back to Warsaw. Thanks to his Polish friends he lived there as an "Aryan" and after the creation of the Polish Workers' Party he became one of the organizers of the People's Guard. It was through him that in February 1942 the Jewish Communists and left-wing Zionists in the Warsaw ghetto established their first contact with the Polish Workers' Party.
  In September 1942 Robb-Narbutt organized the Kielce Region Detachment, the largest People's Guard partisan unit in the Kielce Region made up of Poles, Jews and escaped Soviet prisoners of war, and led it successfully against the Germans. Because of his outstanding abilities as commander and organizer he was next given the task of commanding the People's Guard units in the Częstochowa-Piotrków region. Having again distinguished himself, he was put in command of the People's Guard units in the Warsaw Suburban Left Bank Region. There on August 7, 1943 he commanded the Kazimierz Pułaski Detachment in a classical partisan operation against 2,000 SS men and troops determined to surround his small detachment and wipe it out. Robb-Narbutt extricated his partisan unit after killing twenty-two Germans and losing only six men.
  He was subsequently promoted to a position on the general staff of the People's

Army, which he held until the summer of 1944 when he joined the Polish forces which had entered Poland together with the Red Army. As a colonel he helped General Świerczewski, who had become famous in the Spanish Civil War as General Walter, to organize the Second Polish Army and ended the war in Berlin. After the fall of Berlin he was appointed Government Plenipotentiary for the City of Warsaw, which in effect meant that he was given the task of bringing life back to the most ravaged city in Europe. From that post he was moved to the position of deputy to Świerczewski, who until he was killed by Ukrainian nationalists on March 28, 1947 held the post of a deputy minister of defense. When the railway system became one of the chief targets of the right-wing underground in the Polish civil war that lasted from 1945 to 1948, Robb-Narbutt was given the task of protecting it. Nevertheless, when in 1949 Bierut got rid of Gomułka and his men on the charge of "right-wing nationalist deviation", Robb-Narbutt was among the purged. He died in October 1958, remembered by only a few friends and the partisans he had commanded. (R. Ainsztein, *op. cit.*, pp. 428–30.)

41 Isaac Zuckerman's account in Mark, *op. cit.*, p. 78.

42 Tenenbaum-Tamarof explained why the left-wing Zionists collaborated with the Communists in the following words: "... We looked for contacts and support outside the ghetto. We met the PPR [the Polish Workers' Party], the Communist Party which had organized itself again under the slogan of national unity in the battle for liberation and was ready to collaborate with anybody on the basis of a program of immediate armed struggle against the occupiers. Such a contact was essential to us. Why did we link ourselves with the Communists? The official Polish governmental circles saw the principal direction of their activities in propaganda, training and civil resistance, in particular in the economic field. In every active deed of a ruthless struggle with the occupational authorities they saw a provocation. They argued that the time had not yet come, that one must wait! But we could not wait. Each day brought the likelihood of annihilation. That is why we searched for another ally and we found him in the shape of PPR ..." (Tenenbaum's letter to the Histadrut leaders in Palestine written in April 1943 and forming part of the Bialystok Ghetto Underground Archives, now in the Jewish Historical Institute in Warsaw.)

43 Ringelblum, *op. cit.*, Vol. 1, p. 361.

44 Hersz Berlinski, "Z dziennika członka komendy ŻOB" ("From the Diary of a Member of the ŻOB Command"), *Biuletyn Żydowskiego Instytutu Historycznego*, No. 50, 1964, p. 5; Edelman, *op. cit.*, p. 17.

45 Mark, *Khurves dertseyln (The Ruins Tell their Story)*, pp. 120–22.

46 Edelman, *op. cit.*, pp. 23, 25.

47 *Ibid.*, p. 28.

47a The combined operations for the physical extermination of Polish Jewry were planned and prepared under Reinhard Heydrich's direction. The mass extermination in the death factories of Bełżec, Sobibór, Treblinka, began in March 1942, when the first of the death factories, Bełżec, began operating. It was codenamed *Einsatz Reinhard (Operation Reinhard)* in recognition of Heydrich's role in the Final Solution. In the General-Government the extermination was directed by SS

Gruppenfuehrer (General) Odilo Globocnik and a special staff headed by Hoefle situated in Lublin.

48 *Ibid.*, pp. 28–9.
49 *Ibid.*, p. 31.
50 Berlinski, *op. cit.*, p. 4.
51 Ringelblum, *op. cit.*, Vol. 2, pp. 184–5.
52 Berlinski, *op. cit.*, p. 6.
53 Edelman, *op. cit.*, pp. 30–31.
54 *Ibid.*, pp. 31–2.
55 Tadeusz Bór-Komorowski, *The Secret Army*, p. 99.
56 Ringelblum, *op. cit.*, Vol. 2, pp. 43–4.
57 Edelman, *op. cit.*, pp. 32–3. According to Ringelblum about 20,000 reported for deportation. (*Op. cit.*, Vol. 2, p. 31.)
58 Ringelblum, *op. cit.*, Vol. 2, p. 11.
59 *Trybuna Wolno*ści, No. 14, August 15, 1942. The paper was published by the Polish Workers' Party.
60 *Likwidacja getta warszawskiego. Reportaż*. The reportage was prepared by Antoni Szymanowski and published by the Information and Propaganda Office (BIP) of the Home Army in Warsaw in November 1942.
61 Ringelblum, *op. cit.*, Vol 2, p. 29.
62 *Ibid.*, p. 67.
63 *Ibid.*
64 Mark, *op. cit.*, p. 94.
65 Ringelblum, *op. cit.*, Vol. 2, p. 32. Elsewhere Ringelblum recorded the view that 90 per cent of the hideouts were discovered by the Jewish policemen. The same view of the role played by the Jewish police was taken by other ghetto chroniclers, including Adolf and Barbara Berman in "Zagłada ghetta w Warszawie" ("Annihilation of the Warsaw Ghetto"), *Biuletyn Żydowskiego Instytutu Historycznego*, Nos. 45–6, 1963, and by A. Berman in "Ruch oporu w getcie warszawskim" ("The Resistance Movement in the Warsaw Ghetto"), in No. 29, 1959, of the same publication.
66 *Ibid.*, pp. 67–8.
67 *Ibid.*, p. 36
68 Edelman, *op. cit.*, pp. 41–2.
69 Ringelblum, *op. cit.*, Vol. 2, pp. 47–8.
70 Hilberg, *The Destruction of the European Jews*, p. 320.
71 Ringelblum, "Stosunki polsko-żydowskie w czasie drugiej wojny światowej," *Biuletyn Żydowskiego Instytutu Historycznego*, No. 30, 1959, p. 55.
72 Bór-Komorowski, *op. cit.*, p. 100.
73 *Polskie Siły Zbrojne*, Vol. 3, p. 448.
74 This is how the Pole Władysław Bartoszewski describes the attempts of the Jews to meet representatives of the Home Army: "The official liaison man of the Jewish Fighting Organization with the Polish underground was, however, the previously mentioned Arie Wilner, of Hashomer Hatzair, who had already tried to contact the military authorities in August 1942 in order to obtain their assistance in the organization of armed resistance inside the ghetto. He reached, it is true, certain Home Army cells, but they were not competent to make such important decisions.

The news of 'Jurek's' [i.e. Wilner's] mission did not reach at all the relevant authorities in the Home Army High Command. Another attempt to establish contacts, made in September 1942 through the medium of Aleksander Kamiński, was successful. 'Jurek' met 'Wacław' on whom he made a favorable impression." (W. Bartoszewski, Z. Lewinówna, *Ten jest z ojczyzny mojej*, p. 21.) No mention of "Wacław" entering the ghetto and meeting "the Jewish leaders."

75 Henryk Woliński (alias Wacław and Zakrzewski), "Przegląd działalności Referatu Spraw Żydowskich" ("Review of the Activities of the Jewish Affairs Section"), quoted in full by Mark in *Powstanie w getcie warszawskim*, 1963 edition, pp. 342–3.

76 *Ibid.*, p. 343.

77 Central Archives of the Polish Ministry of Internal Affairs in Warsaw, Home Army Documents, Radiogram No. 354.

78 *Ibid.*, Radiogram No. 803.

79 The attitude of the members of this organization to Jews was shaped by the traditional Catholic teachings on the position of Jews in Christian society. The more liberal were affected by the ideas of people like Jacques Maritain, but many, although they rejected the Nazi treatment of Jews, saw the Jews in terms not unlike those of the medieval popes and people like St. Bernard of Clairvaux or Peter the Venerable, who opposed the killing of all Jews by the Crusaders on the grounds that it was God's will that a miserable remnant of them should survive as proof of the truthfulness of the Christian doctrines. Consequently, in April 1943, at the time of the Warsaw Uprising, *Walka Młodych (The Struggle of the Young)*, an underground publication of the Front of Polish Renaissance, published the following comment on the destruction of the last remnant of Polish Jewry: "The last time the Jews fought was 1800 years ago. . . . Since then the Jews have lived as parasites on the organism of the European peoples and have been hated and despised everywhere. They have fought against everybody, but always by underhand methods, never openly, never with arms in their hands. They have been the cause, the driving power of three-quarters of all the wars that have taken place in Europe between various peoples. We Catholics understand the greatness of the events. Hearing the cries of agony of the murdered, seeing the reflection of the ghetto fires, we cannot remain passive. Our duty is to help the persecuted Jews irrespective of whether they will repay us for our help now or in the future. Our help cannot be confined to material things. We must give them at the same time spiritual assistance. We must pray for those who are dying and open their eyes to the truth, so that from their present sufferings they can build a sacrificial altar that will bring nearer their rebirth, which will free the once Chosen People of the curse afflicting it. We must teach the Jews that by will-power they can achieve redemption in the face of death by conversion and acceptance of the true faith. . . . Their souls will be purified and redeemed by the act of conversion." The link between the author of the article and the Catholic inquisitors who during the Middle Ages burnt and massacred millions of heretics and thousands of Jews *to save their souls* is unmistakable. Or one might call it, like Jacques Maritain, an example of "a psychopathically disguised Christophobia." Such, indeed, were the *friends* of the Jews!

80 Archives of the Polish Ministry of Internal Affairs, Antyk Papers, *Wolność*, No. 6, August 15, 1942, and "Sprawa zydowska w Polsce."

81 B. Mark, *Tsum tsentn yortog fun oifshtand fun Varshever Geto. Dokumentn un materyaln (On the Tenth Anniversary of the Warsaw Ghetto Uprising: Documents and Materials)*, p. 83.

82 Antyk Papers, note on assistance to Jews dated November 28, 1942. The full role and activities of Antyk became known only after its archives were discovered in 1956 by Polish workers who were digging the foundations for a building in Warsaw. About 500 pages of documents referred to or dealt with Jews. Antyk was founded by Henryk Glass, who after the Polish-German treaty in 1934 became the head of the Nazi-financed press agency of the "Polish Institute for the Scientific Study of Communism" founded by the Catholic priest Kwiatkowski, which closely collaborated with the Goebbelsian "Anti-Comintern." After Poland's defeat in September 1939, Glass used his extensive personal files to denounce Polish left-wingers and Communists to the Gestapo. Following the outbreak of the German-Soviet war the London Government's Delegate found Glass' work so useful that he provided him with funds and Antyk was able to expand its activities from the Warsaw region to most of occupied Poland.

From the documents it is clear that Antyk welcomed the creation of the ghettoes and consistently advocated the total extermination of the Jews, fearing that some might survive inside the ghettoes and labor camps. In 1941, before the course of the Final Solution could be known, Antyk published "Materials for the guidance of the (Polish) intelligentsia," in which it warned that the Jews in the ghettoes and labor camps must be watched in case some survived. "Be ready," the instructions said, "to destroy physically the units of Jewish forced laborers and the Jewish quarters in the towns in case the Jews attempt to push us into the abyss of revolution and hand us over into the grip of the Bolsheviks." When the work of the Einsatzgruppen in the occupied territories of the Soviet Union became known to Antyk, Glass described the murder of one-and-a-half million Jews as "an elemental reaction" of the populations of the Baltic republics, Byelorussia and the Ukraine, from which the Germans learnt the need for the Final Solution. When the death factories began to operate on Polish territory and Poland became one gigantic slaughterhouse, Antyk welcomed them and attacked Poles who saved or helped Jews. Glass wrote that Majdanek, Treblinka and Oświęcim were necessary because "The Hitlerites must defend themselves against their relentless and powerful enemy, the Jews."

Thousands of Jews who could have survived on the "Aryan" side were denounced or betrayed to the Germans as a result of the Antyk's activities. Hundreds of Poles who hid or helped Jews in other ways met a similar fate. A typical example of Antyk's methods in dealing with such Poles is provided by the following note in the documents discovered in the ruins of Warsaw: "Lipowski's flat serves as a meeting point for young Jews and Jewish girls. He is angry with Poles for having allowed the Warsaw ghetto to be destroyed." (Abraham Wien, "Der Antyk in eyn rey mit di hitleristishe talyonim," *Folks Shtime*, April 18, 1959.)

83 Central Archives of the Polish Ministry of Internal Affairs, Home Army Documents, Radiogram. No. 4349.

84 *Op. cit.*, p. 344.

85 *Ibid.*, p. 345.

Himmler Defied

1 Wdowiński, *op. cit.*, p. 76.
2 Mark, *Walka i zagłada warszawskiego getta*, pp. 136–7.
3 "Stosunki polsko-żydowskie," *Biuletyn Żydowskiego Instytutu Historycznego*, No. 30, 1959, p. 56.
4 Mark, *op. cit.*, pp. 139–40. The Political Committee of the Jewish Fighting Organization in its report on the Great Liquidation dated November 25, 1942 concluded that the chief responsibility for the absence of mass resistance lay with the Judenrat and the ghetto police: "The monumental betrayal of the Warsaw Judenrat, which assumed the form of assent to the 'resettlement' and which consisted in completely ignoring or pretending to ignore the real situation, will forever remain, next to the betrayal of the ghetto police, an unremovable stain on the Jewish ghetto authority. But while branding it with this deed, one must nevertheless stress that the Jewish ghetto authority, a creation of the occupational conditions, did not reflect the feelings and attitudes of the population." (Mark, *Tsum tsentn yortog*, etc. pp. 79–80.)
5 Edelman, *op. cit.*, p. 39.
6 Kotlicki's account in Mark's *Tsum Tsentn yortog*, etc. p. 87.
7 Mark, *Walka i zagłada warszawskiego getta*, p. 104. A member of Hashomer Hatzair, she escaped when being taken from the Pawiak Prison to the *Umschlagplatz* and took part in the Ghetto Uprising, where at the age of twenty-two she was killed fighting in the Toebbens factory. (*Sefer Hapartizanim Hayehudim*, Vol. 2, p. 714.)
8 Mark, *op. cit.*, p. 105.
9 *Ibid*.
10 Bartoszewski, Lewinówna, *op. cit.*, pp. 497–500.
11 From the middle of 1940 until January 31, 1941, 798,000 Poles were deported to work in Germany. From March to June 1942 800,000 Poles were deported to Germany as slave labor from the General-Government alone and in August 1942 Sauckel, the Reich Plenipotentiary for Labor, ordered that a further 140,000 Polish workers be supplied from the General-Government. As most of the deported Polish workers came from the countryside, this caused an acute shortage of agricultural laborers. Consequently, in the agriculturally rich Lublin region the German authorities began in March 1942 forcibly to employ Jews in farming and allowed Jewish volunteers from other areas to find work with local Polish landowners. A few thousand Jews thus became agricultural workers in the Lublin and other areas of the General-Government until they too were engulfed by the Final Solution in the final months of 1942. (Artur Eisenbach, *Hitlerowska polityka zagłady Żydów*, p. 342.)
12 Wdowiński, *op. cit.*, pp. 81–2.
13 *Ibid.*, p. 80.
14 The two Revisionist historians of the Jewish Military Union, Wdowiński (*op. cit.*, p. 83) and Lazar (*op. cit.*, p. 205), wrongly ascribe the execution of First to the ŻZW. This is because they confuse David Szulman, a member of Dror and seventeen years old when he and his two comrades killed First, with the lawyer David Szulman, born in 1907, who was one of the leaders of the ŻZW.
15 Mark, *Powstanie w getcie warszawskim*, 1963 edition, p. 29; Lazar, *op. cit.*, p. 177.

16 Artur Szarfer, "Lekcja życia" ("A Lesson of Life"), *Folks Shtime*, October 24, 1970.
17 *Ibid.*
18 Mark, *Walka i zagłada warszawskiego getta*, p. 155.
19 *Op. cit.*, p. 50.
20 Ringelblum, "Stosunki polsko-żydowskie," *Biuletyn Żydowskiego Instytutu Historycznego*, No. 30, 1959, p. 58.
21 *Polskie Siły Zbrojne*, Vol. 3, p. 327; Stefan Krakowski, "Stosunek sił w powstaniu w getcie waszawskim" ("Relationship of Forces in the Warsaw Ghetto Uprising"), *Biuletyn Żydowskiego Instytutu Historycznego*, No. 62, 1967, p. 35.
22 Woliński's memorandum to Home Army Command and the Government Delegate's office dated December 3, 1942, Central Archives of the Polish Ministry of Internal Affairs, Government Delegate's Papers, File 458, p. 84, quoted in full by Mark in *Powstanie w getcie warszawskim*, 1963 edition, pp. 199–200.
23 Central Archives of the Polish Ministry of Internal Affairs, Home Army Papers, Radiogram No. 1124/1.
24 *Polskie Siły Zbrojne*, Vol. 3, p. 234.
25 Józef Garliński, *Poland, SOE and the Allies*, pp. 91, 235–6.
26 Lesław M. Bartelski, "Bez Antygony" ("Without Antigone"), *Nowa Kultura*, No. 31, Warsaw, August 2, 1959.
27 *Ibid.*
28 Bartoszewski, Lewinówna, *op. cit.*, p. 22.
29 Woliński's report in Mark's *Powstanie w getcie warszawskim*, 1963 edition, p. 345.
30 Eisenbach, *op. cit.*, pp. 343, 348–9, 358–9.
31 *Ibid.*, p. 314.
32 *Ibid.*, p. 362.
33 *Ibid.*, p. 430.
34 *Akta procesu Stroopa i Konrada (The Trial of Stroop and Konrad)*, Vol. 4, pp. 768–9, Warsaw, 1951.
35 Mark, *Walka i zagłada warszawskiego getta*, p. 134.
36 *Ibid.*
37 Reitlinger, *The Final Solution*, p. 272. The author mistakenly describes Himmler's visit as having occurred on January 14.
38 *Wiadomości*, No. 6, January 9–15 1943.
39 *Akta procesu Stroopa i Konrada*, Vol. 1, p. 150.
40 *Głos Warszawy*, No. 5, January 1943. The paper was published by the Polish Workers' Party. Other Polish reports estimated the number of Nazis at 600.
41 Edelman, *op. cit.*, p. 47.
42 Berlinski, *Wspomnienia (Reminiscences)*, p. 21. The Yiddish original is in the possession of the Jewish Historical Institute in Warsaw.
43 Mark, *op. cit.*, p. 189.
44 *Ibid.*, p. 190.
45 *Ibid.*
46 *Ibid.*, pp. 190–91.
47 Edelman, *op. cit.*, p. 47.
48 Bór-Komorowski, *op. cit.*, p. 105.

49 Hilberg, *op. cit.*, p. 323.
50 Edelman, *op. cit.*, p. 47.
51 From Anielewicz's letter to the Home Army Command and the Government Delegate's Office dated March 13, 1943. Jewish National Committee Papers in the Archives of the Jewish Historical Institute in Warsaw.
52 *Gwardzista*, No. 12, February 15, 1943.
53 Mark, *op. cit.*, p. 198.
54 Minutes of the Council for Helping Jews, meeting of January 29, 1943, Archives of the Jewish Historical Institute in Warsaw.
55 Edelman, *op. cit.*, p. 48; Woliński's report on the activities of the Jewish Section in Mark's *Powstanie w getcie warszawskim*, 1963 edition, p. 346.
56 Woliński's report, p. 350.
57 *Ibid.*, p. 346.
58 See note 51.
59 Anielewicz's letter to Zuckerman on April 23, 1943, quoted in full in Mark's *Tsum tsentn yortog*, etc. p. 173.
60 According to Captain Władysław Żarski-Zajdler, Iwański's second-in-command, in "Ramię przy ramieniu w walce przeciwko hitlerowcom" ("Shoulder to Shoulder in the Struggle against the Nazis"), *Trybuna Ludu*, Warsaw, March 31, 1969.
61 Mark, *Walka i zagłada warszawskiego getta*, p. 249. The PLAN officer in charge of assistance to the ŻZW was Captain Cezary Ketling, whose *noms de guerre* were Szemley and Arpad. (Lazar Litai, *op. cit.*, pp. 173, 177, 180.)
62 *Bulletin of the Council for Helping Jews* for August 1943, Archives of the Jewish Historical Institute in Warsaw. The damaged text quoted in Mark's *Tsum Tsentn yortog*, etc., p. 273.
63 Ringelblum, "Stosunki polsko-żydowskie," *Biuletyn Żydowskiego Instytutu Historycznego*, No. 30, 1959, p. 54.
64 Mark, *Walka i zagłada warszawskiego getta*, pp. 247–8. Also Mark, *Powstanie w getcie warszawskim, (The Uprising in the Warsaw Ghetto)*, Warsaw, 1954, p. 259.
65 Chruściel's letter to Mark from the United States dated January 25, 1958, in *Powstanie w getcie warszawskim*, 1963 edition, p. 273.
66 Mark, *Walka i zagłada warszawskiego getta*, p. 214.
67 Edelman, *op.cit.*, pp.48–9; Mark, *op. cit.*, p. 214
68 Dorka Goldkorn, *Wspomnienia uczestniczki powstania w getcie warszawskim (Reminiscences of a Participant in the Warsaw Ghetto Uprising)*, pp. 20–21.
69 Mark, *ibid.*, pp. 206–7; *Powstanie w getcie warszawskim*, 1963 edition, p. 217.
70 ŻOB's warning to traitors dated March 3, 1943, Central Archives of the Polish Ministry of Internal Affairs, Government Delegate's Papers, File 458, p. 255. Full text in Mark's *Powstanie w getcie warszawskim*, 1963 edition, p. 218.
71 *Ibid.*
72 *Ibid.*; also p. 29.
73 *Akta procesu Stroopa i Konrada*, Vol. 5, p. 777.
74 Edelman, *op. cit.*, p. 49.
75 *Ibid.*, p. 50; Mark, *Walka i zagłada warszawskiego getta*, pp. 215–16.
76 Mark, *ibid.*, pp. 216–18.

77 *Ibid.*, pp. 219–20.
78 *Ibid.*, p. 220.
79 Archives of the Jewish Historical Institute in Warsaw, Ringelblum Papers II, text in Mark's *Powstanie w getcie warszawskim*, 1963 edition, pp. 233–4.

The Uprising

1 Mark, *Walka i zagłada warszawskiego getta*, pp. 231–2.
2 *Ibid.*, pp. 228–30. In September 1943 Stroop was transferred by Himmler from Warsaw to Greece, where as the Higher SS and Police Leader he helped General Speidel to combat the growing partisan movement in that country. In 1944 he was chief of police in the Western March, where he had a number of American parachutists shot. Sentenced to death in 1947 in the American Zone of Occupation, he was handed over the same year to Poland and tried in Warsaw in 1951, where he was again sentenced to death and hanged.
3 Dr. R. Walewski, "Derinerungen un refleksn" ("Reminiscences and Reflections"), *Folks Shtime*, April 19, 1958.
4 *Ibid.*
5 The ŻOB combat groups were commanded, according to the same report: (1) In the Central Ghetto by Zachariah Artsztejn (Dror), Ber Braudo (Dror), Aaron Bryskin (People's Guard), Joseph Farber (Hashomer Hatzair), Mordecai Growas (Hashomer Hatzair), Leyb Gruzalc (Bund), Leyb Rotblat (Akiba), Benjamin Wald (Dror), Henryk Zylberberg (People's Guard). In overall command was Israel Kanał (Akiba). There were also two groups not mentioned in the report: one in the Stawki area commanded by Fondamiński (PPR) and another in Miła Street commanded by Simon Kaufman (PPR). (2) In the Brush Workshops Area the combat groups were commanded by Hirsh Berlinski (Left-Wing Poale Zion), Jurek Blones (Bund) and Jacob Praszker (Hanoar Hatzioni). Edelman (Bund) was in overall command. (3) In the Factories Area the commanders were Isaac Blausztejn (Dror), Hersh Kawe (People's Guard), Meir Majerowicz (Socialist Zionists Group), David Nowodworski (Hashomer Hatzair), Wolf Rozowski (Bund) and Joshua Winogron (Hashomer Hatzair). Eleazar Geller (Gordonia) was in overall command. There was also a group led by Adam Szwarcfus (People's Guard), not mentioned in the report.
6 Edelman, *op. cit.*, p. 51.
7 Mark, *Powstanie w getcie warszawskim*, 1963 edition, p. 27. According to Haim Lazar Litai (*op. cit.*, p. 219) the membership of the ŻZW on the eve of the uprising was 1,200 and included Bundists, Communists, followers of Agudath Israel and Jews without any party affiliations. But membership did not necessarily mean living in barrack conditions, as was the case with the 400 fighters.
8 Mark, *op. cit.*, p. 38
9 Mark, *Khurves dertseylen*, pp. 382–3. About twenty young Hassidim of the group were employed at a Luftwaffe depot outside the ghetto, from where they stole arms, mostly grenades, and smuggled them into the ghetto. During the uprising the group

found itself outside the ghetto, in Bielany near the Gdańsk Railway Station, but its members continued to bring weapons into the ghetto. One day at the height of the uprising the Germans caught Mandel, a member of the group, with a sack full of weapons, but he managed to escape. Convinced that he was a Pole, the Germans rounded up the Polish inhabitants of the nearby houses and demanded that the Jews point out the fugitive among them. The Jews refused to save their lives by singling out an innocent Pole and the Germans shot two of them. Drejzin was one of the group and on May 8, when the group was ordered to climb into lorries that took them to the *Umschlagplatz* in Stawki Street, he refused to budge and was shot dead on the spot. Other members of the group, who were inside the ghetto, fought in Nalewki Street where they had had their *yeshiva*.

10 Bartoszewski, Lewinówna, *op. cit.*, pp. 503–13.

11 Ringelblum has left us a description of the underground ghetto in his *Ksavim fun geto*, Vol. 2, pp. 48–53. A detailed description of an underground hideout is given by B. Goldman, an architect who specialized in their construction, in his account "75 dni w płonącym getcie warszawskim" ("Seventy-Five Days in the Burning Warsaw Ghetto"), *Biuletyn Żydowskiego Instytutu Historycznego*, No. 42, 1962, p. 94. At the end of January 1943 he began to build an underground hideout capable of taking 25 to 30 persons for a group of well-to-do people, who each contributed 10,000 zlotys to the costs. The hideout was underneath a courtyard, and was eight meters long, eight meters wide and three meters high. It had a sleeping compartment, storing space, a kitchen and a living compartment. The kitchen had two electric heaters and a coal stove, the chimney of which travelled a long way underground. To deal with emergencies there was a water pump, a well and a manually operated dynamo providing electric lighting in an emergency. Otherwise water came from the mains and electric power, which was also used for working the air-supply system, came from a cable which supplied power to houses on the "Aryan" side of the walls. The entry to the hideout was in a cellar and was hidden by a movable wall weighing two tons. The hideout was completed by the end of February 1943 and discovered by the Germans on May 10.

12 Kazimierz Moczarski, "Rozmowy z katem" ("Conversations with the Executioner"), *Odra*, Wroclaw, April 1973. Moczarski was a member of the Home Army and being a lawyer acted as a judge who passed sentences on Polish traitors and collaborators. He was arrested by the Polish Security Police on suspicion of having been responsible for the murder of several Communists during the German occupation by the Home Army. To place Nazis, Soviet collaborators and Communists or others, who had spent most of their lives fighting against the Nazi menace, in the same cells or concentration camps was the established Soviet practice. In Poland this practice ceased only after 1956. Moczarski states in his book that he spent 225 days in the same cell with Stroop. Gustav Schielke was employed in the office of SS Oberführer (Brigadier-General) Dr. Walther Bierkamp, the commander of the Sicherheitspolizei and Sicherheitsdienst in the General-Government, which was situated in Cracow, and was therefore exceptionally well informed on what happend during the Warsaw Ghetto Uprising.

13 *Ibid.*, *Odra*, March 1973.

14 Hersh Wasser, "Słup ognisty bohaterstwa" ("The Flaming Pillar of Heroism.")

The author was the secretary of the Underground Ghetto Archives. His account is in the archives of the Jewish Historical Institute in Warsaw. Quoted by Mark in *Walka i zagłada warszawskiego getta*, pp. 235–6.

15 Juergen Stroop's report on the annihilation of the Warsaw ghetto, which SS Obergruppenführer and General of the Police Krueger presented to Himmler on June 2, 1943, was entitled by Stroop "There is no longer a Jewish District in Warsaw." The report opens with an introduction dated May 16, 1943, which summarizes the story of the Warsaw ghetto and its final annihilation. The summary is followed by the daily reports on the fighting and the extermination of the Jews sent by Stroop to Krueger in Cracow. The first report was sent on April 20 and covered Sammern-Frankenegg's unsuccessful attempt to liquidate the ghetto. Another report covering Stroop's own activities followed later on the same day.

16 Stroop's statement at his trial in Warsaw quoted in Mark's *Tsum Tsentn Yortog*, etc., pp. 386–8.

17 *Ibid*.

18 The firemen's task was to prevent the fires spreading to the "Aryan" part of the city, and, in some cases, to save factories set on fire by the Jews from which the Germans wanted to remove machinery or raw materials. A few of the firemen helped the Jews. Thus Henryk Empmacher, a member of Iwański's Security Corps, saved fifty Jews in the Nazi sense—that is, Poles of Jewish origin—from the cellars of the Holiest Madonna Church in Leszno Street (Bartoszewski, Lewinówna, p. 134). But there were some who used the opportunity to finish off wounded Jews and rob them. The Home Army intelligence report No. 441, preserved in the Archives of the Polish Ministry of Internal Affairs, quotes the names of Komoda, Derman, Stańczak and Sztelcer who did precisely that. (Mark, *Walka i zagłada warszawskiego getta*, p. 252.)

19 Stroop told an American officer investigating his role in the destruction of the Warsaw ghetto that "The Security Service [Sicherheitsdienst] had already been active for some time on the territory of the ghetto. During the Aktion its duty was to accompany the SS units. In groups of six to eight they performed the role of guides and experts in ghetto matters. The commander of the Security Police at the time was Obersturmbannführer [Lieutenant-Colonel] Dr. Hahn. He issued orders to the Security Police concerning its tasks in the operation." Dr. Ludwig Hahn was in command of the Warsaw SD—of which the Gestapo was only a section—from the middle of 1941 to 1944, when he helped to put down the Polish uprising. Few Gestapo headquarters in Nazi occupied Europe witnessed so many atrocities as Dr. Hahn's in Szuch Avenue in Warsaw is said to have done. Nevertheless, although he was arrested in Western Germany in 1960 following the capture of Eichmann, a year later he was released. At the time of his arrest he was a prosperous deputy director of an insurance company. He was again arrested in 1965 and again set free, although 2,000 witnesses came forward to allege his crimes. Hahn was sentenced to life in Hamburg in 1977.

20 The battalion was composed mostly of Ukrainians and trained for its extermination tasks in the Trawniki labor camp for Jews.

21 Kaleske's statement made at Oberursel, US Zone of Occupation, on December 20, 1945. (*Nazi Conspiracy and Aggression*, Vol. 6, p. 776, PS-3841.)

22 Mark, *op. cit.*, p. 284.
23 Krakowski, *op. cit.*, pp. 30–31.
24 Edelman, *op. cit.*, pp. 53–5; Mark, *Walka i zagłada warszawskiego getta*, p. 270.
25 Edelman, *op. cit.*, p. 55.
26 Bartoszewski, Lewinówna, *op. cit.*, pp. 34–5.
27 *Ibid.*, pp. 41–4.
28 *Ibid.*, pp. 44–5.
29 Mark, *op. cit.*, pp. 281–2.
30 Mark, *Powstanie w getcie warszawskim*, 1963 edition, p. 60.
31 "Mówi Major Bystry" ("Major Bystry Speaks"), *Kultura*, Warsaw, April 21, 1968.
32 Mark, *op. cit.*, pp. 62–3.
33 *Ibid.*, p. 62–3.
34 Mark, *Walka i zagłada warszawskiego getta*, p. 295.
35 Account of the fighting in the Brush Workshops Area by an unknown ŻOB fighter in Mark's *Tsum tsentn yortog*, etc., pp. 217–18.
36 Mark, *Powstanie w getcie warszawskim*, 1963 edition, p. 64; Edelman, *op. cit.*, p. 55.
37 Edelman, *ibid.*, p. 56.
38 Mark, *op. cit.*, pp. 71–2; *Walka i zagłada warszawskiego getta*, p. 299.
39 According to Jerzy Duracz, Bartoszek flung a grenade at the SS men. (Bartoszewski, Lewinówna, pp. 513–14.) My account is based on that of Marian Spychalski, a personal friend of Bartoszek and the first chief-of-staff of the People's Guard, who was to become Poland's minister of defense and a marshal. His account, based on Bobowski's report only a few minutes after the action, appeared in the Warsaw *Odrodzenie*, Nos. 13–14, 1945. Bartoszek and Bobowski were both killed by German gendarmes on May 14, 1943, after carrying out an "expropriation" at the Społem Bank in Krakowskie Przedmieście. Both were graduates of the Warsaw Academy of Arts.
40 Yuri Suhl, *They Fought Back*, pp. 51–4.
41 *Polski Ruch Robotniczy*, etc., pp. 238–40, 241–2; Jerzy Duracz's reminiscences of Niuta Tejtelbaum in Mark's *Tsum tsentn yortog*, etc., pp. 286–91.
42 Mark, *Walka i zagłada warszawskiego getta*, p. 324.
43 Edelman, *op. cit.*, pp. 57–8; previously quoted account by unknown fighter in *Tsum tsentn yortog*, etc.
44 Mark, *op. cit.*, p. 331.
45 Lazar Litai, *op. cit.*, pp. 262–3.
46 The communiqués were published by the Council for Helping Jews on the basis of reports from the ghetto supplied by Isaac Zuckerman. The first communiqué issued on April 19, was published in the *Żegota Bulletin* of the council of April 21. The quoted passage in Communiqué No. 4 was introduced as follows: "On Wednesday, at nine p.m., we received the following telephone message from the commander of the Jewish Fighting Organization." (The communiqués are quoted in Mark's *Tsum Tsentn yortog*, etc., pp. 155–62.) The ŻOB Command also issued seven situation reports, the first on April 20 and the last on April 28. (Mark, *op. cit.*, pp. 162–72.)

47 Quoted in the Government Delegate's report on the Warsaw Ghetto Uprising to the Polish Government in London. The name of the underground paper is not mentioned in the report. (Central Archives of the Polish Ministry of Internal Affairs, Government Delegate's Papers, File 458, pp. 336–8. Text in Mark's *Powstanie w getcie warszawskim*, 1963 edition, pp. 333–4.)

48 This is how thirty-four-year-old Pola Elster, a member of the ŻOB, described a few months later what she had seen: "I recall a seventeen-year-old girl, the ends of her legs completely charred. The girl's legs were wrapped in rags and she was screaming in an inhuman voice. Her shriek 'Kill me!' is not easy to forget. Or elsewhere there lay a sister and two brothers, who had also been dragged out of a hideout. Their faces were burned, there was nothing left of their eyes, they lay there moaning. Elsewhere there lay a year-old baby. It was no longer moaning or crying—obviously, it had no more strength left. I shall not forget the child's face as long as I live. It lay there—its little hands and its little legs charred, an inhuman expression of pain on its face. . . . Its mother had a completely burned face and arms, so that she could not hold her child and begged the *askar* [i.e., the non-German SS man] to kill her and the child. The *askar* performed a deed of extraordinary 'humanity': he lowered his rifle and shot dead the mother, but left the child to its agony." (Pola Elster, "Kartki z notatnika" ["Pages from a Notebook"], quoted by Mark from the manuscript in *Walka i zagłada warszawskiego getta*, pp. 337–8.) A member of the Left-Wing Poale Zion, Pola Elster died in the Polish uprising of 1944.

48a Because of his unique role during the ghetto uprising, Józef Małecki (*noms de guerre* Sęk and Witek) deserves our special interest. Born in the Gostyn district in 1902, he took part in the uprising against the Germans in Prussian Poland in 1918 and joined the Communist Party in 1922. After the September Campaign he found himself in the Soviet Union and ended up working in a coal mine at Skopin near Ryazan. In January 1942 he was summoned to Moscow and after training was (at the end of April 1942) parachuted to Poland.

In Warsaw Małecki became involved in the organization and leadership of the People's Guard. His first field command was as chief of the People's Guard units in the Radomsk-Kielce region. Having proved himself he was promoted to chief of the Supplies and Arms Section of the People's Guard General Staff and it was in this capacity that he was put in charge of all operations to help the fighters in the ghetto. At the end of July 1944 he was appointed deputy of the chief of staff of the People's Army in Warsaw—the leadership of the Polish Workers' Party and the command of the People's Army had moved to liberated Lublin—and was thus in overall command of the People's Army units during the Warsaw Uprising. Thus he was responsible, among other things, for the welcome extended to the ŻOB survivors. An idealist and honest man, he made no career after the war. (J. B. Garas, *Oddziały Gwardii Ludowej i Armii Ludowej 1942–1945*, Warsaw 1965; Ryszard Nazarewicz, *Polacy-spadochroniarze wywiadowcy na zapleczu frontu wschodniego*, Warsaw 1974, pp. 77–8.)

49 Colonel Józef Sęk-Małecki, "In eyn kamfs-rey mit di geto-oifshtendler" ("In the Same Battle Ranks with the Ghetto Insurgents"), *Folks Shtime*, April 19, 1958.

50 See note 21.

51 Mark, *Walka i zagłada warszawskiego getta*, p. 325.

52 *Ibid.*, p. 326.

53 *Ibid.*, p. 325; Lazar Litai, *op. cit.*, p. 173.

54 The Buehler Papers, Vol. 11, pp. 33–5, Archives of the Chief Commission for the Investigation of Nazi Crimes in Poland. Dr. Josef Buehler, a Catholic, was the chief of Hans Frank's "government" of the General-Government and owed his position to the fact that he had been Frank's partner in his legal practice before the war. When the General-Government was officially formed on October 26, 1939 with Hans Frank as the governor-general, Arthur Seyss-Inquart became Frank's deputy, holding this post until he became the Reich commissar of occupied Holland in May 1940. Buehler replaced Seyss-Inquart as Frank's deputy and when on December 9, 1940 Hitler allowed Frank to turn his General-Governor's Office into the Government of the General-Government, Buehler became the chief state secretary. He is sometimes confused with Reichsleiter Philip Bouhler, who played a crucial role in the Final Solution.

Hitler maintained four chancelleries. One, under Dr. Meissner, dealt with formal matters pertaining to Hitler's position as head of state. The one under Dr. Hans Lammers dealt with matters pertaining to Hitler's position as chancellor and it was through Lammers that Hitler kept both the government machinery and the party informed of his decisions. Thus, when in the first half of 1941, in anticipation of the Final Solution, the Reich Ministry of the Interior wanted to prepare a legal framework for the extermination of German Jews by depriving them officially of their German citizenship, Hitler through Lammers informed the Ministries of the Interior and Justice, as well as Bormann, that he did not regard such legal formulations necessary. (Hilberg, *op. cit.*, pp. 261–2.) Rudolf Hess and, after his flight to Scotland, Martin Bormann, headed the chancellery dealing with party matters. Finally, there was Hitler's personal chancellery under Philip Bouhler whom he had planned to make the ruler of Madagascar. It was chiefly through Bouhler that Hitler gave direct orders dealing with the extermination of Jews and others. These were invariably oral, so that no trace would remain of Hitler's personal involvement in deeds about the criminality of which he had no doubts.

55 *The Goebbels Diaries*, p. 268.

56 Stroop threw more light on Himmler's order and his own decision when answering questions put to him by representatives of the Jewish Historical Commission in Poland. (Mark, *op. cit.*, p. 348.)

57 Lazar Litai, *op. cit.*, p. 263; Mark, *Powstanie w getcie warszawskim*, 1963 edition, p. 93.

58 Rafal Gerber, "Di poilishe demokratye un der oifshtand in Varshever Geto" ("Polish Democracy and the Warsaw Ghetto Uprising"), *Bleter far Geshikhte*, Warsaw, No. 2, 1948. On July 1, 1943 Sternhel and his men attacked an SA detachment marching through Aleje Ujazdowskie. He was arrested in September 1943 and murdered by the Gestapo.

59 Report of the People's Guard Command of April 23, 1943, in Mark's *Powstanie w getcie warszawskim*, 1963 edition, p. 268.

60 *Ibid.*, pp. 90, 268.

61 Bartoszewski, Lewinówna, *op. cit.*, pp. 45–8.

62 *Ibid.*, pp. 517–20.

63 *Ibid.*, pp. 514–17.
64 Sh. Web, "Di aktsye oif Bonifratn-gas" ("Operation in Bonifraterska Street"), *Folks Shtime*, April 19, 1958.
65 Chruściel's letter to Mark.
66 Mark, *op. cit.*, p. 75.
67 Chruściel's letter to Mark.
68 The Hebrew text of the letter is in Dr. A. Berman's archives of the Jewish National Committee (ŻKN) in Tel Aviv. Another text, in Polish, is in the Central Archives of the Polish Ministry of Internal Affairs, Government Delegate's Papers, File 458, p. 319. In the Polish text Anielewicz's reference to the attacks by the People's Guard on the Germans on April 22 is missing.
69 Mark, *Walka i zagłada warszawskiego getta*, pp. 357–6. The two last communiqués on the course of the uprising in the *Żegota Bulletin* of the Council for Helping Jews and the Situation Report No. 7 dated April 1943 were composed outside the ghetto on the basis of fragmentary information received both from Jews and Poles.
70 Mark, *op. cit.*, pp. 358–60. According to the last ŻOB communiqué, dated April 29, the Jews killed over thirty Nazis in the fighting. One of the ŻOB combat groups was commanded by Shoshana (Rose) Rozenfeld. When their bunker in Leszno Street was invaded by SS men, the girls and men fought until they were all killed. (Dorka Goldkorn, *Wspomnienia*, p. 25.)
71 *The Trial of Stroop and Konrad*, Second Day, p. 180.
72 Moczarski, *Odra*, February 1973.
73 Stroop's report for April 27. According to Mark, the traitor was a member of the Security Corps. (*Powstanie w getcie warszawskim*, 1963 edition, p. 105.)
74 "Mówi Major Bystry," *Kultura*, Warsaw, April 21, 1968.
75 Lazar Litai, *op. cit.*, p. 283.
76 "Mówi Major Bystry," *op. cit.*
77 Lazar Litai, *op. cit.*, pp. 291–6.
78 Mark, *op. cit.*, pp. 365–6; *Powstanie w getcie warszawskim*, 1963 edition, p. 111.
79 Mark, *Powstanie w getcie warszawskim*, 1963 edition, p. 146.
80 *Ibid.*, p. 112.
81 Lazar Litai, *op. cit.*; Wdowiński, *op. cit.*, p. 96. Wdowiński's account is so laconic as to make the events he describes almost incredible: "On the eleventh day of the battle, April 29, the fighting group GHETTO decided to break through the tunnel into the Michalin Forest in the vicinity of Warsaw and continue to fight the enemy from there. Part of this group remained in the ghetto as a cover up. That same night the group arrived in the forest. But it was discovered by the Germans and encircled. Severe fighting ensued. After many hours, the group succeeded in blasting its way through the German ring and into the prepared bunker on the 'Aryan' side in Grzybowska Street." Lazar Litai's account may not convey the impression that the tunnel from 5 to 6 Karmelicka extended to somewhere near Otwock, but being based almost literally on Wdowiński's account is not much more informative.
82 Edelman, *op. cit.*, p. 61.
83 Moczarski, *Odra*, February 1973.
84 *Op. cit.*, p. 62.

85 *Ibid.*; Edelman's Eyewitness Account No. 5002 in the Archives of the Jewish Historical Institute; Tevye Borzykowski, *Tsvishn falndike vent (Between Falling Walls)*, pp. 105–8.
86 *Op. cit.*, p. 273.
87 Quoted by Rachel Auerbach in *Der yidisher oifshtand (The Jewish Uprising)*, pp. 54–5.
88 Moczarski, *Odra*, February 1973.
89 Świętochowski's Eyewitness Account No. 5048 in the Jewish Historical Institute. Yiddish translation in Mark's *Tsum tsentn yortog*, etc., pp. 229–32.
90 The reports of the Polish police are in the Central Archives of the Polish Ministry of Internal Affairs. Those dealing with the Ghetto Uprising are quoted in Mark's *Powstanie w getcie warszawskim*, 1963 edition, pp. 294–301.
91 Moczarski, *Odra*, February and March 1973.
92 Lazar Litai, *op. cit.*, pp. 341–2.
93 *Ibid.*, p. 312.
94 Edelman, *op. cit.*, p. 63.
95 *Trial of Stroop and Konrad*, Second Day, p. 112.
96 Mark, *Walka i zagłada warszawskiego getta*, p. 388. In *Powstanie w getcie warszawskim*, 1963 edition, p. 128, Mark writes that Rotblat gave poison to his mother and then shot himself.
97 Hirsh Berlinski's reminiscences "In dem kanal" ("In the Sewer"), which form part of Dr. A. Berman's archives of the Jewish National Committee; Mark, *Powstanie w getcie warszawskim*, 1963 edition, pp. 148–9. About Gaik, who died a few months later in action against the Germans, in Władysław and Stanisława Legec, "Żołnierze ŻOB-u i ich przyjaciele" ("The ŻOB Soldiers and their Friends"), *Biuletyn Żydowskiego Instytutu Historycznego*, No. 5, 1953.
98 Berlinski's "In dem kanal."
99 *Ibid.*
100 *Ibid.*
101 Colonel Sęk-Małecki, *op. cit.*; W. and S. Legec, *op. cit.*
102 Tsivya Lubetkin, *Akharonim al hakhoma (The Last on the Walls)*, p. 507. The girl was Pnina Zandman, a member of Hashomer Hatzair.
103 Stanisława Legec's Eyewitness Account No. 5082 in the archives of the Jewish Historical Institute. Yiddish translation in Mark's *Tsum tsentn yortog*, etc., pp. 235–6.
104 Lazar Litai, *op. cit.*, p. 312–14.
105 Written on March 17, 1970, at the Ghetto Fighters' House in the Kibbutz Lohamei Hagetatot near Acre.
106 W. and S. Legec, *op. cit.*
107 Bór-Komorowski, *op. cit.*, p. 108.
108 Lazar Litai, *op. cit.*, p. 315.
109 *Ibid.*
110 *Polskie Siły Zbrojne*, Vol. 3, p. 676; General Jerzy Kirchmayer, *Powstanie Warszawskie (The Warsaw Uprising)*, pp. 136, 139.
111 *Polskie Siły Zbrojne*, Vol. 3, pp. 694, 816–17. According to Kirchmayer, the People's Army was only 120-strong. (*Op. cit.*, p. 138.)
112 Sh. Web, see note 64.

113 *Op. cit.*, p. 307.

114 In all his histories of the Warsaw Ghetto Uprising Bernard Mark states that Henryk (Mordecai) Zylberberg died on April 19 while commanding his combat group in the fighting in Nalewki Street. Zylberberg is also on the list of dead Jewish partisans and ghetto fighters in *Sefer Hapartizanim Hayehudim*, Vol. 2, p. 707. Mark's mistake is difficult to understand, for in the previously quoted article by Artur Szarfer ("Lekcja życia," *Folks Shtime*, October 27 and 31, 1970) the author cites File No. 5084 in the Archives of the Jewish Historical Institute in Warsaw, in which Zylberberg's identity as a survivor of the Warsaw Ghetto Uprising is confirmed. My attempts to clear up the mystery by writing to Szarfer and Zylberberg in Poland have so far been unsuccessful. There has been no reply to my letters.

115 Mark, *Walka i zagłada warszawskiego getta*, pp. 398–400.

116 Joseph Lehman, "Der heldisher toit fun Sara Rozenblum" ("The Heroic Death of Sarah Rozenblum"), *Dos Naye Leben*, Lodz, May 18, 1948.

116a The raid of the Red Air Force on Warsaw during the night of May 13 to 14, 1943 remains one of the enigmas of the Ghetto Uprising. Before trying to answer the question whether the Soviet Supreme Command ordered the raid to help the Jews, let us examine the available facts.

Ludwik Landau, the uniquely reliable Polish-Jewish chronicler who lived on the "Aryan" side until murdered by Polish fascists, recorded on May 15: "The effects of the raid are far from over. The number of victims has not yet been established, there is a real air-raid panic that is assuming the form of people leaving for the countryside for longer periods or leaving the city every night ... Warsaw is still without water ... It turns that the rumors that the Bolsheviks dropped leaflets during their raid are no figments of imagination. The leaflets exist, on one side they have the text of Stalin's famous letter to *The Times* correspondent, in which he expressed the wish to see a powerful and independent Poland, and on the other side there is an appeal to Poles to take part in insurrectionary, sabotage and similar actions ... " (Landau, *Kronika lat wojny i okupacji*, II pp. 420.)

The text of the leaflet is important, for Mark in his histories of the ghetto uprising published in 1955 and 1959 claimed that the leaflet called on Poles to help the Jews fighting in the ghetto. I shall therefore quote it in full, especially as very few copies of the leaflet survive. On one side it reads: "What did Stalin say about Poland? Polish Brothers! Mr. Parker, the Moscow correspondent of the American *New York Times* and the English *Times*, sent a letter to Yosif Stalin, the Chairman of the Council of People's Commissars of the USSR, asking him to reply to two questions which interest the American and British peoples. In reply Yosif Stalin sent him the following letter: 'Mr. Parker, on May 3 I received your questions referring to Polish-Soviet relations. I am sending you my answer. *First Question*: Does the Government of the USSR wish to see a strong and independent Poland after the defeat of Nazi Germany? *Answer*: Yes, without any reservations. *Second Question*: On what foundations, in your view, should the relations between Poland and the USSR be based after the war? *Answer*: On lasting, good-neighborly relations and mutual respect or, if the Polish people wants it, on the foundation of a treaty of alliance for mutual assistance against Germany as the main enemy of the Soviet Union and Poland. Respectfully, Yosif Stalin, May 4, 1943.'"

The other side of the leaflet reads: "Polish Nation! The time of revenge for all the German crimes and cruelties committed against the Polish people has come. The Red Army from the East and the Anglo-Americans from the West *are preparing a shattering blow that will break the back of the Nazi beast*. Your struggle, your actions can bring nearer the victory over our common enemy! Poles, the hour of action has struck! Pay the enemy back for the seas of blood and the rivers of Polish tears he has shed! Raise higher the banner of struggle against the vile German occupiers! Intensify your sabotage in the factories and mines! Hide your corn and cattle in the villages! Dismantle railway tracks! Derail German military trains! Join the ranks of Polish partisans! Exterminate the Germans day and night! To battle for your freedom and ours! To battle for a strong and independent Poland!"

Judged by the facts as recorded by Landau, the raid was indubitably assisted by the gigantic conflagrations in the ghetto, but there is nothing in the leaflet to suggest that the raid was intended to help the Jews. On the contrary, while the Kościuszko radio station in Moscow run by the Union of Polish Patriots was calling on Poles to rise in support of the fighting ghetto, the leaflet did not even mention the uprising. On April 24 the Kościuszko radio station appealed: "Listen, Warsaw! Listen, you all over Poland! For several days now the inhabitants of the Warsaw ghetto—our fellow-citizens—have been waging a heroic battle against the German occupiers in defense of their lives . . . Armed Polish detachments have hurried to the assistance of our Jewish fellow-citizens. Units of soldiers of the Polish underground have attacked the German gendarmes and SS from the rear. Many a Nazi thug has already been killed by a Polish bullet. But this is not enough, even though we have done a great deal to help the Jews. The inhabitants of the ghetto are gathering their remaining strength, they are doing their best to defend themselves, but they are unable to defend themselves with their own resources. We must help them—such is our duty as human beings, our conscience orders us to do it, the honor of the Polish people demands it, the interest of Poland demands it. One must be made of stone and not be human to remain passive in face of such a terrifying massacre. One must be blind and deaf not to understand that if we allow them to slaughter today the remaining tens of thousands of martyrs in the ghetto, the Nazi murderers will next proceed to do the same with us. If we remain passive, the Germans will conclude that they can do anything they like with us. The Nazi thugs will not hesitate to mobilize us for their army in order to use us as cannon-fodder; they will not hesitate to make the chains of our slavery even tighter and finally, as forecast by Hitler, exterminate us as they are already doing in the Lublin, Jarosław and Rzeszów regions. We are therefore appealing to you, the workers of Warsaw, to you, our countrymen in Warsaw and all over Poland: Go to the help of the fighting inhabitants of the ghetto. Workers of Warsaw, give them your support by going immediately on strike. . . . Form immediately self-defense detachments and with arms in your hands attack at once the Nazi murderers. Don't allow them to carry out the monstrous massacre of tens of thousands of innocent men, women and children! Not one inhabitant of Warsaw, not one underground military Polish organization, must delay acting for another moment. Let us attack the enemy at once with our united strength. Let us hit the Germans in every street of Warsaw, wherever they are. Let us provide the inhabitants of the ghetto with arms and food by every possible means . . ." (Mark, *Powstanie w Getcie Warszawskim*, Warsaw, 1963, pp. 323–5.)

Five days after the Soviet raid, on May 18, the Kościuszko radio station once again appealed to Poles to rise in defense of the Jews. "It is now almost a month," the broadcast began, "that the Warsaw ghetto has been heroically engaged in a life or death battle. There are not enough words to pay tribute to the courage and determination of the 35,000 remaining Jewish inhabitants of Warsaw in repelling the ferocious attacks of the enraged Nazi murderers . . . The unleashing of the widest possible actions of solidarity, of armed struggle in particular, with the inhabitants of the ghetto must not be delayed. Our Polish sense of honor demands it, but, first and foremost, the honor of the Polish working class. When in 1906 Tsarist executioners tried to organize anti-Jewish pogroms in Warsaw, they met with the determined and organized resistance of Polish workers, who dealt ruthlessly with the Black Hundreds. At this very moment, as the first month of the heroic struggle of our fellow-citizens, the Jews of Warsaw, is almost completed, we appeal once again to the people of Warsaw, to the entire population of our land: Make haste to help the brave ghetto fighters! Organize mass strikes to express your solidarity! Take up arms and attack the Nazi gangsters, don't let them slaughter the defenders of the ghetto, help the ghetto inhabitants escape. Give them shelter, help them join the Polish partisan units . . ." (Mark, *ibid.*, pp. 327–8.)

Such are the facts. Mark in his works *Der Oifshtand in Varshever Geto* published in 1955 and in the revised Polish version *Walka i zagłada Warszawskiego Getta* published in 1959 claimed that the Soviet High Command—i.e., Stalin—ordered the raid to help the Jews. Moreover, in the 1955 version he claimed that the leaflets "called on the Poles to take part in insurgent activities, i.e., in the uprising taking place in Warsaw, in the Ghetto Uprising." (p. 366). This conclusion is modified in the 1959 version where he said in a footnote: "The leaflets did not specify the uprising taking place in the city." (p. 408). Nevertheless, he elaborated his claim that the raid had been ordered in Moscow to help the Jews.

His version of events was based on the testimonies of the Pole Franciszek Karawacki and the Jew Leon Kasman, the editor of *Trybuna Ludu*, the mouthpiece of the Polish United Workers' Party, until his dismissal in 1968. Karawacki was one of the small band of Poles who were unable to conceive a free Poland where Jews were not treated as equals and anti-Semitism was not outlawed. First active in the Independent Peasant Party, Karawacki left it for the Polish Communist Party when his own party joined Wincenty Witos' united Peasant Party with its strong clerical and anti-Semitic tendencies. He was one of the first to join the Polish Workers' Party and became the personal assistant of Paweł Finder, when following Marceli Nowotko's assassination Finder became the leader of the Polish Workers' Party. He also acted in the same capacity to Gomułka when the latter found himself leader of the party following Finder's arrest by the Gestapo. In a statement made for the Jewish Historical Institute in Warsaw and kept in its archives, Karawacki stated that Finder had appealed to Moscow for help to the fighting ghetto and the air raid was the Soviet response. The text of the radio message, as far as he could recall, was: "Warsaw in flames, the Germans have started their bestial extermination of the remnants of the Jewish population in the Warsaw ghetto. Our organization unable to reach the fighting Jews. The PWP is organizing counter-actions against the liquidators of the ghetto and assistance to the fighters ... Retaliation in the form of bombings of a number of military targets and part of the German quarter is called for." (Mark, *op. cit.*, p. 406.)

In an article specially written for the fifteenth anniversary of the Warsaw Ghetto Uprising, Karawacki recalled how the radiogram came to be sent: "On April 20 Jerzy Wieniawski [who liaised between the Central Committee of the Polish Workers' Party and the ghetto RA] proposed that we ask for the dispatch of a Soviet squadron to retaliate for the bestial bombardments of the ghetto by the Germans. 'Let our Polish brothers,' he said, 'who are in the ranks of the Polish Army in the USSR, let our airmen smash the railway stations in Warsaw and other military targets and swoop down upon Szuch Avenue with its Gestapo headquarters. While the raid is taking place detachments of the People's Guard may succeed in breaking through the German lines and help the heroic Jewish fighters escape from the burning trap.' I thought his proposal made sense and therefore I immediately reported it to Comrade Paweł (Finder), who told me to compose without any waste of time the radiogram and transmit it to Moscow. Shortly afterwards it was radioed by our wireless-operator 'Jurek' and he received confirmation that it had been received. As a result of the radiogram squadrons of Soviet planes raided and bombed during the night of May 13 to 14, the munition dumps in the Kazimierz Square, the railway stations and a number of other military targets in Warsaw. Part of the ghetto fighters managed to leave the ghetto during the raid and reached partisan territory. Some of the children and women who escaped from the ghetto found shelter with Polish families in Warsaw or were moved to the Wyszków or other areas where they were protected by the partisans." (Franciszek Karawacki, "Ven mir hobn gerufn tsu hilf di Sovietishe Aviatsye," *Folks Shtime*, April 19, 1958.)

Wieniawski, the liaison man who was probably a Jew, fell into the hands of the Gestapo after the end of the ghetto uprising and was tortured to death. As for the wireless-operator "Jurek," Mark was unable to discover his true identity. However, Mark believed that Karawacki's account was corroborated by Kasman, whose own account No. 5,004 is in the archives of the Jewish Historical Institute. I have been unable to consult his account and must therefore rely on Mark's summary of it: "The radiogram travelled from one partisan base to another, which is confirmed by the partisan Janowski (Leon Kasman's pseudonym RA). The radiogram passed through Janowski's hands ... After some time there was a reply to the effect that the State Committee of Defense in Moscow had received the radiogram and accepted the proposal it contained. A second wireless message from Moscow informed that the air force would soon bomb a number of military targets in Warsaw." (Mark, *Walka i zagłada Warszawskiego Getta*, pp. 406–7).

The weakness in Kasman's testimony, at least as summed up by Mark, is that Kasman was not in a position at the time of the Warsaw Ghetto Uprising to see the wireless messages. For it was only in the last days of April 1943, following Stalin's final breach with Sikorski's government on the 25th, that the Organizational Committee of the Union of Polish Patriots was given the go-ahead by Stalin to create a Polish army on the territory of the Soviet Union. The Union of Polish Patriots then appealed to the Soviet Government to be allowed to form the Tadeusz Kościuszko

Division and received official permission to do so on 9 May. In July the agreement was extended to the organization of a Polish army corps. As part of their plans to organize a powerful Communist-led partisan movement on Polish territory, the Russians now proceeded to train its commanders and Leon Kasman, a veteran of the International Brigades, was one of them. Together with the Jew Aleksander Skotnicki and the Poles Borkowski, Czerwiński and Rózga, Kasman, was dropped by parachute in the Pinsk region of Polesye in territory controlled by Soviet partisans and there trained 100 Polish volunteers in the skills of partisan warfare. Kasman then led the detachment across the Bug and reached the Lublin region in January 1944. There he divided his force into three groups: one under the command of Ignacy Borkowski became the nucleus of the First Lublin People's Army brigade; the second under Skotnicki's command became the backbone of the Hołod People's Army Brigade, which was also known as the Northern Lublin People's Army Brigade. (See Ainsztein, *op. cit.*, pp. 390–1, 422–5. The information on p. 391 that Skotnicki was in the Pinsk ghetto is wrong.) Kasman's own detachment moved into the Parczew forests where it acted, thanks to its powerful radio transmitter, as the link between the Polish Partisan Staff in the Soviet Union and the command of the People's Army. Its chief task was to receive airdrops of arms and to distribute them to the People's Army units.

At that time Kasman was indeed in a position to transmit any messages he liked to Moscow, but obviously could not have dealt with the radio messages sent at the time of the ghetto uprising. Mark must have finally realized the unreliability of Kasman's memory, for in his last version, *Powstanie w Getcie Warszawskim* published in 1963, he made no claim that the Red Air Force had raided Warsaw to help the Jews (p. 138.) On the other hand, there is no reason to doubt Karawacki's account. Mark may have got rid of his final illusions about the purpose of the raid when in the third volume of the official Soviet history of the war published in 1961 he found the handsome tribute to the ghetto fighters, but no claim that the Red Air Force had helped them.

117 In his report Stroop reported that his men had been fired at from the "Aryan" side, but as neither the People's Guard nor the Home Army nor any other Polish organization has claimed to have been active during the night of the Soviet air raid, it must be assumed that the firing was done by Jews.

118 Colonel Sęk-Małecki, *op. cit.*

119 Mark, *op. cit.*, p. 419.

120 Mark, *op. cit.*, pp. 422–3; *Powstanie w getcie warszawskim*, 1963 edition, p. 151.

121 Artur Szarfer, *op. cit.*

122 Daily Reports of the Home Army Intelligence, June 15, 1943. Archives of the Institute of Party History—III.

123 Mark, *Walka i zagłada warszawskiego getta*, p. 424.

124 *Ibid.*, p. 429.

125 "Mówi Major Bystry," *op. cit.*

126 Mark, *op. cit.*, pp. 425–6.

127 *Ibid.*, p. 429.

128 Josef Wulf, *Das Dritte Reich und seine Vollstrecker*, p. 303.

129 Archives of the Chief Commission for the Investigation of Nazi Crimes in Poland, 368/7, pp. 166–7. Full text in Mark's *Powstanie w getcie warszawskim*, 1963

130 Mark, *Walka i zagłada warszawskiego getta*, p. 429.
131 Mark, *Powstanie w getcie warszawskim*, 1963 edition, p. 156.
132 *Ibid.*
133 Reitlinger, *The Final Solution*, p. 277.
134 Hilberg, *op. cit.*, p. 326.
135 Archives of the Institute of Party History, Papers of the Intelligence Section of the Central Committee of the Polish Workers' Party, Report No. 41.
136 *Ibid.*, 202/III-21.
137 Central Archives of the Polish Ministry of Internal Affairs, Antyk Papers.
138 *Ibid.*, Government Delegate's Papers, File 458, pp. 336–8.
139 Major Samuel Erlich-Krakowski, "Di militerishe badaitung fun oifshtand in Varshever Geto" ("The Military Significance of the Warsaw Ghetto Uprising,") *Folks Shtime*, April 13, 1966. Poterański's findings are thus close to the figures of 300 Nazis killed and over 1,000 wounded given by the Jewish National Committee in its telegram to Jewish organizations in New York on May 15, 1943.
140 Moczarski, *Odra*, February 1973. Stroop's report to Himmler is countersigned by Max Jesuiter.
141 *Istoriya Velikoi Otechestvennoi Voiny Sovetskogo Soyuza*, Vol. 3, p. 522.

The Epilogue

1 The 3,000 Jews in the Trawniki labor camp were slaughtered on November 3, 1943. A few days before the massacre the Germans had improved their food, given orders to expand the workshops and brought in large amounts of raw materials to lull the vigilance of the inmates. On the day of the slaughter the men were ordered to dig air-raid shelters and while engaged in their work they were mown down with machine guns. The same was then done with the women. Also on November 3, as part of the Erntfest Aktion (Harvest Operation) in which 42,000 Jews were murdered in the Lublin region camps, the Germans exterminated the 10,000 Jewish prisoners at Poniatowa. There they met with resistance led by the Revisionist David Szulman, one of the ŻZW leaders in the Warsaw ghetto, and overcame it by burning one barrack with the resisting Jews inside it. In his previously quoted report on the activities of the Jewish Section, Woliński said that following Jewish requests for arms the Home Army ". . . undertook unsuccessful preparations for the defense of Poniatowa and Trawniki."

2 Mark, *Powstanie w getcie warszawskim*, 1963 edition, p. 348.

3 Woliński's report.

4 Stefan Rowecki was born at Piotrków in 1895. His great-grandfather had fought in the Polish contingent of Napoleon's armies and his grandfather had taken part in the January Uprising of 1863. Rowecki himself served in Piłsudski's Legions and in the Polish-Soviet war of 1919–20. In the 1930s he became the founder and editor of *Przegląd Wojskowy (Military Review)*, thus displaying much wider intellectual interests than most of the officers who had served in the Legions. Because of his exceptional qualifications he was entrusted in June 1939 with the organization of

the Warsaw Armored and Mechanized Brigade, the only one of its kind in the Polish Army. As he noted in his diary on August 31, 1939, he had only 75 per cent of his strength in men and hardly any of the equipment. Moreover, his officers and men had not yet learnt how to drive at night and could not operate in larger units than troops or squadrons. Having become the commander of the Home Army, Rowecki tried to steer politically a course right of center and to defend General Sikorski's policy of attempting to come to a political understanding with Stalin, which was rejected by most of his fellow-officers. After his arrest by the Gestapo he was taken to Berlin where he spent a year in prison without revealing any of his secrets to the Gestapo. In August 1944 he was murdered at Sachsenhausen. (Andrzej Garliński, "Co nowego w historii?") ["What's New in History?"], *Kultura*, Warsaw, July 1, 1969.)

5 Woliński's report.

6 *Ibid.*

7 Because of their resistance, the 30,000 Jews removed from Sosnowiec and Będzin received special treatment on arriving in Auschwitz. After travelling 100 to a truck for two or three days without water one train was received with machine gun fire from the SS as it steamed In at the Birkenau ramp. Over 2,000 were killed and an unknown number wounded before the trucks were unlocked and the survivors driven into the gas-chambers. Before being crammed into the gas-chambers, the whole transport was treated with a savagery that was exceptional even at Auschwitz. (Ota Kraus and Erich Kulka, *The Death Factory*, pp. 190–91.)

8 Ch. I. Goldstein, *Zibn in bunker (Seven in a Bunker)*, pp. 211–12, 214, 222.

9 Salo Fiszgrund, "Der Varshever Oifshtand un der onteyl fun yidhishe kemfer" ("The Warsaw Uprising and the Participation of Jewish Fighters"), *Folks Shtime*, August 1, 1957. The author, a member of the Bund, took part in the Ghetto Uprising and in the Warsaw Uprising fought in the Polish People's Army.

10 *Polskie Siły Zbrojne*, Vol. 3, p. 820.

11 Archives of the Jewish Historical Institute, Eyewitness Account No. 4443.

12 *Ibid.*, Eyewitness Account No. 3961.

13 *Polskie Siły Zbrojne*, Vol. 3, p. 816.

14 Mark, *Walka i zagłada warszawskiego getta*, p. 468.

15 *Ibid.*

16 Michael Zylberberg, *A Warsaw Diary*, pp. 176–7.

17 Esther Mark, "Yidn in dem Varshever Oifshtand" ("Jews in the Warsaw Uprising"), *Folks Shtime*, August 1, 1964.

18 Archives of the Jewish Historical Institute, Eyewitness Account 5678.

19 Goldstein, *op. cit.*, pp. 127–9.

20 *Ibid.*

21 *Ibid.*, p. 120.

22 *Ibid*, pp. 125–6.

23 *Ibid.*, pp. 274–6.

24 *Ibid.*, pp. 121–3.

25 A. Kwaterko, "Yidn in Varshever Oifshtand" ("Jews in the Warsaw Uprising") *Folks Shtime*, July 27, 1969.

26 *Ibid.*

27 O. Kraus and E. Kulka, *op. cit.*, pp. 30–31.

Selected Bibliography

BASIC SOURCES
Biuletyn Głównej Komisji Badania Zbrodni Hitlerowskich w Polsce, 13 vols., Warsaw 1948–58.
Dokumenty i materiały do dziejów okupacji niemieckiej w Polsce: Vol. 1. *Obozy*, Lodz 1946; Vol. 2. *Akcje i wysiedlenia*, Lodz 1946; Vol. 3. *Ruch podziemny w ghettach i obozach*, Lodz 1946.
Dziennik Hansa Franka (edited by S. Piotrowski), Warsaw 1957.
Eksterminacja Żydów na ziemiach polskich w okresie okupacji hitlerowskiej (edited by T. Berenstein, A. Eisenbach and A. Rutkowski), Warsaw 1957.
Landau, L., *Kronika lat wojny i okupacji*, 3 vols., Warsaw 1962–3.
Ringelblum, E., *Ksavim Fun Geto*, 2 vols., Warsaw 1962–3.
————, *Notes from the Warsaw Ghetto*, New York 1974. (An edited and inadequate version.)

BASIC WORKS
Ainsztein, R., *Jewish Resistance in Nazi-occupied Eastern Europe*, London and New York 1974.
Eisenbach, A., *Hitlerowska polityka zagłady Żydów*, Warsaw 1961.
Hilberg, R., *The Destruction of the European Jews*, Chicago 1961.
Kamiński, A.J., *Hitlerowskie obozy koncentracyjne i ośrodki masowej zaglady w polityce imperializmu niemieckiego*, Poznań 1964.
Madajczyk, Cz., *Polityka III Rzeszy w okupowanej Polsce*, 2 vols., Warsaw 1970.
Piotrowski, S., *Misja Odila Globocnika*, Warsaw 1949.
Reitlinger, G., *The Final Solution*, London and New York 1953, 19.
Sefer Hapartizanim Hayehudim, 2 vols., Merhavia 1958.
Sefer Milkhamot Hagetaot, Ein Harod 1953.
Trunk, I., *Judenrat*, New York 1972.
Weinreich, M., *Hitler's Professors*, New York 1946.

BOOKS QUOTED OR USED
Alef-Bolkowiak, *Gorące dni*, Warsaw 1971.
Auerbach, R., *Oif di felder fun Treblinka*, Warsaw 1946.
————, *Der yidisher oifshtand – Varshe 1943*, Warsaw 1948.
Berg, M., *Warsaw Ghetto*, New York 1945.
Bór-Komorowski, T., *The Secret Army*, London 1950.
Borzykowski, T., *Tsvishn falndike vent*, Warsaw 1949, Ghetto Fighters House, Israel 1976.
Czerniakow, A., *Warsaw Ghetto Diary* (in Hebrew), Jerusalem 1968.
Donat, A., *The Holocaust Kingdom*, New York and London 1965.
Drewnowski, K. and Koźniewski, K., *Pierwsza bitwa z Gestapo*, Warsaw 1965.
Edelman, M., *Getto walczy*, Warsaw-Lodz 1945.

Goldkorn, D., *Wspomnienia uczestniczki powstania w Getcie Warszawskim*, Warsaw 1951.
Hirszfeld, L., *Historia jednego życia*, Warsaw 1957.
Kantorowicz, N., *Di yidishe vidershtand-bavegung in Poiln*, New York 1967.
Kaplan, Ch., *Scroll of Agony*, New York 1965, London 1966.
Kermisz, J. *Powstanie w Getcie Warszawskim*, Lodz 1946.
Litai, H.L., *Muranowska 7*, Tel Aviv 1968.
Lubetkin, Ts., *Akharonim al hakhoma*, Ein Harod 1946.
———, *Biyemei kilayon vemered*, Ein Harod 1947.
Mark, M., *Khurves dertseyln*, Lodz 1947.
———, *Der Oifshtand in Varshever Geto*, Warsaw 1955.
———, *Der Oifshtand in Varshever Geto*, Warsaw 1963.
———, *Powstanie w Getcie Warszawskim*, Warsaw 1954.
———, *Powstanie w Getcie Warszawskim*, Warsaw 1963.
———, (editor), *Tsum tsentn yortog fun Oifshtand in Varshever Getto*, Warsaw 1953.
———, *Walka i zagłada Warszawskiego Getta*, Warsaw 1959.
———, English translation published by Schocken.
Suhl, Y., *They Fought Back*, New York 1967, London 1969.
Tushnet, L., *The Pavement of Hell*, New York 1972.
Wdowiński, D., *And We Are Not Saved*, New York 1963, London 1964.
Wulf, J., *Vom Leben, Kampf und Tod im Ghetto Warschau*, Bonn 1958.
Zylberberg, M., *A Warsaw Diary*, London 1969.

Index

(The ranks of persons given are in most cases the highest reached by them)

Adamowicz, Irena, 23, 28
Agudath Israel 10, 12
AK, see Home Army
Akiba, Zionist right-of-center youth organization, 31, 60, 79, 97
Alef-Bolkowiak, Gustaw, Capt., 32
Altman, Tosia, 145
Andrzejewski, Jerzy, 151
Anielewicz, Mordecai, 29-31, 35-7, 61-3, 76, 79-82, 84, 90-1, 97, 101, 126-8, 144-5, 149, 175
Antyk Agency, 5, 50-1
Apfelbaum, David Mordecai (Moryc), 20, 62, 98, 107, 130, 144
Arciszewski, Tomasz, 25
Artsztejn, Zachary, 77, 90, 102, 152, 155
Auerswald, Heinz, 74
Auschwitz (Oswięcim), 178, 200

Barczyński, Solomon, 135
Barlicki, Norbert, 26
Bartoszek, Franciszek, 115-6, 120
Bartoszewski, Władysław, 71, 109
Beck, Józef, Col., 19, 21, 25
Będzin, extermination and resistance, 35, 177
Bejgelman, Menakhem, 145
Bem, Mieczysław, 22
Berlinski, Hirsh (Hersz), 30, 35-7, 61, 97, 112, 146, 195
Berling, Zygmunt, Gen., 196
Berman, Dr. Adolf, 49, 61
Besztimt, Pinkhas, 112
Białogród, David, 159
Białoskura, ŻZW leader, 20
Bieńkowski, Witold, 71, 80, 83
Binenfeld Leyb, 160, 166
Binsztok, 103
Błaszczak, Stanisław, Major, 194
Blones, Jurek, 112

Blum, Abrasza, 25, 30, 35-37, 61
Bodrowski, Zygmunt, 115
Boraks, Eliyahu (Edek), 17
Bór-Komorowski, Tadeusz, Lieut. Gen., 39, 43-7, 52, 71, 78, 83, 149, 150-6, 167, 177, 185, 195, 199
Bornstein, Stanisław, 23
Borzykowski, Tuvye, 181, 183, 195
Brandt, SS Obersturmführer (Lieut.), 75-6, 90, 122
Brasław, Samuel, 40
Brojdo or Braudo Ber, 64, 103, 145
Bronek, ŻOB fighter, 90
Bryskin, Aaron 103, 146
Brzeziński, Warsaw ghetto police officer, 87
Bund, 18, 24-7, 30-1, 33, 38, 58, 60, 66, 97
Bystry, see Iwański

Chełmno-on-the-Ner (Kulmhof), 17
Chruściel Antoni, Maj. Gen., 128, 134, 150, 176-9
Communists, Jewish, 18, 29-30, 60, 97
Council for Helping Jews, 49-52, 69-71, 80, 82, 175
Cukierman, Isaac, see Zuckerman
Czempel, Moses, 77
Czerniakow, Adam, 9-11, 18, 34, 41

Dąbrowski, Juliusz and Jan, 22-3
Dehmke, Otto, 120
Diament, Abraham, 112
Diehl, SS Lieutenant, 130
Dobrzański, Witold, 99
Drejer, Jacob, 28
Drejzin, Warsaw ghetto fighter, 98
Dror (Freedom), Zionist labor youth organization, 31, 60, 79, 97
Dubois, Stanisław, 26

Dudziec, Jadwiga, 23
Duracz, Jerzy, 115

Edelman, David, 191
Edelman, Marek, 40, 61, 68, 97, 112, 117, 137, 144-7, 200, 204 n. 22
Entin, Shlomo, 17
Eupen-Malmedy, Tneodor von, SS Hauptsturmführer, 75-8

Fajner, Dr. Leon, *see* Feiner
Farber, Joseph, 155
Federbusz, Khaim, 98, 103
Feiner, Dr. Leon, 51, 61, 69
Feinkind, Meilakh, 30
Finder, Paweł, 27-8
Finkel, Pika, 104
First (also Fuerst), Israel, 64
Firstenberg, Jerzy, 87
Fischer, Dr Ludwig, SA Gruppenführer (Lieut. Gen.), 3, 5, 105
Fiszelson, Warsaw ghetto fighter, 31
Fondamiński, Edward, 61, 67, 139, 145
Forelle, Jolanta, 23
Frank, Dr Hans, Governor-General of Poland, 5, 6, 8, 18, 71, 121
Frauendorfer, Dr Max, SS Obersturmbannführer (Lieut. Col.), 72-3
Frenkel, Paweł, 21, 62, 98, 107, 130, 144, 148
Fretter, Colonel, 73-4
Fridman (Frydman), Rabbi Zysie (Zusie), 35-37
Frydrych, Zalman or Zelman, 38, 144-5
Fuchrer, Mira, 145
Fuden, Regina 135, 144

Gaik, Władysław, 134-5, 144, 146-7
Gancwajch, Abraham, *see* Ganzweich
Ganzweich, Abraham, 7-14, 32-3, 41, 88
Garas, Józef Bolesław, 181 n.
Geller, Eleazar, 97
Gens, Jacob 8
Gepner, Abraham, 67
Giterman, Isaac, 35-7
Glicensztajn, Warsaw rabbi, 10
Globocnik, Odilo, SS Gruppenführer, (Lieut. Gen.), 71-2, 74, 85, 121
Goebbels, Dr Josef, 138. 152
Godlewski, Father Marceli, 203, n. 1
Goldstein, Chaim, 190-4
Goldsztein, Motl, 86
Gomulka, Władysław, 28, 170, 195
Gordonia, non-Marxist socialist Zionist youth organization, 60, 79, 97
Granatsztejn, Sarah, 64
Grey Ranks (Szare Szeregi), 124
Grosman, Khaya, 17
Growas, Mordecai, 64, 103, 136
Gruzalc, Leyb, 103, 145
Grynszpan, Jurek, 112
Gustek, Jan, 156
Gutkowski, Elias, 97-8
Gutman, Henokh, 112

Hahn, Dr Ludwig, SS Standartenführer (Col.), 100, 140, 170
Hajduk, Home Army officer, 84
Hamer Group, 117
Handelsman, Marceli, 46
Hanoar Hatzioni, Zionist-Liberal youth organization, 31, 97
Harand, Irena, 8
Hashomer Hatzair, Zionist youth organization of orthodox Marxists, 18, 23, 28, 31, 60, 79, 97
Hekhalutz (Pioneer), joint body of socialist Zionist organizations training future members of kibbutzim, 32
Heller, Zelik, 11-4, 33
Herff, Maximilian von, SS Obergruppenführer (Gen.), 153
Herling-Grudziński, Gustaw, 23
Herman of Warsaw ghetto Judenrat, 10
Herszberg, Rubbleman leader, 18
Hibner, Juliusz, capt., 19
Hilberg, Raul, 44-6, 78, 167-8
Himmler, Heinrich, Reichsführer SS (SS Field-Marshal), 73-5, 85, 88, 95, 121. 140, 168, 169, 178
Hoefle, Hermann, Standartenführer (Col.), 34, 38
Home Army, 19, 20, 29, 80, 82-4, 101, 115, 123, 125, 128, 134, 144, 149-51,

156-7, 165-7, 169, 175-7, 179, 180, 182, 184, 187, 189

Igra, Michał, Sgt. 188
Iwański, Henryk, Maj., 19-20, 24, 62, 67, 83, 98, 111, 114, 130-1, 133, 150, 151, 157; Wiktoria, 130, 158; Roman (son) 130, 134; Zbigniew (son) 158; Wacław (brother), 130-1, 158; Zbigniew (brother), 158

Janiszewski, Major, 84
Jaworski, Bronisław, 77
Jelień, Abraham 165
Jesuiter, Max, SS Sturmbannführer (Major), 169
Jewish Fighting Organization, see ŻOB
Jewish Military Union, see ŻZW
Józefów woods, ŻZW fighters in, 111
Jóźwiak, Franciszek, 28
Justman, Regina (Malka), 58, 66

Kagan, baker, 162-3
Kah, Dr, 140
Kaleske, Karl, SS Capt., 106, 120
Kamiński, Aleksander, 22, 46, 79
Kanał, Israel, 52, 97, 146
Kaplan, Joseph, ZOB leader, 30-31
Kapler, Jacob, 128-9
Kaufman, Simon, 5
Kawe, Hirsh, 86
Kazimierczuk, Zygmunt, Capt. 166
KB, 19, 83, 98, 111, 132-3, 135, 181
Kempner, Israel, 17
Kern-Jędrychowski, Tadeusz, Lieut., 135
Ketling, Cezary, 21, 62, 67, 83, 98, 133, 150, 151
KIMB, 22-3, 28, 46, 61-2
Kirchmayer, Jerzy, Brig. Gen., 170-1
Kirszenbaum, Menakhem, 35, 37
Kisielew, Nazi informer 31
Klepfisz, Michał, 66-7
Kliszko, Zenon, 195
Klostermayer, of the Warsaw ghetto SD, 86

Kneibel, Warsaw ghetto gendarme, 65
Kobyliński, Lech, 181-4
Kohn, Adolf, Dr. 169
Koluszko, Stefan, 131
Kon, Maurycy, 11-14, 33
Konrad, Franz, SS Obersturmführer (Lieut.), 139
Korman, Dr. 161-2
Korn, Leah, 135
Kossak-Szczucka, Zofia, 49-50
Kotlicki, Henryk, 58-9
Kott, Andrzej, 23-4
Kowalski, Bolesław, Major, 181
Koźniewski, Kazimierz, 24
Krahelska-Filipowiczowa, Wanda, 49
Kreński, Rubbleman leader, 152
Krueger, Friedrich Wilhelm, SS Obergruppenführer (Gen.), 73, 74, 88, 95, 104, 114, 118-9, 121, 137, 138, 139, 140, 142, 144, 151, 153, 154, 169, 170
Kruk, Herman, 30
Krzywonos, Wild Group leader, 98
Kurland, Stanisław, Capt. 182
Kuryłowicz, Adam, 28
Kwaterko, Abraham, 183 n.

Lammers, Dr Hans Dietrich, SS Obergruppenführer (Gen.), 121
Landau, Aleksander, 35-7, 64
Landau, Emilia, 64, 76
Lanota, Edward, Capt. 182
Lederman, Henryk, 187
Lejbgot, Benjamin, 77
Lejbman, Leyb, Serg., 130
Lejewski, Józef, 111
Lejkin, Jacob, 41-2, 64
Lerner (Lerski), Jerzy, 116-8, 122-3
Lewartowski, Joseph, 28-30, 35-37, 61
Lewin, Lazar, 29-30
Lewiński, Jerzy, Capt., 122
Lichtenbaum, Maksymilian, 10, 69
Lipszyc, Henryk, 20, 98
Łomianki woods, shelters ŻOB survivors, 135, 147-8
Łopata, Khaim, 98, 112
Lowther, Gerard 15
Lubetkin, Tsivya, 62, 77, 146, 195

Makowiecki, Jerzy, 49
Mark, Esther, 179 n
Małecki, Józef, Col., 119, 134, 144, 147, 154, 184
Matywiecki, Manashe (Anastazy), Major, 182-3
Mazurkiewicz, Jan, Lieut.-Col. 194, 197
Melamud, Ephraim, 68
Mellon, Simon 154, 158
Mendelson, Kalman, 20
Meretik, Adam, 28-31
Merin, Moses, 8
Międzyrzec, 31
Moczarski, Kazimierz, 99, 160, 169
Mołojec, Bolesław and Zygmunt, 27-8
Morgensztern, Yokhanan, 30, 61
Morro, Jerzy, Lieut., 124, 190, 194
Moselman, Rysiek, 134, 147-8
Moses the Bolshevik, 157
Myzia, Wacław, Major, 186

Niedzielski, Mieczysław, Lieut.-Col., 198-9
Nosak, Gestapo agent, 86
Nossig, Dr Alfred, 14-16, 87
Nowicki, Stanisław, Major, 182,
Nowotko, Marceli, 27-8
NSZ, 111, 157, 177

Ohlenbusch, Dr Wilhelm, 8
Olszewski, Tadeusz, 181
Orzech, Maurycy, 25, 30, 35, 37, 60
Osóbka, Edward, 26
OZN, 21

PAL, 134, 150, 186
PLAN, 21-25, 83, 120, 136, 150
Pełczyński, Tadeusz, Col. 179, 185
Petrykowski, Andrzej, Col., 19, 20
Pińczewski, 17
Podkański, Józef, 120
Poterański, Wacław, 169
Praszke, Jacob, 112
Próchnik, Adam, 26
Prużanski, Gestapo agent, 86
Prywes, Rubbleman leader, 152
PS, 26-7, 33, 38, 66, 111

Pszenny, Józef, Capt., 107-8, 123
Pużak, Kazimierz, 25

Raabe, Leszek, 27, 66
Rakower, Wild Group leader, 125
Ratajzer, Simkha, 144-6
Revisionists, right-wing Zionist followers of Vladimir Jabotinsky 18, 29, 62, 97
Ringelblum, Emanuel, 11, 13, 16-7, 35, 37, 40, 41-4, 57-8, 83, 154, 201 n. 23
Robb-Narbutt, Ignacy, Col., 28, 31
Rodal, Abraham, 98, 112, 136, 143; Leon, 62, 98, 107, 131
Rojzenfeld, Michał, 61, 97, 145-6
Romanowicz, Warsaw ŻOB fighter, 117
Rossum, Fritz, Lieut. Gen., 105
Rotblat, Leyb (Lutek), 102, 145; Halina, 145; Maria, 145
Rowecki, Stefan, Maj. Gen., 43-5, 47, 49-52, 69-71, 83, 149, 175-6
Różański, Elijah, 64
Rozenblum, Sarah, 153
Rozłubirski, Edwin, 180-4 186
RPPS, 26
Rubblemen, 156
Rudnicki, Adolf, 108
Rutkiewicz, Maria, 27
Rydz-Śmigły, Edward, Marshal, 19, 21, 25

Rzepecki, Jan, Col., 46, 49

Sagan, Shakhno Ephraim, 30, 35-7
Sak, Joseph, 30
Salek, ŻOB fighter, 86
Sammern-Frankenegg, Ferdinand von, SS Oberführer (Brig. Gen.), 75-6, 78, 85, 89, 95, 101-2, 105, 113
Sawicka, Hanna Szapiro-, 181
Schielke, Gustav, 99, 143, 169
Schindler, Max, Lieut. Gen., 72-3
Schipper, Dr Isaac, 18, 35-7
Schultz, K. G., 56, 81, 85-6, 89, 113, 117, 169
SD, 99, 120
Sikorski, Władysław, Lieut. Gen., 19-20, 25-6, 48, 51, 69-71, 177
Singer, Gestapo agent, 86

Skif, Bund youth organization, 38
Skokowski, Julian, Col., 186
Skoniecki, Czesław, 27
Skosowski, Gestapo agent, 86
Śledziewski, Wacław 144
Skupieński, Jerzy, Lieut, 123
Smakowski, Jacob, 103, 132, 160, 166
Sokołów, siding to Treblinka, 38
Sokołow, Nakhum, 20
Sombart, Werner, 15
Sosnkowski, Kazimierz, Gen., 177
Sosnowiec, 35, 177
Speer, Albert, 74
Spiegler, Henryk, Dr., 188
Spilker, Alfred, SS Hauptsturmführer (Capt.), 142
Spychalski, Marian, Marshal, 170
Stach, ŻOB fighter, 86
Stalin, Y.V., 28
Stalkowski, Zbigniew, Sub-Ensign, 123
Staniewicz, Lazar 98, 103
Stein, Leonard, 15
Sterling, Jan, 23
Sternhel, Henryk, Dr. (Gustaw) 122-130
Stroop, Juergen, SS Brigadeführer (Major. Gen.), 95-6, 99, 102, 104-8, 113-4, 117-21, 126-8, 131, 137-44, 150-1, 153-4, 167-71.
Strykowski, Dr. Michał, 62
Strzelecki, Ryszard, Capt., 184
Strzeszewski, Jan, 181
Sukiennik, ŻOB fighter, 77
Sym, Igo, 24
Świętochowski, Władysław, 141
Świtał, Dr., 200
Szajn, Adam, 88
Szaniawski, Jan, Capt., 195, 199
Szejngut, Tevye, 134-5
Szelubski, Jan, Maj., 148
Szermans, Rubbleman leaders, 152
Szerszen, Lazar, 152
Szeryński, Józef Andrzej, 6, 7, 10, 41, 59, 64, 204 n. 23
Szlakman, Solomon, 147
Szmerling, Warsaw ghetto policeman, 42
Szmidt, Andrzej, 27-31
Sznajderman, Tamara, 17

Sztajngold, Munik, 32
Szternfeld, Ganzweich's assistant, 10, 13
Szulkaper, Nehemiah, 186
Szulman, David, Warsaw ŻOB fighter 64
Szulman, David, ŻZW leader, 98
Szymanowski, Antoni, 56

Tarczyński, Stanisław, 135, 147
Tatar, Stanisław, Brig. Gen., 170-1
Taub, Pinkhas, 98, 118
Tejtelbaum, Niuta, 66, 115-6
Tenenbaum-Tamarof, Mordecai, 6, 17, 28-31, 67
Tetmajer, Michał, 122
Toebbens, Walther, 56, 75, 85-6, 89-90, 95, 113, 117, 169
Trawniki, 86, 155, 177
Treblinka II, 11, 38-40, 42, 44, 55-7, 74-5, 120, 128
Tryfon, Ryszard, 135
Tsukunft, Bund youth organization, 38
Tuwim, Andrzej, 23

Umschuetz, Gęsia prison SS man 178

Wagner, Eduard, Gen., 74
Wajnsztok, Roman, 98
Wald, Benjamin, 155
Walewski, Dr Ryszard, 96-7
Wallach from Treblinka, 39
Warsaw ghetto: creation 1, end, 154; population, 1-5, 56-7, 105; size, 1, 56; Judenrat, 5, 9-10, 34-5, 39, 56, 59, 64, 87; Jewish police, 5, 12, 34, 40-2, 64, 87; Nazi agencies of treachery and corruption, 1-6, 33; extermination, 5-6, 16, 30-35, 38-42, 55-6, 72-8, 89, 90, 153, 170; resistance, 7-11, 33-6, 38-40, 51, 58-63, 76-79, 84-91; arms, 26-7, 29, 35, 38, 51, 57-8, 64-72, 81-4; partisans from, 32
Warsaw Ghetto Uprising: arms, 97-8, 112; battle plans, 101-2; bunkers and tunnels, 97-9, 145-6; Jewish fighters, 97-8, 152; Polish assistance, 108-9, 115-6, 120-5; German forces, 105-8, 120, 133, 167-8; German losses, 112,

168-9; fighting, first phase, 105-133; second phase, 133-151; third phase, 151-159; number of Jews, 178; number of Jewish combatants 179-80; Home Army and the Jews, 175-8, 179; 181-2, 184; People's Army and the Jews, 178-9; Security Corps, PAL and the Jews, 179; Polish anti-Semitism, 180-4

Wasilewski, Antoni, 23
Wdowiński, Dr David 18, 62
Weber, Stanisław, Maj., 81, 84, 176
Węgrower, Yehuda, 145-6
Weiss, Eugeniusz, 187
Widerszal, Dr Ludwik, 46
Więckowski, PLAN commander, 120
Wiegand, Arpad, SS Brigadeführer (Maj. Gen.), 6
Wilner, Arye (Jurek), 17, 45-7, 51, 61, 69, 80-1, 145
Witek, Lieut., 183, 199-200
Włosko, David, 31
Wojciechowski, Czesław, 144
Woliński, Henryk, 46-7, 49, 51-2, 89
Woźniak, Henryk, Capt., 184

WRN. 25-6, 31, 66
Wyszyński, Warsaw ŻOB fighter, 66

Yankel ŻZW child-fighter, 13

Zajdler-Żarski, Władysław, 130
Zaremba, Zygmunt, 25
ŻKK, 50-5, 176
ŻKN, 58-9
ŻOB, 60-2, 64, 67-8, 71, 75, 77-8, 80-3, 86-90, 96-9, 101, 103, 105, 107, 109, 112-3, 118, 120, 126-8, 133-4, 138-9, 144-5, 149, 151-2, 175-7, 180, 184
Zołotow, Jurek, 134, 147-8
Zuchowicz, Tadeusz, 124-5, 157, 190-1
Zuckerman, Isaac, 30, 58-9, 77, 81-3, 98, 125-7, 134, 144, 147-8, 175, 177
Zylberberg, Henryk, 65-6, 102, 152, 155-6
Zylberberg, Michael, 189-90
ŻZW, 62, 64-5, 67-9, 76, 83, 86-90, 96-9, 104, 107, 110-4, 117-8, 120, 126-7, 130, 133, 136, 143-4, 148, 150-1, 155, 175.

WITHDRAWN FROM CLARK UNIVERSITY LIBRARY